GROUPS: Facilitating Individual Growth and Societal Change

GROUPS: Facilitating Individual Growth and Societal Change

by
WALTER M. LIFTON
Professor of Education, State University
of New York at Albany

and a specially prepared
Bibliography of References in Group Work
by
DAVID G. ZIMPFER
Associate Professor, College of Education,
University of Rochester, New York

John Wiley & Sons, Inc.
New York • London • Sydney • Toronto

Preface

Some time ago I reexamined my textbook, *Working with Groups,* to determine where updating was needed. I discovered that the changes were so many that in reality I had to write a new book. At an earlier time users of *Working with Groups* provided me with reactions about the strengths and weaknesses of that text. Guided by those comments (for which I am grateful), I have retained in this present book the sections that were considered useful.

Readers who are familiar with my earlier books will notice three new emphases in *Groups: Facilitating Individual Growth and Societal Change.* I am deeply concerned over the movement in our society which believes that values and philosophy are not basic to skill in a helping relationship. Because of the pronounced effect of sensitivity groups and their numerous cousins, I have tried to rescue the contributions arising from this movement, which are partially obscured by the sensationalism and incompetent behavior found in many people who call themselves group leaders or facilitators.

Finally, I have spotlighted an area of group behavior rarely taught or studied, but that is being experienced with increasing frequency by frightened members of our society. More and more we recognize the need for social change, but we evade the threat which that change implies. The nonchangers are being confronted by change agents using techniques that are little understood and against which few know how to react. I hope to make readers aware of the ferment in urban settings and to provide suggestions as to how they can clarify their own role in a changing society.

In this book, whenever I refer to a helping person who in other settings might be called a group worker, leader, facilitator, or therapist, I use the term counselor. No one label is truly descriptive.

Walter M. Lifton
December 1971

v

Acknowledgments

If an author has the temerity to include in the title of his text ". . . facilitating social change," he better be sure even his preface reflects current attitudes. Arlie Hochschild in the November/December 1970 issue of *Transaction* (The American Woman: Another Idol of Social Science), documents the put down of women when even books conclude with ("And lastly to my wife, etc."). Accordingly let me start by making as clear as I can that a marriage of over thirty years has produced more than children and books. It supplied a climate of love and affection along with an insistence that anger and differences could be worked out, if only we had the courage to face them.

This book obviously couldn't have been written if I did not have meaningful experiences which I think others might find of interest and maybe of help.

For all of us, the family is our nuclear group. From a group of four we are now seven, including David who at the time of this writing hasn't weathered his first year. Although I have learned much from my two children, Robert and Hazel, I owe a special indication of my debt to their mates Judy and Bill. It is hard to understand how we considered ourself a family before they joined our group. With each addition we have added both diversity and strength. Recently, my wife in writing to our children said that I was working on another book and it was as difficult as having a baby.

I acknowledge a special debt to Alan Klein of the State University of New York at Albany, School of Social Welfare. He has helped me include in this text many contributions from the field of social work. If the helping person of tomorrow uses the combined contributions of many disciplines, he will reflect the efforts of people like Alan Klein who are willing to join hands across disciplines, for the common good. Also, helpful comments were given by Edward Christensen, David Hartley, Floyd Brewer, David Zimpfer, and Gerald Gladstein. I am also grateful to the many publishers who granted me permission to quote from their publications.

The following people served as models for photographs used to show nonverbal communication: Raymond Antil, Elia Christensen, Natalie Cobb, Joseph Gaffigan, Sister Rosemary Hoodack, William McGinnis, Mary McKearn, Frederick Moran, Christine and Mark Palinski, Robert Schwartz, Concetta Terranova, Donald Welch, Nancy Guarelia, and photographer Norman Shartzer. I appreciate their willingness to help me try this approach to learning.

Finally, I acknowledge the help of Jean Kruckow who had the least rewarding task of typing and collating the manuscript.

W.M.L.

Contents

1 Group Characteristics and the Needs of Society

*"The World is too dangerous
for anything but the truth
and too small
for anything but brotherhood"*

ADLAI STEVENSON

THE EFFECTS OF SOCIAL CONDITIONS ON GROUP TECHNIQUES

There was a time when a textbook about working with groups could be expected to be a scholarly work, rather dry, and of interest only to professionals in the field.

Today groups and group process are the topics of best sellers. Nude Marathons, the John Birch Society, and changing public values have caused any discussion of groups to cover topics as widely divergent as sex and politics.

In the not-too-distant past, when using groups to help people was not yet in style, advocates of group techniques obtained acceptance only when they showed the economy of working with several clients at once, or when they worked with people who were deviant enough that society was prepared to accept any approach that promised success. Much of the pressure for working with groups of patients developed during World War II when the neuropsychiatric casualty rate exceeded the available personnel to provide therapy.

It is not possible to exactly pinpoint when group approaches became popular, but two influences are clearly apparent. As behavioral scientists became more effective in helping people secure a more satisfying life, and as attention turned from an earlier preoccupation with pathology to ways in which normal people could improve their lives, there arose in the United States those whose focus was on increasing the effectiveness of groups working together to accomplish a task.

In retrospect it appears clear that the development of groups designed to help people live more gratifying lives, or what Maslow termed "engage in self-actualization," depended on a society that was affluent enough that the more basic needs had been met and people could, therefore, afford to turn their attention to less pressing needs.

Working then in this type of social setting, Kurt Lewin discovered when working with groups, that a "feedback" or report about how they behaved or functioned enabled the members of a group to refine their relationships with each other and to move more rapidly toward achieving the desired group goal.

As a result Leland Bradford, then director of the Adult Education Division of the National Education Association, together with Ronald Lippitt, of the University of Michigan, and Kenneth Benne, of the Boston University Human Relations Center, established the first training center more than two decades ago at Bethel, Maine, and founded the National Training Laboratories (NTL). It was Bradford's (1,2) tough and dogged fight against strong opposition within education that finally won support for human relations training, first from industry, then from the social and behavioral scientists, and finally from the education hierarchy.

In the early 1940s a strong movement developed in the field of psychology, which had its roots in helping people solve problems based on discussions of the "here and now" instead of the past and which focused on the uniqueness of each man's view of life and reality. This phenomenological approach was given tremendous impetus by the work of Carl Rogers (3), who developed an approach for helping people which appeared equally useful with normally anxious people as it was with more seriously disturbed individuals. Although supporters of different points of view argued about the relative merits of the approaches, those techniques used with less disturbed people tended to be called group counseling instead of group therapy.

In the 1950s there were many studies like those by Gorlow, Hoch, and Teschow (4) designed to produce greater understanding of these new approaches. This period after the war reflected society's preoccupation with the effect of authoritarian dictatorships on society. It is not surprising, therefore, that the counseling techniques of this period showed a major concern with insuring that any helping process not foster dependency nor permit leader control over directions or goals of the group. This emphasis on a materialistic, pragmatic, effective group with its leadership developed within democratic limits really defines the place where the NTL began. It is best summarized by a review of the group roles described by Benne and Sheats (5), which were the focus of concern at that time. See Table I p. 4.

Let us see how this type of group might function. The newspapers announce that there will be a meeting of all citizens interested in helping to promote the local bond issue. Mrs. Smith decides that this is just the kind of volunteer work she would like to do. She is tired of being cooped up in the house and aches for someone to talk to. At the meeting that night, Mrs. Smith pitches in with enthusiasm. She has found that to understand an idea she must put it in her own words. Since she is not very clear about the idea, and since she likes to talk, she unwittingly monopolizes the meeting. At the end of the session, the group process-observer points up the way in which her behavior slowed down the group. Since Mrs. Smith really wants friends, and since she is concerned about the group goal, she sits quietly through the next couple of meetings.

How can we evaluate what has happened? The group has exercised control over its members to insure maximum movement. Mrs. Smith has learned what not to do, but no longer knows how to participate, since her normal method of functioning brings group disapproval. The group has achieved conformity at the expense of a member's individual growth.

Although in earlier days Mrs. Smith, in a T group, would get her feedback from the process observer, today in an encounter group she might be jumped on during the session by all the group members who do not like her way of acting. The attention the group would shower on her would be rewarding, but it still would not give her the knowledge about alternate behaviors nor the security to use them.

For most citizens in the United States, the 1960s and early 1970s were experienced as years of relative economic security while psychological questions of survival in an atomic and polluted society grew more pressing. The disenchantment with intellectuals who produced bombs and ignored the effect on people helped spur an anti-intellectual bias where seeking pleasure today because tomorrow might not come seemed logical. Concurrently there is a growing dismay over the way organizations influence peoples' lives. An anarchistic feeling, that no one has the right to influence another's life, results in a society where each individual strives "to do his own thing." It is predicated on the belief that man is basically good and if left alone his choices will make for a better life for all. These pressures, along with a growing recognition by the people at NTL that they had paid inadequate attention to the needs or feelings of individuals in the group caused a shift in emphasis toward greater concern about feelings, affect, and the messages being communicated on a nonverbal level. Several new types of groups arose bearing names like T (for Training) group, Sensitivity group, or Encounter groups. These groups have a common philosophy but with three distinct styles.

TABLE 1. Member Roles in Groups Attempting to Identify, Select, and Solve Common Problems

A. Group Task Roles.   Facilitation and coordination of group problem solving activities.

  1. *Initiator contributor.* Offers new ideas or changed ways of regarding group problem or goal. Suggests solutions. How to handle group difficulty. New procedure for group. New organization for group.
  2. *Information seeker.* Seeks clarification of suggestions in terms of factual adequacy and/or authoritative information and pertinent facts.
  3. *Opinion seeker.* Seeks clarification of values pertinent to what group is undertaking or values involved in suggestions made.
  4. *Information giver.* Offers facts or generalizations which are "authoritative" or relates own experience *pertinently* to group problem.
  5. *Opinion giver.* States belief or opinion pertinently to suggestions. Emphasis on his proposal of what should become group's views of pertinent values.
  6. *Elaborator.* Gives examples or develops meanings, offers rationale for suggestions made before, and tries to deduce how ideas might work out.
  7. *Coordinator.* Clarifies relationships among ideas and suggestions, pulls ideas and suggestions together, or tries to coordinate activities of members of subgroups.
  8. *Orienter.* Defines position of group with respect to goals. Summarizes. Shows departures from agreed directions or goals. Questions direction of discussion.
  9. *Evalvator.* Subjects accomplishment of group to "standards" of group functioning. May evaluate or question "practicability," "logic," "facts," or "procedure" of a suggestion or of some unit of group discussion.
  10. *Energizer.* Prods group to action or decision. Tries to stimulate group to "greater" or "higher quality" activity.
  11. *Procedural technician.* Performs routine tasks (distributes materials, etc.) or manipulates objects for group (rearranging chairs, etc.)
  12. *Recorder.* Writes down suggestions, group decision, or products of discussion. "Group memory."

B. Group Growing and Vitalizing Roles.   Building group-centered attitudes and orientation.

  13. *Encourager.* Praises, agrees with, and accepts others' ideas. Indicates warmth and solidarity in his attitude toward members.
  14. *Harmonizer.* Mediates intragroup scraps. Relieves tensions.
  15. *Compromiser.* Operates from within a conflict in which his idea or position is involved. May yield status, admit error, discipline himself, "come halfway."

TABLE 1.   (Cont.)

16. *Gatekeeper and expediter.* Encourages and facilitates participation of others. Let's hear. . . . Why not limit length of contributions so all can react to problem?
17. *Standard setter or ego ideal.* Expresses standards for group to attempt to achieve in its functioning or applies standards in evaluating the quality of group processes.
18. *Group observer and commentator.* Keeps records of group processes and contributes these data with proposed interpretations into group's evaluation of its own procedures.
19. *Follower.* Goes along somewhat passively. Is friendly audience.

C. Antigroup Roles. Tries to meet felt individual needs at expense of group health rather than through cooperation with group.

20. *Aggressor.* Deflates status of others. Expresses disapproval of values, acts, or feelings of others. Attacks group or problem. Jokes aggressively, shows envy by trying to take credit for other's idea.
21. *Blocker.* Negativistic. Stubbornly and unreasoningly resistant. Tries to bring back issue group intentionally rejected or bypassed.
22. *Recognition-seeker.* Tries to call attention to himself. May boast, report on personal achievements, and in unusual ways, struggle to prevent being placed in "inferior" position, etc.
23. *Self-confessor.* Uses group to express personal, non-group oriented, "feeling," "insight," "ideology," etc.
24. *Playboy.* Displays lack of involvement in group's work. Actions may take form of cynicism, nonchalance, horseplay, or other more or less studied out of "field behavior."
25. *Dominator.* Tries to assert authority in manipulating group or some individuals in group. May be flattery, assertion of superior status or right to attention, giving of directions authoritatively, interrupting contributions of others, etc.
26. *Help-seeker.* Tries to get "sympathy" response from others through expressions of insecurity, personal confusion or depreciation of himself beyond "reason."
27. *Special interest pleader.* Verbally for "small business man," "grass roots" community, "housewife," "labor," etc. Actually cloaking own prejudices or biases on stereotype which best fits his individual need.

GROUPS AND DEMOCRACY

The appealing concept of using groups to improve our democracy has had some interesting implications recently. In earlier times, institutions in our society were developed by people in the power structure, and clients' abilities to get their needs met depended on the way the agency chose to define its purpose and goal. With the advent of the Economic Opportunity Act a new concept appeared on the social scene. It stemmed from a requirement that any project to be funded needed "maximum feasible participation" of the poor. A new guideline developed. Agencies were now seen as the servants of their clients, and goals, procedures, and operating style depended on client approval for justification. With this movement of "power to the people" also came an awareness that experts were not the only ones who could be helpful and, in fact, in some settings because of the experts' own backgrounds, were unable to really perceive problems through the eyes of their clients. With this movement there developed an associated drive toward using paraprofessionals wherever possible.

The negation of the need for trained leadership finds itself represented in ultimate form by the presence on the market today of games and tapes, which imply that if instructions are followed, they can produce increased understanding and better social relationships for the participants (6,7,8).

If any reader doubts that 1984 has already arrived, he should visit some schools or churches where people are grouped around a tape recorder waiting for a voice on tape to tell them what to do and when to do it. Obviously, if in the process of going through these motions an individual gets disturbed or acts in an unpredictable way, there is no one assigned the responsibility for coping with the situation. The implication is that a group of people will contain within it all the expertise needed to handle any situation that might develop. This is the height of anti-intellectualism, of loss of responsibility, and of emphasis on behaviors, with no attempt to help people to relate their experiences to situations they can cope with in real life.

Facing this issue Miller (9) in an article "On Turning Psychology over to the Unwashed," indicates that the needs of our society are too great to restrict psychological knowledge to the professional. Recognizing that those who control the stimuli can also control the resulting behavior, he notes that changing behavior is pointless in the absence of a plan of how it should be done. He spotlights the public's concern for the impact of the *process* used on the final result. Humane applications of behavior control must be based on professional ability to diagnose personal and social problems. Given the facts, society then might be in a position to truly make choices.

A GROUP VERSUS A MASS

For many people any grouping of people carries with it the concept of the loss of individual responsibility and identity. Freud (10) in describing the effect of group behavior on people, was particularly con-

cerned with the tendency for people to reinforce in each other the needs
of an antisocial nature that could be expressed, since a person's identity
in a group was lost from view. This concept is not unlike that which
we see in a lynch mob. The concept of a "group mind" as a unique
entity that is the sum of the people involved, but responsible to no one
certainly has not become obsolete in popular thinking.

The definition of the characteristics of a group described by Loeser (11)
is of interest in the light of our desire in some way to differentiate the
labels we apply to numbers of people. Loeser states that groups have:

1. Dynamic interaction among members.
2. A common goal.
3. A relationship between size and function.
4. Volition and consent.
5. A capacity for self-direction.

Applying these concepts to a group of theatergoers, one could possibly
find every defined characteristic except the group's capacity for self-
direction. As long as they are all reacting on an individual basis to the
show they are watching, even if they are aware of other people, they
more aptly could be called a crowd or a mass. They do not become a
group until there is an awareness of their dependence on each other to
accomplish a goal and an acceptance of their responsibility to each other
in the process. An educative or therapeutic group demands that there be
continual awareness of each person's behavior in the group and the
acceptance by each person of responsibility for his own actions. Fundamental in a democracy to the use of any group technique is a concern
over the rights and needs of the individual.

There can be little question that group processes such as those employed in the concentration camps can modify behavior and attitudes.
However, when the pressures for achievement must arise from within
each individual, it becomes very relevant that these motivating needs reflect the intrinsic values of each group member as he shares in developing group goals. Within this context, each term describing group techniques has to be considered as it relates to the way it facilitates or hinders
individual growth. Within such a context, for example, group guidance
is evaluated in terms of the conditions under which people develop the
need for information and the environment that best facilitates the incorporation of the desired information.

THE ROLE OF THE GROUP IN SOCIETY

One of the easiest ways to pick a fight in our society is to imply that
the larger group takes precedence over the individual. As a nation dedi-
cated to the right of each person to find happiness in his own way, we

tend to look with suspicion on any organization where the individual becomes submerged and the group becomes more important. This strong preoccupation with the individual has been equally present in the field of mental health. Convinced that the road to a healthy society depends on treating people in a one-to-one relationship, many professions have predicted the need for additional personnel, based on their estimates of how many people each professional can treat.

The incidence of people needing help grows larger, and the gap in available professional workers grows. Even if by some miracle suitable people could be located, trained, and employed, the dimension of the problem suggests that other approaches must be explored (12). There can be no doubt that we must reassess ways in which people can be helped. It is also time for us to question the validity of the belief that using group processes necessarily robs people of their individuality.

Let's face it. The values we cherish in our society are apparently contradictory. On the one hand, we value our heritage of rugged individualism; on the other, we are proud of the picture of ourselves as the champions of democracy.

Contradictions provoke controversies. We need but to glance at some major controversies in our society—labor-management-government interrelations, integration-segregation problems, national defense needs, the role of government in health, education, welfare, and science—and we see that they stem from this common contradiction of values.

Is this apparent contradiction of values real? Is the point at which the rights of the individual end and society's rights begin a never-never land of inevitable conflict? It seems unlikely. A major premise of this textbook is that there is no necessary contradiction between individual growth and societal, or group, process. And it follows that as the speed of communication increases, so also it becomes increasingly imperative that we find a way to communicate how group action can be a source and a means of freeing the individual instead of enslaving him.

GROUPS, POLITICS, AND VALUES

The role of the group in politics represents a major present concern. The freedom of the mob to express their hostility under the cover of lost identity, the right of a property owner to decide who his neighbors will be, the use of laws and government to change behavior, even when they cannot affect feelings—all these represent examples of why the day-to-day experiences of the average man have left him with a mistrust of groups. Few people have experienced truly democratic groups. Until they do, it will be hard for them to realize that along with the rights granted to people in a democracy there is also responsibility—responsibility not only for oneself but also for one's neighbor.

It has been stressed that true learning takes place only when a person feels secure in the setting. One of the first things that any group seeks to discover is the dividing line between what is acceptable and what is not. There are two kinds of limits, those imposed by society and those internal ones we impose on ourselves. Society has the responsibility continually of determining which of its rules are unyielding and which require change. The setting in which the group meets, the question of voluntary or forced membership, the societal expectations of the purpose of a group, all will influence where the limit is set and how it is interpreted. People need security to see how the group can be useful to them and they to it. The group has the responsibility of setting limits to what it can offer; some needs ought to be met elsewhere.

Although each individual must clarify his own beliefs, these beliefs cannot be considered in a vacuum. The salvation of the democratic way of life depends basically on our skill in teaching people how to use the group process as a means to preserve an environment not only where all may live, but also where individual difference is valued and where each person's happiness is truly believed to be the vital concern of all. This teaching process ought to be felt in all aspects of our lives; it cannot be limited to the school setting. Church groups, social agencies, industrial organizations, all contribute to the flavor and operating philosophy of a society. Value systems do not develop in people at a specific age but grow and change from infancy on. Hence this book directs itself to the group experiences found in the entire spectrum of society, regardless of age or setting.

THE FORCES FOR CHANGE

It is not enough to help people adjust to society. We also need to help them learn how to change their environment. How then do we get change? Tillich (13) tells us that man cares enough for himself to act in behalf of himself even when such actions challenge his self-esteem and self-integration. May (14) feels that man becomes truly human at the moment of decision. Allport (15,16) states that much of our behavior involves seeking of challenges and tensions. And Frenkel-Brunswick (17) has shown that the antidemocratic authoritarian personality, when faced with anxiety, tends to avoid activities involving self-exploration or introspection. For the "authoritarian personality," consideration of his relationship with peers, friends, or family is threatening.

Our society includes both democratic and antidemocratic elements.

Both elements seek help, and in both cases they need help from the leader they select. The basic responsibility of the initial group leader is to be responsive to the real goals of the group, including those not as yet articulated. Since the security of group members depends on clearly defined limits, the group leader defines the initial purpose of the group. Because under stress people tend to be unable to communicate, it is the leader's role to help the group develop and use their resources to provide support to group members.

One of the major differences in the role of the leader in a democratic society from other types is that he derives his authority from the group. At any point where his perception of group goals deviates beyond the limits of group acceptance, he is no longer able to function. Therefore, it is the group's responsibility to give the leader the help he needs to shoulder the roles required by the group. It is also their responsibility constantly to share their ideas and feelings so that the hidden agenda can come to light.

How do we help man transcend himself? My answer is both humanistic and existential. Since society cannot depend on answers coming from all people in every situation, leadership must be delegated. One of the most difficult roles of this leadership is to set limits that reflect society's wish for change, even when readiness is not reflected by the sounds of the loudest voices.

To the degree that we can use a group setting to help people gain the support they need to face stress from within and without, to that degree we make it possible for democracy to succeed.

As a nation we face some unprecedented changes. We are becoming increasingly mobile, heterogeneous, and technically oriented. Some of the guideposts that used to come from tradition will have to be redefined by each group as they cope with new conditions.

Concern over the effects of our rapidly growing technology and its effects on man was concisely stated by Rollo May (18) in a speech entitled "Freedom and Responsibility Reexamined":

". . . if we accept the proposal sometimes made in psychological conferences that our computers can set our goals and our technicians determine our policies, we are in my judgment making the most serious error of all. For we are abdicating in the face of our lack of goals and values. The one thing our computers cannot tell us is what our goals ought to be. In this day when we and all sensitive contemporary people are so confused and anxious, it is not surprising we tend to abdicate in favor of the machine. We then tend more and more to ask only the questions the machine can answer, we teach more and more only the things the machine can teach, and limit our research to the quantitative work the machine can do. There then is bound to emerge a real and inexorable tendency to make our image of man over into the image of the very machine by which we study and control him."

ACCOUNTABILITY

There has developed another aspect of our materialistic society that in some ways could have even more serious impact on our way of life than technology. Originating in the military establishment where they were concerned with obtaining "the biggest bang for the buck," new budgeting systems were developed to insure that each person was accountable for producing revenue or results equal to the investment. The Program, Planning, Budgeting System (PPBS) logically asks that goals be set and that evaluation take place to prove the goals are met. Ability to secure funds depends on ability to demonstrate achievement. Given that setting, there is a tendency to set objective goals and avoid ethical or value goals that are almost impossible to measure. It is easy to show that you get people to behave in approved ways (cut down absenteeism); it is hard to show carryover of this learning to later life.

Many of our major concerns today seem to be wrapped up in the term "manpower utilization." Regardless of the reasons for this concern, society finds itself seeking means of motivating people to make optimal use of their educational and occupational potentials. The underachiever, whether his behavior stems from cultural or from psychological factors, needs to be helped to gain the higher rewards that are available and are given in our society to productive citizens. Much of our concern, unfortunately, has not come from our interest in the specific individual. Rather, looking at the aggregate of our potential, we seek security in a world of conflicting political ideologies by stressing material productivity. This concern with things instead of with people has led to some panaceas which may well cure the symptom but kill the patient.

In a book on counseling, Fullmer and Bernard (19) raised the basic issue of whether we should learn from the communists and employ their techniques of brainwashing. We, of course, would use it to propagandize for democracy. This approach, at the opposite end of the continuum from Freud, rejects self-knowledge or insight as the main source of change. Learning theory and the development of systems of rewards and punishments to control behavior have particular appeal to a technologically oriented society (20). This may account for their recent rapid growth. Apparently, however, we have not yet learned that the means determine the end. We also seem to be confused over ways of developing instrinsic instead of extrinsic rewards for behavior.

For democracy to achieve the efficiency we seek, we obviously must develop skills in having our society's goals reflect the consensus of the needs of individuals. We must also help each individual to clarify his personal goals and to relate them to the objectives of the community. This "I–We" dialogue develops best when the individual can test his ideas against those of his peers.

Even at age levels where we have long recognized the importance of the group to the individual, we have been extremely slow in using socio- logical and psychiatric insights that employ the group as a vehicle for therapeutic change.

Social workers and sociologists have had much to tell us about gangs, juvenile delinquency, peer-group pressures, and group-work process. Psychiatrists looking at the developmental stages of man have stressed the need for children to belong to clubs and peer groups as part of their search for identity. Within the last 20 years the message seems to be getting through. There is a swell of demand for people trained to work in group settings.

This demand for group work skills did not stem purely from a desire for economy of effort or from a desire to relieve staff shortages. The de- mand also stems from a growing awareness—an awareness that there are some peculiar growth experiences available to individuals in groups that are not present in a one-to-one relationship.

GROUP LABELS

Group Guidance, Group Counseling, and Group Therapy. Almost all of the labels used to describe groups prior to the establishment of the NTL reflected a concern with helping sick people get well. The major

TABLE 2.

Structured	Some Structure	No Structure

Group guidance
Micro laboratories
Achievement motivation
   groups
Human potential groups
	Group counseling
	Sensitivity training groups
	Organizational develop-
	   ment groups (T group)
	Confrontation groups
		Group therapy
		Encounter groups

Emphasis on improving
   communication skills
   and providing infor-
   mation
	Emphasis on developing
	   sensitivity to one's
	   impact on others and
	   their impact on you
		Emphasis on personal
		   growth and develop-
		   ment; improvement
		   of mental health

exceptions today are the human potential groups and "group guidance," which is seen as an economical way of providing people with information or needed experiences in formal settings.

Floyd Brewer has conceptualized the relationship of various techniques along a continuum defined in terms of structure. Table 2 represents his conception of the relative structure involved in various types of groups.

Clarence Mahler (21,22) in summarizing definitions established for group guidance, group counseling, and group therapy, differentiates these labels in terms of:

- The initially defined purpose of the group.
- The size of the group.
- The management of the content.
- The length of the group's life.
- The responsibility of the leader.
- The severity of the problem.
- The competency of the leader.

Mahler sees group guidance as primarily focused toward information dispensing, and with major responsibility for content and direction being focused on the teacher or leader.

The major difference between group guidance and group counseling, according to Mahler, is that in group counseling the focus is on each group member, not on the topic being discussed, and on changing each individual's behavior. He sees group counseling as a social experience, dealing with developmental problems and attitudes of people, *in a secure setting* (italics mine). He includes sensitivity and encounter groups as variations of group counseling. In earlier days many similar activities performed by social workers were called "group work."

Group therapy is one step further along the continuum since it is more concerned with unconscious motivation. It is aimed at disturbed individuals and, therefore, may last over a long period of time. Group psychotherapy had many of its roots in the work of Freud, and most of the initial forms of group therapy had their base in psychoanalytic theory. Most of the early practitioners worked within a medical frame of reference. The works of Slavson (23), Moreno (24), and Klapman (25) are illustrative of this period.

Table 3, dealing with the area of family relationships, demonstrates the differences in the application of the different types of groups.

These definitions carry current popular appeal. Unfortunately, they are based on a static view of schools and on psychological theories that

TABLE 3. Family Relationships

Unit	Size	Frequency of Meetings	Approach	Goals	Methods
Class (group guidance)	30	Extended homeroom program unit for one, two, or three weeks.	Unit outline prepared as part of course.	Understand roles of various family members, sibling relationships, parent-child relationships.	Text Outside readings Class discussion Individual projects Films on family life Speakers Role playing Group projects Attitude surveys
Large group (group guidance or counseling depending on emphasis)	10–20	Usually a period a week for a semester. Frequency varies considerably depending on goals.	Topic comes up only if a an area of concern.	Understand oneself in context of family relationships.	No text Outside readings Personal logs or autobiographical writings Group discussion Attitude surveys
Small group (group counseling)	2–10	One or two hours a week for semester or school year.	Topic chosen by group as student brings it up. Group may or may not work on it for a whole period.	Understand oneself in context of family relationships.	Primarily group discussion Role playing Sociodrama
Therapy group	2–8	One or two hours a week for school year.	Topic may come up at any time a group member feels inclined to talk about his own family relationships.	Understand oneself and family better. Experience catharsis of feelings involved in a particular situation.	Primarily group discussion Role playing Psychodrama

From Clarence A. Mahler and Edson Caldwell, *Group Counseling in the Secondary Schools*, Chicago: Science Research Associates, Inc., 1961, p. 25.

posit unconscious factors in human behavior. As Chapter 2 will demonstrate, many current philosophies doubt the need for either the use of insight, dealing with past events, or requiring long-term relationships. There are some who even question if severely disturbed people reflect their own maladjustment or the problems of society.

Group guidance, or disseminating information for educational purposes, is now being attacked along with the rest of education. The brunt of the attack is on the use of group approaches that obscure the unique needs, readiness, or motivation of the individual. The growth of the many new media of instruction and the new technologies of information storage and retrieval raises provocative questions about their effect on instruction and group orientation procedures. As machines facilitate some phases of individual instruction and as computers become a ready and accurate resource, some of the traditional roles found in learning groups may disappear.

Group guidance in many places involves a variety of nonhuman devices. Increasingly, society will search for places where the mass of information being spewed forth can be incorporated. It will also seek ways to enable the individual to use and to have access to data at the time *he* needs it most.

It is not the purpose of this text to discuss the nature of the classroom and the factors within a class that militate against the security necessary for a therapeutic experience. Suffice it to say that where the teacher's role represents that of an evaluative authority figure, and where the individual will lose status within the group or within the community by exploring negative feelings or ideas, it is impossible for therapeutic growth to take place (26,27,28). Wieder, for example (29), has supplied evidence which suggests that this difference is a genuine one. He compared a classroom group led according to nondirective group-therapy procedures with another group taught according to traditional lecture methods. His results indicated that the "therapy group" measurably modified attitudes associated with racial, religious, and ethnic prejudice; the group taught according to traditional methods did not significantly modify these same attitudes.

The educator's role and the learning process are basically psychological problems. For the educator to function adequately, it is important for him to know the philosophy of the agency within which he works, the limits of behavior that will be tolerated by the community, his own ability to tolerate differences with his own value system, and probably most crucial of all, the kind of behavior he exhibits as contrasted with the things he would like to be doing.

Encounter, Sensitivity, and T-Groups. Most attempts to help groups of people today tend to be subsumed under the heading of "group-counseling." Because the NTL groups—T-groups, sensitivity groups, and encounter groups—are most common, they will be discussed in detail.

Charles Seashore of the National Training Laboratories (30), Institute for Applied Behavioral Science described the underlying assumptions behind T-group training as follows.

The learning processes that distinguish group training from other more traditional models of learning are:

1. *Learning responsibility.* Each participant is responsible for his own learning. What a person learns depends upon his own style, readiness, and the relationships he develops with other members of the group.

2. *Staff role.* The staff person's role is to facilitate the examination and understanding of the experiences in the group. He helps participants to focus on the way the group is working, the style of an individual's participation, or the issues that are facing the group.

3. *Experience and conceptualization.* Most learning is a combination of experience and conceptualization. A major T-group aim is to provide a setting in which individuals are encouraged to examine their experiences together in enough detail so that valid generalizations can be drawn.

4. *Authentic relations and learning.* A person is most free to learn when he establishes authentic relationships with other people and therapy increases his sense of self-esteem and decreases his defensiveness. In authentic relationships persons can be open, honest, and direct with one another so that they are communicating what they are actually feeling rather than masking their feelings.

5. *Skill acquisition and values.* The development of new skills in working with people is maximized as a person examines the basic values underlying his behavior as he acquires appropriate concepts and theory and as he is able to practice new behavior and obtain feedback on the degree to which his behavior produces the intended impact.

Encounter groups are sometimes called "personal growth labs" and focus on the individual, seeking to instill in him a sense of self-awareness. They rely heavily on nonverbal ("touch and feel") techniques. This is a form of sensitivity training and is most common today. The group is usually composed of from 6 to 12 members. It has no preset agenda, but focuses strongly on the feelings presented within the group. The emphasis is on an atmosphere of openness and honesty in communicating with each other (31). Encounter group is a term used more commonly on the West Coast of the United States and refers primarily to sensitivity groups.

T-group, the older original method, uses more verbal exercises and emphasizes the relationship of each group member to what is happening in the group at that time. It assists members to see how others in the group perceive them and, like its sister the "Organizational Development Group," it focuses on helping members of an organized body function more effectively as a team.

The last popular group label arising from this movement is the confrontation group. As described by Max Birnbaum (32)

"Confrontation sessions are usually contrived racial encounters in which militant blacks literally "confront" members of the white community (teachers, police, industrial management, etc.) with their angry reaction to white racism, discrimination, and prejudice. The theoretical basis for this type of experience is that the social conditions requiring this form of learning demand a maximum dose of aggression and hostility in order to convince the targets—the whites—of the seriousness of the personal situation. (Because most confrontation sessions of this kind are not part of a plan for organizational change, they usually end as paratherapeutic experiences rather than training.)"

One other contribution of this movement is a series of other terms and jargon, which are used to describe the types of format being used or the behaviors of group members. There also are several different time lengths for sensitivity programs. The shortest form is a three-hour "microlab." More often encounter or T-group labs run from two days to two or more weeks. Another version is the "marathon," a continuous, exhaustive session that may last for 24 or 48 consecutive hours. The T-group has a special language of its own, a mixture of hippie talk and social-science jargon. People are "hungup" or "uptight," trying to discover "where I'm at." They don't talk; they "have a dyad." In one exercise, half the group listens to the others and then gives its impression of what it has heard. This is not called "talking" and "criticizing"—it is known as "input" and "feedback." (Some sophisticated T-groups get "feedback" through videotaped replays (33). Today it might even be called rapping.

If the various groups which now claim NTL as their parent were to select a motto it might be "Don't think—feel!"

The phenomenal growth of the various forms of sensitivity groups is felt by many to reflect the degree of alienation in our society as well as man's search to relieve his loneliness and lack of meaningful contacts with others. Few people are as close to others as they would like to be. They distrust the truthfulness of the emotions they experience in their daily lives. With the breakdown of formal religion and churches as the source of renewal and both human and spiritual support, crowds flock to settings that promise easy intimacy, honest relations, and in some groups, sexually tinged physical relationships without fear or guilt.

Considerable space has been spent in describing the NTL and its offshoots because the popularity of these groups coupled with the equally strong rejection by parts of society could easily once again reverse the pendulum and cause society to reject all groups, not just those guilty of excesses.

It is important to examine some of the criticisms being expressed so the contributions arising from the activities of these groups will be recognized. If we truly understand the issues involved we won't have to throw out the baby with the bath water. The most serious charges against some groups appear to be the lack of insistence on trained leadership, the autocratic nature of the process which does not truly permit participants the freedom to select the areas or acts in which they want to be involved, the pressures toward conformity, and in some groups, the emphasis on style or behavior with no attempt to help people relate this to causes or situations outside the group's life (34).

It is very important to recognize that few people would criticize the goals of these groups, the effectiveness of the techniques, or their potential usefulness if some of the present abuses were faced.

June Howard (35), in a very readable book entitled *Please Touch*, describes her experiences as she moved from one encounter group to another. She recognizes the fears of the far right that these sensitivity groups are part of a conspiracy to weaken the moral fiber of United States citizens. These she rejects as groundless. Summarized, her review of the more serious charges include the following. The statements are Howard's, the comments are those of this author.

1. *The group can be run by charlatans who are corrupt or mediocre or both.*   While this is seen as true, it is not seen as a basis for not permitting ethical people to function.

2. *The groups are a hotbed of junkies and dope addicts.*   Howard points out that most groups are focused on expanding human potential without the use of drugs. Many groups specifically fight drug addiction (for example, Synanon).

3. *The groups invade privacy.*   Although people in the encounter groups are not forced to confess, group pressure makes it hard to retain areas of personal privacy. This criticism will be discussed in greater de-

tail later because it forms the basis for much opposition to these types of groups.

4. *The groups foster sexual promiscuity.*   Howard believes this to be partially true, but questions if this is all bad.

5. *The groups encourage physical violence.*   Although they do encourage people to express hostile feelings, they do not permit people to be seriously physically hurt.

6. *Groups can be fatal.*   This one is hard to prove. The NTL officials state that less than one percent of the persons who have been in their sessions suffered psychological damage and most of those already had emotional problems. This question is related to the absence of any type of screening and the use of inadequately trained leaders in some groups.

7. *Groups do psychological damage.*   As indicated above, they can, but it is a function of leadership skills.

8. *Groups hypnotize their members.*   Some do.

9. *Groups are anti-intellectual.*   Frequently true. The focus is on "gut-level feelings."

10. *The group cheapens real emotion.*   Sometimes true. People who learn to act as others want them to, but don't really feel it, learn how to act but not feel.

11. *The groups themselves are guilty of the failings they most chastise in their members—phoniness.*   Could be true.

12. *The groups lead to emotional elitism.*   Very true. People who are more overt and act out feelings are seen as better than others.

13. *The groups have ridiculous jargon.*   True.

14. *The groups may get to be a cult.*   Actually the cults already exist with real between-groups rivalry.

15. *The groups are pointless.*   Hard to answer. Evaluation depends on whether subjugating oneself to the group with loss of identity is good.

16. *The groups may indeed cause stirring and wonderful things to happen, but these effects are not valid because they don't last.*   This is open to debate, but there is little evidence of the ability of group members to transfer learnings to other situations.

One of the more objective evaluations of encounter groups appeared in *The New York Times Magazine,* January 3, 1971 in an article by Dr. Bruce Maliver (36).

His major concern is directed toward the quality of leadership. He emphasizes the degree to which the therapist's personality may be his most important tool. Therefore training of therapists requires not only a recognition of pathology and group techniques, but also an understanding of his own needs as a prerequisite to permitting him to serve in the group leadership professional role. Concern for potential medical conditions, psychotic behavior, and the effect of group scapegoating of specific patients require both trained understanding and skill.

One of the hang-ups of the encounter group advocates is that in their desire to facilitate emotional spontaneity they feel people with academic training tend to be overly intellectual. The fallacy here of course is that academic training need not be permitted to proceed in that direction. Maliver (36) points out that

"To put down all talk as useless is absurd. Analysts aim at a synthesis of emotion and cognition; that is, they try to bring the adult capacities to bear on the emotional situations that were not well handled in childhood (p. 40)."

Maliver also notes that

"Many simply turn to encounter groups to experience what they miss in their own lives and to raise the emotional intensity level—they want to get "turned on." The need for stimulation is a basic life force, but it has an interesting quirk: the more you get, the more you need."

Moreover, since it is easier to get your charge through a controlled group, we are developing a generation of people who turn repeatedly to these groups to get easily what they won't try to accomplish themselves in the other areas of their lives.

For this author, Maliver's most devastating criticism comes from description of the degree of control exercised by the facilitators. Encounter groups contain the essence of emotional fascism. This reflects not political values, but a climate that enforces emotional conformity, that demands the correct behavior and the correct emotion at the designated time, and that suppresses criticism (36, p. 43).

Readers of Robert Lifton's *Thought Reform and the Psychology of Totalism* cannot help but recognize the elements of brainwashing found in some encounter groups (37).

Gordon (38) describing the typical need of the adolescent to discover where his individuality begins and ends, is distressed by the notion that one can only really discover himself by losing himself in the other. He states that "If one loses one's self in the other, if one no longer has anything private he can call his own, if all thoughts and feelings and attitudes are shared, have we not moved to a collective mind, an opening wedge to 1984?" He goes on to say "I would hope that adolescents are able to develop some equilibrium in the resolution of this conflict without moving to either pole, either retreat into a solitary existence or a surrender to the group. I hope they resolve the identity crisis so that they have an individuality but feel related to all of man."

Blanchard (39), writing under the provocative title of "Ecstacy Without Agony is Baloney," makes the point that many seeking heightened awareness are not aware of where the process can lead them. Deep awareness may permit the perceiver to discover much that is horrible about himself and the world. As a result he will find it difficult to keep his distance from injustice and will be unable to continue to pretend there is nothing he can do about it. Awareness makes a person keenly sensitive to his interdependence on others and his areas of similarity with all other men.

The quality of emphasis on the "here and now" found in encounter groups is examined by Halleck (40), who points out that our current orientation toward life in the present is not necessarily bad. A .person who focuses on today need not feel guilty for past mistakes or drive himself toward previously selected unrealistic goals. Unfortunately, however, a total emphasis on the present can be destructive. At its worst, it leads to an emphasis on style, on concern with problem solving divorced from the content of the problem itself and it rewards people for going through socially approved behaviors instead of seeking solutions. He feels that extreme reliance on style can produce nothing ultimately but despair. Halleck feels we are becoming a protest-oriented nation where gratification is coming from the protest itself. The gratification involved in the act of protesting sometimes causes it to continue long after the original demands are met. There is great tragedy inherent in this. Society desperately needs change, but change will not occur if protesters forget their original objective. He also makes a very significant point that emphasis on style can lead dissent to get out of hand.

THE COMMON DENOMINATOR IN GROUPS

Common in most groups is the feeling that basic to the development of any meaningful decisions or changes in behavior is the awareness and acceptance by group members of the needs or feelings that motivate their actions. Although groups may differ in the techniques they employ to facilitate self-understanding, all would accept the following concepts.

1. People need security in the group before they can afford to look at the underlying bases for their actions.

2. Topics form the basis for the group to pull together, but they are a vehicle instead of an end in itself. Therefore, "digressions" are not seen as such, but rather an attempt is made to see what need the new topic is representing, and how it relates to the one it followed.

3. The group strives to put across the feeling that indicates a continued acceptance of the individual despite possible rejection of his behavior or idea. This concept reflects the epitome of the successful group. When group members can feel the continued interest and concern in them as people and not feel rejected when others disagree with their ideas, the group has achieved the kind of security that maximizes spontaneity and puts the premium on individual difference. Jung (41) has stated the basic concept here in clear terms:

"I fully approve of the integration of the individual into society. However, I want to defend the inalienable rights of the individual; for individuality alone is the bearer of life and is, in these times, gravely threatened by degradation. Even in the smallest group the individual is acceptable only if he appears acceptable to the majority. He has to be content with toleration. But mere toleration does not improve the individual; on the contrary, toleration causes a sense of insecurity, by which the lonely individual who has something to champion may be seriously hindered. Without intrinsic value social relations have no importance."

4. The group is a place to test the reality of an idea and it is the role of the leader or other members to react honestly.

5. Group members will present their feelings not only through the words they use but also by physical behavior.

6. The more a member participates in a group the more he gets out of it.

7. The group is strengthened by recognizing individual differences instead of merely focusing on the bases of similarity or consensus.

8. People react in terms of their present perception of a situation. This perception, however, is based on past experiences. To the degree that present perceptions can be related to the past, it is possible for the person to determine if he wishes to continue in the same direction for the future.

These are but a few of the common denominators to be found among groups that see the major reason for group life as being the means for most effectively recognizing and gratifying the needs of the individual. Like it or not, none of us lives in a vacuum. The ultimate lesson we have to learn is that we can find ourselves only as we relate to others.

WHY THIS BOOK WAS WRITTEN

The need for group workers is clear and present. How, then, do we go about training in group work skills? One cannot train people to help others with just a book. The process is too complicated. A counselor not only has to try to understand one person, but, as is more vital in a group, he must also be aware of the interplay between several people. Obviously the demands on the counselor or group leader are for an extremely high level of skill and sensitivity.

But every day, laymen and professionals alike find themselves thrust into group environments. And they have to do the best job they can under the circumstances. Increasingly, they call for help in understanding the problems involved in group process. They want also a clear statement of appropriate techniques to employ. Therefore, this book is intended both to provide some immediate help for the beginner and to help potential group workers to recognize their need for formal professional training.

PHILOSOPHY OF TEXT

My philosophy is biased toward describing personality as an ever-changing thing. I believe that in dealing with an individual it is impossible to divide your relationship into levels. Accordingly, it is possible to use terms like teaching, counseling, or psychotherapy interchangeably without doing violence to the kinds of relationships that need to be developed in a group to achieve the goal of individual growth (42). With this point of view we can draw from the fields of education, social work, and psychology in our attempts to explore the problems and skills associated with group leadership. The following hypotheses about the nature of personality and the way to achieve behavior change represent my theoretical position.

1. To help people we need to start with their perception of a situation.
2. Help is most useful if it is initially directed toward the problem causing an individual (or group) the most immediate concern.
3. Individuals (groups) have an innate capacity to heal themselves, *if they are provided a setting where they can feel secure enough to examine their problems.*
4. As an individual (group) is helped to feel more secure, his need to shut out unwanted bits of information decreases. As he broadens his perceptions of the problem, he must by necessity include the values and attitudes expressed by society. Particularly in a group setting, this means that the solution to a problem, although it starts out as egocentric, must

ultimately resolve the paradox that man can only get his needs met through others.

5. A change in any part of an individual's life affects all other aspects of his being. A new perception today can cause all past experiences to have a new and different meaning.

Certainly these assumptions are not original. They can be traced back to the works of such people as Rogers, Wertheimer, Rank, Taft, Bergson, and Rousseau.

I have accepted as my concept of man a philosophy based on man's positive growth potential. Within this frame of reference, it is possible to start with the society we now have, including its many faults, and to try to help the individual perceive realistically what he can get from his environment. But of greater importance for social change, this point of view helps the counselor assist the individual in developing the security that he needs when he begins to investigate the ways in which he can modify his own environment. Under a democratic educational setting, youngsters learn to be responsible for their own behavior. However, as they grow to be more responsible, they also begin to recognize the ways in which the society that their parents have developed does not necessarily represent their own needs and goals. Probably the greatest failure of this democratic framework is that in it our leadership has not helped people learn a new kind of security that will go along with the changing environment which is now being created.

George Sharp, in his book, *Curriculum Development as Reeducation of the Teacher* (43), stated rather well the ethical and social problems involved in acting as a change agent.

> . . . he must realize that he is embarking on a program aimed at the deliberate change of society and individuals, and as he has no sanction to do either, he must work to develop the insights of others instead of imposing his own views. He must have a working knowledge of the dynamics of behavioral change not only in terms of theory but in terms of human behavior. Finally, he must understand the ethical and psychological requirements of the role he is to play and be able to control his own behavior in accordance with these requirements (p. 38).

SUMMARY

This chapter has traced the relationship of various types of groups to the social climate where they operate. It has defined different types of groups and has paid special emphasis to those groups currently most popular. Some of their strengths and weaknesses were explored.

The belief was presented that the appropriate type of group can foster a democratic society and allow for social change, yet permitting the individual to retain his uniqueness and integrity. The relationship of the leader's values, philosophy, and techniques to the type of group that will emerge was explored. Since it is believed any person seeking to develop leadership skills must first examine his beliefs and values, Chapter 2 explores the effect of different philosophical and psychological systems on the relationship the helping person will have with those he seeks to help.

Bibliography

1. Birnbaum, M. "Sense About Sensitivity Training," *Saturday Review of Literature,* November 15, 1969, p. 82.
2. Bradford, L., Gibb, J., and Benne, K. *T-Group Theory and Laboratory Method,* New York: Wiley, 1964.
3. Rogers, C. *Counseling and Psychotherapy,* Mass.: Houghton Mifflin, 1942.
4. Gorlow, L., Hoch, E., and Telschow, E. *The Nature of Nondirective Group Psychotherapy,* New York: T. C. Bureau of Publications, 1952.
5. Benne, K., and Sheats, P. "Functional Roles of Group Members," *Journal of Social Issues,* Vol. 4, 42–47, Spring 1948.
6. *Encounter Tapes,* Human Development Institute, Atlanta, Georgia.
7. *Body Talk—The Game of Feelings and Expression,* Psychology Today Games, Los Angeles, California.
8. *Blacks and Whites,* Psychology Today Games, Los Angeles, California.
9. Miller, G. A. "On Turning Psychology over to the Unwashed," *Psychology Today,* December 1969, pp. 53, 66.
10. Freud, S. *Group Psychology and the Analysis of the Ego,* London: International Psychoanalytic Press, 1922.
11. Loeser, L. *International Journal of Group Psychotherapy,* **VII,** No. 1, 5–19, January 1957.
12. Hollister, W. G. "Current Trends in Mental Health Programming in the Classroom," *Journal of Social Issues,* **15,** No. 1, 51–52, 1959.
13. Tillich, P. *The Courage To Be,* New Haven: Yale University Press, 1952.
14. May, R. "Existential Psychiatry, an Evaluation," *Journal of Religion and Health,* **I,** No. 1, 1961.
15. Allport, G. W. *Becoming,* New Haven: Yale University Press, 1955.
16. Allport, G. W. "Psychological Needs for Guidance," *Harvard Educational Review,* **32,** No. 4, 373–381, Fall 1962.
17. Frenkel-Brunswick, E., et al. "The Anti-Democratic Personality." In T. Newcomb, E. Maccoby, and L. Hartly (Eds.), *Readings in Social Psychology,* New York: Henry Holt, 1958.
18. May, R. "Freedom and Responsibility Reexamined," Speech 1962, APGA Convention, Chicago, Illinois.
19. Fullmer, D., and Bernard, H. *Counseling Content and Process,* Chicago: SRA, 1964.

20. Haley, J. *Strategies of Psychotherapy,* New York: Grove and Stratton, 1963.

21. Mahler, C. "Group Counseling," *The Personnel and Guidance Journal,* Vol. 49, No. 8, 601–610, April 1971.

22. Mahler, C., and Caldwell, E. *Group Counseling in the Secondary Schools,* Chicago: SRA, 1961, p. 25.

23. Slavson, S. R. *The Practice of Group Psychotherapy,* New York: International Universities Press, 1947.

24. Moreno, J. L. (Ed.). *Group Psychotherapy: A Symposium,* New York: Beacon House, 1946.

25. Klapman, J. W. *Group Psychotherapy: Theory and Practice,* New York: Grove and Stratton, 1946.

26. Laycock, S. R. "Mental Hygiene of Classroom Teaching," *Understanding the Child,* **16,** 39–43, April 1947.

27. Lifton, W. M. "Group Classroom Techniques," *Progressive Education,* **30,** 210–213, May 1953.

28. Super, D. E. "Group Techniques in the Guidance Program," *Educational and Psychological Measurement,* **9,** 496–510, Autumn 1949.

29. Wieder, G. S. *A Comparative Study of the Relative Effectiveness of Two Methods of Teaching a Thirty-Hour Course in Psychology in Modifying Attitudes Associated with Racial, Religious, and Ethnic Prejudice,* New York: New York University, 1951 (Doctor's thesis), Abstract: Dissertation Abstracts, 12, 163, No. 2, 1952.

30. Lake, D. "Sensitivity Training: Some Cautions and Hopes," in *Psychological Humanistic Education,* New York: State Department of Education, Fall 1969, p. 157.

31. Schutz, W. C. *Joy—Expanding Human Awareness,* New York: Grove Press, 1967.

32. Birnbaum, M. "Sense and Nonsense About Sensitivity Training," *Saturday Review,* November 15, 1969, p. 83.

33. Rakstis, T. "Sensitivity Training: Fad, Fraud or New Frontier," *Today's Health,* January 1970, p. 24.

34. Lakin, M. "Some Ethical Issues in Sensitivity Training," Paper presented at the meeting of Southeastern Psychological Association, New Orleans, February 1969.

35. Howard, J. *Please Touch,* New York: McGraw-Hill, 1970.

36. Maliver, B. "Encounter Groupers Up Against The Wall," *The New York Times Magazine,* January 3, 1971.

37. Lifton, R. J. *Thought Reform and the Psychology of Totalism,* New York: Norton, 1963.

38. Gordon, I. "The Needs of Children and Youth," Speech given at USOE Leadership Training Conference, Atlanta, Georgia, January 1970.

39. Blanchard, W. H. "Ecstacy Without Agony is Baloney," *Psychology Today*, January 1970, p. 64.

40. Halleck, S. "You Can Go to Hell with Style," *Psychology Today*, November 1969, p. 16.

41. Illing, H. A. "C. G. Jung on the Present Trends in Group Psychotherapy," *Human Relations*, **10**, 77–84, 1957.

42. Journal of the National Association of Deans of Women. "Counseling and Group Work," **X**, No. 3, 99–124, March 1947.

43. Sharp, G. *Curriculum Development as Reeducation of the Teacher*, New York: T. C. Bureau of Publications, 1951.

2 The Interdependence of Theory and Action

In our pragmatic society there is great appeal for counseling approaches that can be taught mechanistically and that can function without the need for the user to understand the dynamics of the approach. In a time when there is strong need for people who can offer helping relationships, and when great attention is being focused on the use of paraprofessionals, it is easy to see why drilling people in specific responses empathic or otherwise, without attention to theory, seems both logical and necessary (1). However, let us transfer this concept to another area more familiar to most of us and let us see if the logic holds up.

A family is stranded in a remote area and has been starving for days. They are rescued and brought to your house. Does it matter what food you offer them? Suppose you started with highly seasoned and rich foods. It is likely that despite their hunger the victims' stomachs would violently reject the food.

Suppose you find a person who has been exposed to severe cold and is suffering from frostbite. Would you compensate for the cold by applying equal amounts of heat? Our training in first aid teaches us that restoring circulation through gentle massage and lukewarm water is best.

The point of these illustrations is to demonstrate that in most situations alternative solutions are possible, that "common sense" does not always provide the best answers, and that past experiences or knowledge about how problems like these can be solved is very necessary. A person desiring to work with groups must ultimately understand his own value system and the approach which permits him to fulfill this system most

29

effectively. Then and only then does he have a yardstick he can use to evaluate his effectiveness or to plan subsequent action.

It is quite true that no one can yet prove the way the mind works. No one can demonstrate universal truths about concepts of soul or the nature of man. From earliest days man has coped with these questions by developing religions and ethical beliefs that they accept as true and then use as guidelines to determine future actions at decision-making points.

Years ago university psychology departments and philosophy departments were one. There is a logic to this, since the root of psychology still rests on questions of psyche—or soul. Psychology can become very scientific in its application of methodology, but it cannot divorce itself from the fact that the systems of psychology ultimately rest on different conceptions about the nature of man and where responsibility rests in deciding on appropriate actions or goals.

Because people strive for consistency, it is important that they recognize that assuming helping roles in society does not enable them to reject the assumptions they have accepted about man, values, and "what is right" in the other areas of their life. It is for this reason that the author some time ago traced the relationships between popular religions in our western culture and the counseling philosophies most closely associated with them (2).

THEORIES EXPLORED

Each person seeking to perfect his skill in a helping role needs to examine his own beliefs about:

- What is man, mind, and personality?
- What yardsticks need to be applied to decide if a decision is right?
- Does the desired end or goal justify the means used to attain it or, conversely, will the process used in a helping role determine the possible goal?
- Where do the rights of a person end and the rights of society begin (3)?

THEORIES OF PERSONALITY

Readers trying to answer questions about the nature of man, mind, and personality may find *Theories of Personality* by Calvin Hall and Gardner Lindzey (New York: John Wiley) helpful. In the beginning of their book as they explore various theories of personality, they set forth attributes that serve to differentiate one theory of personality from the next. Included are the following:

1. Is man purposeful in his life or are his actions just mechanical reactions based upon learned patterns acquired early in life?

2. Is man's behavior determined by conscious or unconscious motives? Or, as a third possibility, is normality really a function of the degree to which man is aware of his needs and motives?

3. To what degree is man's behavior a function of seeking rewards? A corollary of this question is the concept that the only responses that will be learned are those accompanied by a reward or reinforcement.

4. Does the theory focus on the outcomes of learning rather than on the learning process itself?

5. How critical are the effects of early childhood experiences? Is personality an ever-changing thing or is it jelled early in life?

6. Is there an objective reality that we all can perceive or is a person's perception a unique subjective experience?

SOCIAL FORCES

Each author recommends books he has found helpful to him in broadening his horizon. Few authors have done as comprehensive a job as Carroll E. Kennedy in relating readings to basic questions human relations workers have to face. With the kind permission of both Carroll E. Kennedy and the publishers of *Counselor Education and Supervision,* we are reprinting here excerpts from an article entitled "Considering the Social Processes in Human Development."

The writer has observed that consideration of the social processes of human development often finds students asking questions somewhat along the lines of the ten questions listed below.

"1. *What Does It Mean to Be Human?* Is there such a characteristic as humanness to distinguish man from other animals? How do we make this distinction? Is such a distinction a matter of degree—of quantity or quality? Are there criteria for humanness? If so, are they universal or does the concept humanness vary with time and nation? Are we more human today than we were two hundred or two thousand years ago?

2. *What Are Some Physical Influences in Social Development?* How does our native endowment influence our personality and performance? Are some people at birth more emotional than others? Are some races more intelligent than others? In what way does his physiological inheritance limit an individual? Can we predict and prescribe an individual's physiological inheritance? Are you happy or unhappy about this?

3. *What Do We Inherit Socially?* What of the social milieu into which a child is born? In what ways do the sounds, sights, people and plans surrounding an individual influence what he is or becomes? To what extent would an individual be the same regardless of where he was born? How true is it that culture gives us eyes to see with, tongues to speak with and hearts with which to feel? To what extent do we inherit a social niche and to what extent is ours a classless society?

4. *How Do We Appropriate Our Social Inheritance?* By what mechanism does what is outside the individual get into or direct the organism? Are there principles that can describe the ways in which the behavior of an individual is changed through contact with his environment?

5. *What Are the Forces That Shape the Socialization Process?* If there is a social flux or enveloping climate which shapes the individual, how does this climate change? Does the physiology and personality of the individual have any influence upon the effectiveness of the environment—does either change the characteristics of the environment? To what extent is the socialization process independent of geological and technological processes in the environment?

6. *What Are the Evidences of Socialization?* Is there a uniformity of behavior or a consistency of expectation that reflects the socialization process? How do the ways of perceiving and believing resulting from socialization processes in this country differ from those of other countries? Along what continua can we note social difference among the people of our own country?

7. *What Is the Significance of the Family as a Socialization Agent?* To what extent does emotional climate of the family parallel the emotional pattern of the child? In what respects is the socialization function of the family unique? Who determines the objectives of the family's socialization program—to what extent is this possible or desirable?

8. *What Is the Significance of Religious and Ethnic Factors as Socializing Agents?* To what extent are these factors an extension of the family? To what extent is it possible and helpful to identify distinctive socializing effects of religious and ethnic groups? What are some ways in which the preservation of ethnic differences adds to a nation's richness? How may such uniqueness retard development?

9. *What Is the Significance of School and Community Organizations as Socializing Agents?* To what extent is school distinct from home

and other community organizations as a socializing agent? How may the community activities influence self-concept? What are some socializing functions of government agencies? What concerns do urbanization raise? Are there any respects in which the State may be seen as a large self?

10. *What Is the Significance of Peers and Associates as Socializing Agents?* In what areas of the socialization process are these influences most critical? What socializing functions do peers perform that others may not do so well? Are there some individuals who would be more influenced by peers than others would? Under what circumstances might we expect these influences to be most significant?"

The ten questions listed above are simply one way of summarizing some of the kinds of ideas with which students are concerned in their thinking through of the processes of socialization. Similar types of questions are developed in discussion of physical and self-processes in human development.

The main point of Kennedy's article is that counselors are working with social beings in a social context. It is important that *as students* they be encouraged in the lifelong task of attempting to gain some awareness of the process of socialization and some appreciation for its subtle beauty and far-reaching implications. Such experiences seem to lead students to an increased sensitivity to and acceptance of themselves and others in the human situation.

HISTORICAL PERSPECTIVE

Any person striving to survey the multitude of answers and philosophies developed to answer questions about man and how he functions can rapidly become overwhelmed. Because the range is great, any attempts at summary of necessity do violence to the ideas being surveyed. Therefore, the reader is urged to use this chapter only as a springboard for further inquiry. At the end of this chapter there is a bibliography of books that deal more extensively with the individual approaches. The reader is also cautioned to recognize that because philosophies differ any attempt at grouping must reflect subjective judgment on the part of the author. Summaries do not neatly reflect the degrees of overlap among the theories grouped together.

Except for religions which believe that man's fate is predetermined, most include an element of human control over destiny. Whether the label used is "free will," or "instinct," or "humanistic self-determination," there is implied some force within the individual that affects his future.

TABLE 1. Common Elements in Psychological Theories

		Mind-Body Relationships	
		McDougall (4) James-Lange (5) Cannon (6)	
Emphasis on Emotions and Affect		Emphasis on Tasks and Behavior	
Analytic—looking into history for causes→ data→analysis→diagnosis→prognosis→ treatment[a]	Situational—Phenomeno-logical here and now—posits life force, homeostasis	Genetic Theorists	Rationalists and Learning Theorists
Freud (7) Adler (8) Jung (9) Horney (10) Sullivan (11) Erikson (12)	Titchener (13) Rank (14) Taft (15) Rogers (16) Snygg & Combs (17) Maslow (18) Prescott (19) Lecky (20) May (45)	Sheldon (12) Kraeplin (22) Eysenck (23) Cattell (24) Jung (9) Salter (25) Murphy (26) (Bio-Social)	Ellis (27) Pavlov (28) Dollard and Miller (29) Mowrer (30) Skinner (31) Kelly (32) Glasser (33) (Reality Therapy) Otto (Human Potential) (34) Lewin (Field Theory) (35) Korzybski (36) (Semantics) Wolpe (37)

Philosophical and/or Religious Values Closely Related

Orthodox Fundamental Religions— Judaism, Catholicism and Protestantism	Bergson (Elan Vital) Rousseau Chasidim (Jewish) Zen Unitarianism Universalism Humanists Existentialists	Predetermination in some Protestant beliefs	Pragmatism Communism

[a] Counselor has major role in setting goals and directions of relationship.

Many have chosen to divide these forces into two camps—those of the mind and those of the body. This dualistic thinking persists today. Table 1 graphically represents the way this dichotomy is expressed in the varied theories of man and the associated implied therapeutic approaches dealing with man in trouble.

Philosophies Emphasizing Emotions and Affect.   Although no philosophy deals exclusively with affect or cognition, on the left side of Table 1 are those philosophies that place an *emphasis* on emotions and affect. They are divided into two groups. One group is composed of those theories that place a primal emphasis on early childhood experiences and believe a resolution of problems initiated at those times require approaches that seek to help the patient recall and relive the crisis points in their life. The other group places their emphasis on dealing with the feelings and emotions experienced by the client today. They believe that by reshaping the client's perceptions of situations he is currently experiencing, it is also possible to help him reperceive and react differently to past experiences. One of the other major differences between these two groups comes from the relative activity and degree of control exercised by the counselor.

TABLE 2.   Major Emphasis in Psychological Theories

Man Is Purposive	Major Role of Reward	Importance of Self-Individual (Ego?)	Centrality of Society (Environment)	Unconscious Motivation
Allport	Dollard	Adler	Lewin	Freud
Murray	Miller	Rogers	Rogers	Jung
Goldstein	Freud (Pleasure Principle)			
		Allport	Allport	Murray
Rogers	Murphy (Canalization)	Lecky (Self-consistency)	Murray	
Angyal	Learning Theories	Fromm		
Adler		Lewin		
		Otto (Human Potential)		

Table 2 groups the psychological theories on the basis of major emphasis. Not too long ago philosophies were categorized as being either directive or nondirective, terms used to imply whether it was the counselor or the client who held control of the direction, pace, and content of sessions. Research studies demonstrated clearly that in any interaction between two people both were always affected by the other's behavior, whether it was verbal or nonverbal. It became apparent that even in choosing from the material presented by the client, counselor values and professional opinion were operating. By paying attention to some areas while ignoring others the counselor was subtly able to influence client behavior. As a result of these studies concern has shifted from questions of counselor versus client control to questions about the degree to which the counselor is aware of the way in which his behavior is serving as a stimulus to which the client responds. With this shift in focus has come associated concerns about the counselor's awareness of his own needs.

Current differentiation between counselor approaches has shifted to the ways in which the counselor is open and honest. Focus is on the counselor sharing with clients his awareness of the degree to which his (the counselor's) values are affecting his ability to respond to the client in ways that truly permit the client freedom of choice.

Returning to Table 1, let us see how counselor values affect counselor function. Distinctions between the two groups found on the "mind" side of the chart can best be seen if one examines the religions believed most congruent with the different frames of reference presented (38).

Religious fundamentalists are best characterized by beliefs about the unitary nature of truth (usually God given), the responsibility of the priest or religious intermediary to help people proceed in the paths of righteousness, and the hierarchical nature of responsibility—man is his brother's keeper. Many religions in this group also posit negative drives in man that can lead to destruction if they are not controlled. Man is basically animal, sinful, and needs to be saved from the forces of evil within him.

In opposition, the other group includes philosophies that see a positive life-giving force in man which strives (if permitted) to move him toward a more meaningful and satisfying existence. Whether this force is termed "a spark of the divine in man," or "homeostasis," or the "élan vital" the concept is similar. If man can be helped to truly consider what he believes will make him happy, he will choose the best answers both for himself and for society.

The role of the priest or religious leader in these religions is to serve as a catalyst to insure a secure setting where man can be freed enough from pressures so he can attend to his own innermost strivings for within them lie the answers to his questions. Instead of seeing feelings and senses as bad, they are seen as the key to existence. Accordingly, many counseling approaches developed from this group of philosophies focus on sensations and the pleasure principle in life. Later, in this text, there is a discussion of the way in which some of these approaches can lead either to an egocentric preoccupation or can help people discover how to meet their needs within a society of other men with whom they are interdependent. The movement of self to others occurs in the following way. A person thinks to himself:

> I want what I want.
>
> I want you to give me what I want.
>
> But you won't give me what I want unless I give you what you want.
>
> Therefore I can only meet my needs through recognizing and meeting the needs of others.

Philosophies Emphasizing Tasks and Behavior (see right side of Table 1). Many major philosophies today depend on a view of man as a reactive mechanism. Some focus on innate characteristics that predetermine the nature of responses which can be expected. Others view man somewhat like a computer who is being progressively programmed to respond to specific stimuli in specified ways. Most in this category focus on obtaining socially desired responses. The techniques primarily consider how best to insure getting a man to respond in the desired ways. The counselor in some ways acts somewhat like an offstage stage manager serving to the best of his ability to insure that clients like the right or appropriate societally approved responses. It should be immediately obvious that this conditioned-response approach makes the role of the agency deciding on "the" correct response very critical. Individual needs are considered only to the degree that they do not conflict with obtaining the desired response.

The genetic theorists operate from predetermined ideas about the relationship of specific body types on defined personality patterns. Therefore, they tend to assist the client in accepting the limitations that his particular heritage imposes. The client decides within these limitations how best to meet his desired needs.

The rationalists and learning theorists introduce another major dimension. They separate man from other animals by his ability to think. By this they mean that man's ability to translate acts, thoughts, and feelings into symbolic form (words), permits him to examine these concepts, external to himself and, understanding the laws of logic, he is then able to examine which of the lines of thought provide the most rational result. A recent advertisement for a book published by one advocate of this point of view was headed by the statement "You feel the way you think." The task of the counselor within this framework is to teach the client how to manipulate verbal symbols or behaviors so that he arrives at the most socially approved response. Some of the theorists within this grouping place the major stimulus to which clients respond as arising from "society," "the environment," or "the field" where the client finds himself. Accordingly counselors of this persuasion find it appropriate to manipulate the environment to obtain the stimulus they desire, to insure the preferred client response.

In describing these philosophies the term "preferred response" has been used frequently. Unlike previous groups discussed, where goals came from above or from the individual, the rationalists and learning theorists are dependent on "society" for determination of what are to be the desired goals. Within this framework one can go from the brain-washing used by totalitarian societies to a consensual determination as to what will be accepted as "good" or "real."

Importance of Philosophy not Technique.   The preceding discussion focused on theory or matters of faith. There are those who consider such issues unimportant. They adopt as their yardstick the pragmatic question "Does it work?"

A carpenter who doesn't know how to use tools could easily use his wrench as a hammer. Because it is not shaped properly it may not be very effective and may gouge the wood in the process. If all that mattered was to drive the nail in, the damage to the wood surface would be immaterial. "Does it work" then must be answered qualitatively.

In helping people, however, we like to feel we know the results of our efforts. Moreover, if we are ethical people, we feel responsible for the effect of our efforts on our client. Inescapably then we find ourselves seeking yardsticks to measure the success of our approach.

At this point the counselor soon realizes he can adopt at least three criterion measures for use in evaluation of the counseling as a helping process.

1. Does the client behave, think, or act as the counselor desires?
2. Does the client feel satisfied with the conclusion he has reached for himself?
3. Does the client's decision coincide with important societal values?

Wherever the term client is used one could substitute the word "group."

Eclecticism—What It Is and What It Is Not.   To insure clarity it is important to state that this text accepts an eclectic approach to the use of techniques, but believes that there cannot be an eclectic philosophy or value system.

Man rarely is comfortable with limits. He much prefers to feel free to meet each situation and to use the approach that fits best. This idealistic objective assumes that the counselor in his counseling role is quite capable of not only changing his way of behaving with each client, but also of changing value systems. Here of course is the rub. How does one determine that "this" client hasn't the capacity to accept responsibility for his life but the next client does? Such an approach not only demands a differential diagnosis for each client and assumes the counselor's ability to function within a wide range of counseling models but, by raising the question itself, it also conveys the counselor's inability to truly believe in the worth and potential of *all* clients.

Move this situation into the religious field. Should the counselor be able to act as priest, rabbi, or zen buddhist with equal ability and conviction? Is one set of beliefs antithetical to another?

A close examination of writers who fight for an eclectic approach quickly reveals that they, like every man, have a preferred value system they use to decide the appropriateness of their actions.

What then is the role of eclecticism? An examination of the way effective counselors *function* demonstrates an amazing similarity of techniques employed and relationships used. The desired eclecticism then is in freedom to use a wide range of tools and techniques, while employing them consistently within an operating framework. Fiedler (39) found that therapists from different schools agreed on the characteristics which make for an ideal therapeutic relationship. All seem to agree on the importance of the helping person being able to be empathic, understanding, have a strong interest in the client and a desire to help him, openness (genuineness, self-congruence) or as it now is frequently labeled—authenticity in his relationships with clients, and confidence in the theory or method he uses.

Carl Rogers (40) many years ago presented a discussion of the differences between rigidity and consistency. He pointed out that you can never know if an approach or theory works until you have tried it out. If you quit halfway you will never know the results you would have achieved if you had followed the theory consistently. When you do complete your exploration, then, and only then, should you decide if the results suggest modification. At this point, an inability to modify based on proven error points to rigidity. The consistent person will modify his theory and then hold to it until it has had an equal trial before revision is considered again.

Theories, like oil and water, are not always compatible. The competent behavioral scientist will use all tools available that are consistent with his philosophical value system.

One last comment for those free souls who dislike being forced to recognize that they cannot, like a chameleon, change colors to fit their surroundings. Even if they could shift techniques and relationships easily they could, just as easily, lose their clients. Part of a client's willingness to submit to the relationship is based on the results he hopes will occur.

The client's security in the situation depends on knowing what takes place in the counseling setting. When the counselor shifts from session to session in his roles, the client must spend time figuring out the response needed to cope with the new game rules. The confused client who does not know if the counselor will offer fish, flesh, or good red herring, stalls and waits until he can be sure another shift will not come before he has adjusted to the latest one. Client security determines the speed of movement in the counseling setting. Movement will occur best when the limits of the relationship remain stable and understandable.

Brammer (41), in a closely reasoned article on eclecticism, defines eclecticism as an openness to all research findings on counseling. His review of Shostrom and Riley (42), Raskin (43), and Sundland and Barker (44), suggests that good therapists have much in common, but that differences come from matters of emphasis. As shown below, Brammer sees the counselor going through three steps. First, he needs conceptual "hooks" on which to hang his observations and experiences. Second, he needs to review past knowledge to develop his own point of view. And third, he needs to know his own personality thoroughly so that his counseling style reflects *his* stated theory and methods.

Observation, experiment, and reflection on client relationships. plus Familiarization with historical and contemporary points of view on theory and experience with rationally selected methods. plus Awareness of one's unique personhood.	→	An emerging eclectic view unique to each counselor and psychotherapist—an individual style.	→	Ultimately, a general theory of personality structure and behavior change.

FIGURE 1.   Development of a unique style of counseling and psychotherapy.

Group Approaches Follow Psychological Theories.   The preceding material dealing with the variety of philosophies about the nature of man has included references to "schools" of thought usually named after the person who developed the theory. Although many eminent social psychologists have explored group dynamics, such as Lippitt (46, power), Cattell (47, group leadership), Cartwright (48, group pressures), Guetzkow

(49, group roles), and Hare, Borgatta, and Bales (50, group counseling, small groups, social interaction), most of the operational techniques in group counseling tend to be offshoots of theories about personality and techniques to effect personality or behavior change.

Readers seeking to discover more about the application of specific theories to group practice may find the following list a beginning point for further exploration. Each practitioner, of course, has modified the general theory in his own way.

Theory	Group Worker
Freud (7, unconscious motivation)	Slavson (51), Bach (52), Shostrom (53)
Adler (8, ego psychology)	Dreikurs (50), Otto (34), Dinkmeyer (54), Edelson (60)
May (45) and Rogers (16) (existentialism, humanism)	Rogers (55), Moustakis (56), Lifton
Jung (9, gestalt)	Perls (57)
Skinner (31, behaviorism, conditioning)	Wolpe (37), Rose (61)
Lewin (35, field theory)	Glasser (33)
Murphy (26, biosocial)	Schutz (58)

SUMMARY

Every person has adopted beliefs about the nature of man and the way his behavior is determined. These beliefs seen in an individual's religion or ethical value system are found equally present in the helping relationship as in other areas of a person's life. It is important for a person to know himself and what he believes in because only then can he select approaches which are most congruent with his beliefs.

Tools and techniques used to facilitate human growth are essentially neuter in their character. It is only when they are applied for a specific purpose or to achieve a defined goal that tools become a part of a philosophy or psychological system.

The following chapter describes a wide variety of techniques and tools used to help either clients or groups clarify their goals or change their behavior. Although some techniques are used slightly differently in group settings, their characteristics and limitations remain basically the same.

Bibliography

1. Carkhuff, R. R., and Truax, C. B. "Lay Mental Health Counseling: The Effects of Lay Group Counseling," *Journal of Consulting Psychology*, 1965, **29**, pp. 426–431.

2. Lifton, W. M. "Counseling and the Religious View of Man," *The Personnel and Guidance Journal*, March 1953, pp. 366–367.

3. Kennedy, C. E. "Considering the Social Processes in Human Development," *Counselor Education and Supervision*, Vol. III, No. 2, Winter 1964, pp. 84–97.

4. McDougall, W. *An Introduction to Social Psychology*, Boston: Luce, 1908.

5. Lange, J. W. *Psychology, Briefer Course*, New York: Holt, 1892.

6. Cannon, W. B. *The Wisdom of the Body*, New York: Norton, 1939.

7. Freud, S. *The Basic Writings of Sigmund Freud*, New York: Random House, 1938.

8. Adler, A. *Practise and Theory of Individual Psychology*, New York: Harcourt Brace, 1927.

9. Jung, C. G. *Psychological Types*, New York: Harcourt Brace, 1923.

10. Horney, K. *Neurosis and Human Growth*, New York: Norton, 1950.

11. Sullivan, H. S. *The Interpersonal Theory of Psychiatry*, New York: Norton, 1953.

12. Erikson, E. H. *Childhood and Society*, New York: Norton, 1964.

13. Titchener, E. B. in C. Hall and G. Lindzey, *Theories of Personality*, New York: Wiley, 1957, p. 5.

14. Rank, O. *Will Therapy and Truth and Reality*, New York: Knopf, 1947.

15. Taft, J. *The Dynamics of Therapy in a Controlled Relationship*, New York: Macmillan, 1933.

16. Rogers, C. *On Becoming a Person*, Boston: Houghton Mifflin, 1961.

17. Snygg, D., and Combs, A. *Individual Behavior*, 2nd ed., New York: Harper & Row, 1959.

18. Maslow, A. H. *Motivation and Personality*, 2nd ed., New York: Harper & Row, 1970.

19. Prescott, D. A. *Emotion and the Educative Process*, Washington, D.C.: Council on Education, 1938.

20. Lecky, P. *Self Consistency*, New York: Island Press, 1945.

21. Sheldon, W. H. *The Varieties of Temperament,* New York: Harper, 1942.

22. Kretschmer, E. *Physique and Character,* New York: Harcourt Brace, 1925.

23. Eysenck, H. J. *Dimensions of Personality,* London: Rootlodge and Kegan Paul, 1947.

24. Cattell, R. B. *Personality: A Systematic, Theoretical and Factual Study,* New York: McGraw-Hill, 1950.

25. Salter A. *Conditioned Reflex Therapy,* New York: Creative Age Press, 1949.

26. Murphy, G. *Historical Introductions to Modern Psychology,* New York: Harcourt Brace, 1949.

27. Ellis, A. *Reason and Emotion in Psychotherapy,* New York: Stuart, 1970.

28. Pavlov, I. *Conditioned Reflexes and Psychiatry,* New York: International Publishers, 1941.

29. Dollard, J., and Miller, N. *Personality and Psychotherapy,* New York: McGraw-Hill, 1950.

30. Mowrer, O. H. *Psychotherapy: Theory and Research,* New York: Ronald Press, 1953.

31. Skinner, B. F. "Two Types of Conditioned Reflex and a Pseudotype," *J. Gene Psychol,* 1935, **12**, 66–77.

32. Kelly, G. *The Psychology of Personal Constructs,* New York: Norton, 1955.

33. Glasser, W. *Reality Therapy,* New York: Harper & Row, 1965.

34. Otto, H. *Human Potentialities: The Challenge and the Promise,* St. Louis: Green, 1968.

35. Lewin, K. *Principles of Topological Psychology,* New York: McGraw-Hill, 1936.

36. Korzybski, A. *Science and Sanity,* Lancaster, Pa.: Science Press, 1941.

37. Wolpe, J. *Psychotherapy by Reciprocal Inhibition,* Stanford, Cal.: Stanford University Press, 1958.

38. DeGrazia, S. *Errors in Psychotherapy and Religion,* Garden City, N.Y.: Doubleday, 1952.

39. Fiedler, F. "The Concept of an Ideal Therapeutic Relationship," *Journal Consult Psych,* 1950, 14, 235–245.

40. Rogers, C. *Client Centered Therapy,* Boston: Houghton Mifflin, 1951.

41. Brammer, L. M. "Eclecticism Revisited," *Personnel and Guidance Journal,* Vol. 48, No. 3, November 1969, pp. 192–197.

42. Shostrom, E. L. and Riley, C. M. "Parametric analysis of psychotherapy." Unpublished manuscript, Institute of Therapeutic Psychology, 1967.

43. Raskin, N. J. The psychotherapy research project of the American Acadamy of Psychotherapists. Proceedings of the American Psychological Association Convention. Washington, D.C.: APA, 1965. Pp. 353–354.

44. Sundland, D. M., and Barker, E. N. "The Orientations of Psychotherapists," *Journal of Consulting Psychology,* 1962, **26**, 201–202.

45. May, R. *Love and Will,* New York: Norton, 1969.

46. Lippitt, R., Polansky, N., and Rosen, S. "The Dynamics of Power: A Field Study of Social Influence in Groups of Children," *Human Relations,* 1952, 5, 37–64.

47. Cattell, R. B. "New Concepts for Measuring Leadership in Terms of Group Syntality," *Human Relations,* 1951, 4, 161–184.

48. Cartwright, D. "Achieving Change in People: Some Applications of Group Dynamics Theory," *Human Relations,* 1951, 4, 381–392.

49. Guetzkow, H. (Ed.) *Groups, Leadership and Men: Research in Human Relations,* Pittsburgh: Carnegie Press, 1951.

50. Hare, P. A., Borgatta, E. F., and Bales, R. (Eds.). *Small Groups: Studies in Social Interaction,* New York: Knopf, 1955.

51. Slavson, S. R. *A Textbook in Analytic Group Psychotherapy,* New York: International Universities Press, 1964.

52. Bach, G. R. *Intensive Group Psychotherapy,* New York: Ronald Press, 1954.

53. Shostrom, E., and Brammer, L. *Therapeutic Psychology,* 2nd ed., New Jersey: Prentice Hall, 1968 (Chapter XI, Group Principles and Methods).

54. Dinkmeyer, D. C., and Muro, J. *Group Counseling Theory and Practice,* Illinois: F. E. Peacock, 1971.

55. Rogers, C. *Carl Rogers on Encounter Groups,* New York: Harper & Row, 1970.

56. Moustakas, C. *Individuality and Encounter,* Cambridge, Mass.: Doyle, 1968.

57. Perls, F. S. *Gestalt Therapy Verbatim,* Lafayette, Cal.: Real People Press, 1969.

58. Schutz, W. *Joy,* New York: Grove Press, 1967 (Chapter 2, The Body).

59. Dreikurs, R. *Group Psychotherapy and Group Approaches: Collected Papers,* Chicago: Alfred Adler Institute, 1960.

60. Edelson, M. *Ego-Psychology, Group Dynamics and the Therapeutic Community,* New York: Grune & Stratton, 1964.

61. Rose, S. "A Behavioral Approach to Group Treatment with Children," *The Socio-Behavioral Approach to Social Work,* New York: Council on Social Work Education, 1969.

3 The Tools and Techniques Involved in the Helping Process

"No man can reveal to you aught but that which already lies half asleep in the dawning of your knowledge."

FROM THE PROPHET BY KAHLIL GIBRAN[1]

The degree of similarity between a two-person learning situation and a three-person or group situation is great. Much of the theory of how people learn and how to effect change has equal applicability in both settings. However, as was described in Chapter 1, groups do contain some unique characteristics. Through the sharing of perceptions, groups provide the vehicle for:

· Reduction of anxiety.

· A setting for reality testing.

· The establishment of a consensual validity.

· The dissemination of information.

· The development of skills.

· Emotional support to face threat.

Consistent with the above characteristics, groups typically are formed initially with at least one of the following objectives in mind:

· Information dispensing.

· Skill development.

· Decision making.

· Self-understanding.

[1]Reprinted from *The Prophet* by Kahlil Gibran with permission of the publisher, Alfred A. Knopf, Inc. Copyright 1923 by Kahlil Gibran; renewal copyright 1937 by Administrators C. T. A. of Kahlil Gibran Estate, and Mary G. Gibran.

- Reality testing.
- Task orientation.
- Power base to effect change.

If one avoids the semantic traps associated with specific philosophies discussed in Chapter 2, it is quite correct to view the task of the group, regardless of function, as an educational learning problem.

COMMUNICATION

Before examining some of the more basic techniques, it is important to have a prior understanding of the way communication provides the key to the learning process. Essentially the major problem in our society is a breakdown in communication. Not only do people have trouble understanding each other, but frequently a person is not sure of himself. The first and hardest lesson for the beginner to learn is that you cannot assume that the other person meant what you assumed his words to mean. Not only do words frequently have a variety of meanings, but also the way in which they are said can vastly alter their intent. Shakespeare understood this well when he had one of his characters say, "The lady doth protest too much, methinks." One of the skills most desired by maturing youth is to know whether a girl really means no when she says it. To review, then, words are defined with a variety of meanings in the dictionary, they change meaning according to the setting, and they can reflect the exact reverse of their stated meanings. To further compilicate the issue, people use ideas to express feelings that are important to them. It is almost as if words were a car, with the feelings being its passenger, and with the passenger being more vital than the car itself. The major problem, then, is to see how one can learn what the other person is trying to convey. Until one understands the feelings, one cannot begin to help him (or them) face the issue to be solved.

The first place where anyone can start is with his own experience. "What could the words I hear possibly mean?" Having explored the range of possible alternatives, a person next tries to examine the context in which the words occurred to select the most likely meaning. He still cannot be sure that his own needs are not causing him to distort what he has heard, so that ultimately all he can do is to check if his idea is what the other person actually meant.

Sometimes, however, understanding the meaning one has given to a word is not enough. In some situations, insight may depend on experiences as yet unknown to the person. Words can cause insights to develop only if they can rearrange prior meanings into a new format (1).

This attempt at precision of meaning is really at the very heart of the helping process in which several things are going on at once. To clarify the relationship in the helping process, the person being helped will be called the client. For the client who hears from another his idea exactly as he meant it, there is the wonderful feeling of being understood, of not being alone in the world, and of having someone else available who can help him see if he is getting across to others the things he desires. For the client who sees someone else trying to understand, but who finds that his words do not seem to convey the exact meaning he desires, there is still the opportunity to try to redefine himself. In this process of re-definition—this attempt to clear away ambiguity—frequently the speaker becomes clearer not only about what he wants to say, but also about what his true feelings really are (2).

The skilled group worker needs more than a text to train his sensitivities to hearing and responding to others. The group leader not only needs to have knowledge of others, but also has to be sure his own house is in order. We do not hear others say things which, if we recognize them, would force us to see unacceptable things in ourselves. The more we need to block out from hearing, the less we can help others. Although this chapter can discuss techniques, no true learning can take place for the reader until he has a chance to see if he can use the ideas himself. He also needs help from others who can call his attention to the things he typically doesn't hear or respond to.

Thus, the primary goal in the helping process is to assist others in examining their words or behavior to see if they represented what the client wished to communicate. With this as our goal let's explore some tools which help people to clarify their thoughts. The process of re-flecting back to the client the literal dictionary meaning of what he says is called "reflection of content."

Obviously, in order to understand the literal meaning of words, one must have a broad education not always achieved in school. Kinsey reported that knowing the meaning of the phrase "to turn a trick" spelled the difference between success and failure in his interviews with prostitutes. Today, it is equally important to understand the language of the hippie or the black. As one measure of your sophistication try the following test on yourself.

Black Vocabulary Test

Directions: Choose the word or words that best complete the following statements or answers to the following questions.

1. To say "Give me a play" means to give (a) a chance (b) a handshake (c) an invitation (d) encouragement

2. To say that something is good, blacks say that it is (a) mellow (b) groovy (c) lovely (d) straight
3. A common way blacks address a girl is (a) good morning (b) hey chick (c) say hammer (d) hey beautiful
4. When blacks say they are "rapping" they mean (a) hitting someone (b) talking (c) knocking (d) prison term
5. To be well dressed is to be (a) pressed (b) draped (c) clean (d) conditioned
6. To say someone is "sidditty" is to imply that he thinks he is (a) better (b) good looking (c) rich (d) superior
7. What is a "set"? (a) a group (b) a party (c) a gang (d) a stage
8. When someone's "jaws are tight" he is (a) fearful (b) angry (c) strong (d) hungry
9. To say someone is "heavy" means he is (a) overweight (b) thin (c) intelligent (d) good looking
10. A synonym for car is (a) wheels (b) short (c) ride (d) machine
11. A "box" is a (a) car (b) casket (c) wooden box (d) a hi fi
12. A very attractive female is (a) a babe (b) a cutie (c) a swinger (d) a fox
13. To describe a girl with a beautiful figure it is said she is (a) a looker (b) hip (c) a swinger (d) fat (phat)
14. Which word is most out of place? (a) squib (b) blood (c) gray (d) spook
15. A "jam" is (a) a fix (b) shoes (c) a dance (d) a record

Answers: 10. (b); 11. (d); 12. (d); 13. (d); 14. (c); 15. (d).
1. (c); 2. (a); 3. (c); 4. (b); 5. (c); 6. (d); 7. (b); 8. (b); 9. (c);

When we reflect back to the person what he is *trying* to say, or the latent desires in his words, the process is called *"reflection of feeling."* Reflection of feeling is particularly tricky. If we can help put into words a feeling of which the person was dimly aware, but had not found a clear way to state, we will help him by this clarifying process. If, however, we pick up feelings which we feel are there but which the client is either not ready to examine or which represent our distortion of his feelings, we may be in for trouble. The attempt to reflect these unconscious needs or to link up past experiences with present behavior is called *"interpretation."* Since any linking of past with present or any predicting of future behavior has to come from the perceiver's own experiences or logic, the success of this technique will be vitally dependent upon its accuracy and the concurrent help given to the person to face frightening or unacceptable ideas. Since interpretation is so dependent on a vast experience and an ability to judge a person's readiness for threatening material, it is a device best reserved for only the more skilled person.

Recently, the term *confrontation* has become quite popular. It is used in different ways. The lay concept refers to open, overt, hostile taking of a position in opposition to others. In therapeutic settings it tends to refer to a process designed to face people with the way they are perceived by others, as contrasted with what the client would like to believe others are seeing. Brammer and Shostrom (3) develop a continuum that reflects levels of client awareness. Their five levels are reflection, clarification, reflectation (counselor moves to point client has reached implicitly *but* beyond his conscious awareness), confrontation (counselor moves to point client has reached implicitly *but* unconsciously), and finally depth interpretation.

Since most helping relationships demand ways of relating that are not part of the typical social situation, a technique called *"structuring"* is used. In essence, "structuring" involves either a statement of the rules of the helping process or an understanding of such rules by the way the therapist or group leader does or does not act in specific situations. In a group setting, the initial group leader may take the responsibility of indicating the limits to be imposed on the group by the setting in which they are meeting or by the nature of the group. In other words, he is indicating the outside limits imposed by society. Rules developed inside the group reflect a philosophy along with its concept of how the leader can be most helpful. In this book, the leader's role in "structuring" is seen as that of assisting the group to become aware of problems they need to solve and helping them learn to work together in setting up the rules by which they will function together.

Because many people coming into a helping situation expect the expert to take over, it is important that the initial leader make clear early in the sessions what the group can or cannot expect from him. Since the group will be more responsive to his behavior than his words, it is vital that there be consistency between what he says and does. The leader or counselor has been referred to as the initial leader because, as early as possible, it is the leader's objective to have members of the group assume responsibility for directing and assisting their fellow members. The initial group leader not only provides a model for the leadership role, but frequently will live out other group member roles too, thereby providing a range of group role models.

In the initial sessions of a group, structuring will include, among many others, such questions as, "What is the group going to do?" "What is the leader's role?" "How are people treated here?" "What are the acceptable things to talk about?" "How confidential will the contents of group sessions be?" "Isn't it a sign of weakness to admit confusion over ideas or goals?" Although most of the structuring occurs early in the group's life, structuring can continue as long as the group needs to develop ways of handling new situations.

Other more common tools that all of us have had a chance to experience include *questioning, supplying information, clarifying an idea* (summarizing all the points raised that bear on each other), and (probably most important of all) the use of *silence* to allow the other person to think his own thoughts in his own way.

Recently there has been a tendency in the field of counseling to believe that probably none of these tools in itself is of great importance. The touchstone of the helping process is, now more than ever, felt to be the way the person who is trying to help indicates to another that he really cares about him. It is a relationship that cannot be faked. One way to let others know that you feel that what they say is really important is to constantly look at them. To actually understand them, you need to see the facial expressions and gestures that go along with their words. Try the following experiment yourself.

Knowing that constant eye contact is helpful, try this on a friend: Tell him that you wish to have him help you learn how to convey interest in a client. Ask him to let you know when he feels you are with him and when he feels you are wool-gathering. For the first few moments try your hardest to listen to the feelings the client is expressing. Then, while still focusing your eyes on the client's face imagine a scene taking place behind him, and, in a sense, look right through him to the scene beyond. Return again to a real attempt to listen. This time, however, spend your time thinking of how you would like to answer him. In other words, although you are concerned with his problem, your major attention is on what it means to you. If you are successful in playing these roles you will discover to your dismay that when you are not really listening to what he is trying to express, you are fooling no one but yourself.

NONVERBAL COMMUNICATION

People often communicate by their behavior feelings that contradict the words they are using. The saying "action speaks louder than words" holds equally true in the group situation. Since the objective in most groups is to facilitate communication, the initial group leader needs to help the group learn to read and label behaviors they observe, so that this level of communication is not overlooked.

Behavioral cues seem to fall into at least three categories: cues that reflect avoidance behavior; cues that signify tension, concern, or other emotions; and cues that have symbolic meaning within a cultural context and which to be understood demand an awareness of their meaning to the individual, based on his background and previous experience. I would like to examine each of these categories (4).

Probably the easiest cues for a group or the leader to recognize are those that reflect emotions of pleasure or anger. From earliest infancy we have learned to respond to the meaning of a smile, a frown, the clenching of teeth, the making of a fist, the upraised hand as if to strike, the beckoning motion that precedes being caressed, or the upraised eyebrow which we tend to interpret as questioning. Less apparent to the observer are physical cues signifying the internal pressure felt by the individual. Perspiration on the brow is fairly visible, but the individual who wraps his arms around himself as if to hold his body in place, or who presses one hand against the other so that the knuckles whiten, or who in a seated position has one knee over the other and begins to swing his leg almost like a metronome, pacing the swings to the degree of tension— these and other similar characteristics, although easily observable, tend not to be so frequently noticed.

The second group of cues dealing with avoidance behavior tend to be more subtle. Since their very purpose is to avoid notice, they tend to involve activities which do not intrude on others but, by their very nature, inhibit interaction with other members of the group. From the very socially acceptable constant writing of notes so that there is no eye contact with other members of the group, to the mouthful of gum or pencils which prevents speech, or in even less obvious fashion, the movement by an individual of his chair out of the circle by thrusting his chair back just a few inches, all signify ways of moving out of reach and minimizing involvement. The member who buries his face in his hands or gazes off into space is also obviously avoiding eye contact.

Even less noticeable than these behaviors are those that are socially acceptable but that by their nature assist the person in avoiding open involvement in group discussion. The individual who takes notes for the group, volunteers to serve the food, answers the doorbell, or provides a variety of housekeeping functions, signifies by his behavior his desire to be helpful and liked by group members, yet in the process also successfully avoids personal involvement.

Less socially acceptable behaviors include either late arrival or early departure, and activities which tend to set up physical barriers between group members. Books stacked in front of people, obstructing their view, or clothing, a brief case, or other inanimate objects lined up between chairs, thereby creating physical distance, are examples of behavior which symbolically offers protection from the threat presented by other group members.

Probably the most difficult types of behaviors to interpret are those which carry their symbolic meaning within the context of a specific culture or social group. The young girl, who as she talks with the group unconsciously buttons and unbuttons her blouse, or who flutters her eyelashes, certainly can easily be seen as engaging in sexually provocative and seductive behavior. Either of these acts could and do occur for a variety of reasons. So too with other behaviors. Their meaning is frequently determined by the setting. Consider the amazement of Americans when they see Russian leaders applauding in unison with their audience. Recently those in the know have come to realize that in hippie circles snapping your fingers is a sign of approval, not a request for help from a waiter or a gesture of disdain.

The fact that a black or brown child does not look into the eyes of the person speaking to them is often misunderstood. Instead of recognizing the act as one of learned deference, it is sometimes perceived as shyness or subtle hostility.

For counselors who now find themselves increasingly involved in helping people from the inner city or from lower socioeconomic groups where acting out feelings is much more acceptable and customary, an awareness of the meaning of certain physical gestures can certainly facilitate the incorporation of this additional means of communicating into the life of the group. Included in these behaviors are many that are obscene in purpose, expressing hostility by implying degrading acts. Within this group would be included the upthrust pointing finger, the making of horns through extended two fingers of the fist (symbolizing that the person is a cuckold), the striking of a forearm that has been flexed by the other hand, and so on. As children we learned a variety of other signs that tend to have rather common meaning. Sticking out your tongue, circling your ear with your finger and pointing to the other individual, and pinching your nose, all suggest that the other individual is considerably less than acceptable.

Obviously, this list of nonverbal cues could be extended indefinitely. The real question, however, is what is to be done with them and how they are to be recognized. If the group leader is to truly serve the linking function described by Gordon as basic to group process, the more effectively he can help all of the members of the group perceive how they are reacting to one another either on a verbal or physical level, the faster the group will move and the greater will be their security in the group situation. Just as words carry latent and manifest meanings, so too nonverbal cues can be dealt with by reflecting the manifest feelings involved or could be interpreted to help the individual and the group understand the motivation behind the action.

No rule of thumb can be given as to when it is helpful to clarify the silent client's involvement through calling the group's attention to the client's feeling, as demonstrated by his behavior.

Since for me the major role of the group leader is to facilitate group awareness of the interaction between group members or their need to cope with a problem which is affecting the group climate, nonverbal behavior will be reflected when it affects either of these two situations.

An example might help. The leader says, "John and Mary have said they favor the plan, but Jim and Betty seemed to be shaking their heads in disagreement." Obviously, if the group leader read Jim and Betty's head movement incorrectly, they still had a chance to correct his interpretation. Just as words can be misunderstood, so too the silent client needs to realize that his unconscious physical cues can also be misunderstood and that he needs to take responsibility for correcting misperceptions if he is concerned about how others feel about him.

One illustration of the difference in meaning of behavior when it is shared by the group versus when it reflects just an individual's point of view, can be seen in the illustration of the group member who almost unconsciously begins to shuffle his feet, making sufficient noise so that the person talking may have difficulty in being heard or, at the very least, is distracted. When this feeling on the part of the individual member is then taken up by the entire group, with all of them shuffling or stamping their feet, the meaning of that shared group behavior certainly carries a tone and a quality that is far different. For the speaker it demonstrates group rejection; for the restless shoe shuffler it communicates group support for his feeling.

One of the limitations of using a book to teach group process is that it focuses unduly on verbal cues. In an attempt to overcome this restriction, the reader is encouraged to examine the series of photographs that follow.

In each picture at least one group member is involved in an activity that may warrant being called to the group's attention by the leader or another group member. To sharpen the reader's skill, the reader is encouraged to write the type of confronting verbal message that might be directed toward the group member or members involved to help them recognize their behavior. Included with each picture is one possible leader response to the problem being presented.

For readers who find "reading" nonverbal cues unfamiliar, several references would be worth exploring.

FIGURE 1.   Person in group with seat pushed back.

"I get the feeling Ray is moving away from us, I wonder why?"

FIGURE 2.   Person surrounded by physical walls (books, pocketbook, ash tray).

"It's hard to see you, hear you, or reach you when you build walls around yourself."

FIGURE 3. Hand over face.

"Some things are harder to face than others. Don seems to want to avoid seeing what's going on."

FIGURE 4. Person serving food.

"Have you noticed Chris always chooses to serve us. She seems to want to show she cares for us, but by being on the outside she doesn't have to be involved."

FIGURE 5. Person standing.

"You've got us all looking up to you. Does that make it easier for you?"

FIGURE 6. Two people facing each other in conversation, ignoring group.

"Conny and Elia seem to have something private going on. How do you all feel about being left out?"

56

FIGURE 7. One person talking, others yawning.

"It looks as if many of us are turning Bill off."

FIGURE 8. All group members not looking at each other.

"We all seem to be working hard at not looking at each other. I wonder why?"

Ruesch and Kees (5) suggest actions may be viewed and categorized as follows:

1. *Expressive movements*: all glandular, vascular, and intestinal manifestations, along with all voluntary and involuntary gestures, including any other purposive, nonverbal actions that have communicative value.

2. *Adaptive behavior as a form of language*: silent action as well as the spoken and written word, and gestures, might be considered here.

3. *Symbolic movements that cannot in themselves satisfy any immediate bodily needs*: gestures necessarily used along with speech to illustrate, to emphasize, to point, or to interrupt.

4. *Traces that action leaves on people*: callouses on feet of those who walk barefoot, occupational stigmata from physical and mechanical causes that mark workers' hands: grease stains on mechanics' hands; callouses on clerical workers' fingers from holding pens or pencils, and the like.

5. *Hypertrophy or atrophy of muscles resulting from usage or disuse*: trombonists' or violinists' well-developed arm and shoulder muscles, for example.

6. *Posture*: an index of the body's past action and a predictor of the body's future performance. Erect bearing, for example, is associated with soldiers, doormen, and butlers.

7. *Appearance*: beauty or ugliness may convey either false or correct impressions about a person, even though different cultures and different historical periods vary in their aesthetic reactions.

8. *Clothing*: a person's identity and taste may be indicated by his apparel, which may conform to current styles, the season, occupational status, and the like; may be used to conceal defects in bodily structure.

Although one might observe that these categories and viewpoints are not exhaustive or mutually exclusive, the authors point out that even those who ignore nonverbal signals and language systems must rely on these to communicate at all.

Mehrabian (6), in a provocative article on "Communication Without Words," suggests that the total impact of a message is composed of 0.07 verbal $+$ 0.38 vocal and 0.55 facial. By using an electronic filter that makes words unintelligible but retained the other vocal qualities, Mehrabian found judges could easily tell how much people like each other by the quality of the message. He reports on a study by George Mahl of Yale University who found that errors of speech, including stuttering and omission of words, become more frequent as the speaker's anxiety increases.

Timing in speech, too, is significant. When one speaks to someone whose status is perceived as higher than one's own, the longer the higher status person nods his head, the longer his partner's utterances last. If the higher status person changes his pattern of speech to either longer or shorter segments, the other person follows suit. If the higher status person interrupts frequently or allows long silences, the other person becomes uncomfortable.

Negative attitude is also shown through verbal distance. References to "those people" is more remote, than "these people," which in turn is more remote than "Sam and I."

Gross bodily shifts may communicate negative feelings toward the person talking.

The tension or relaxed position of the body indicates both feelings of liking and of status.

> . . . Relaxation of posture is a good indicator of both attitude and status, and one that we have been able to measure quite precisely. Three categories have been established for relaxation in a seated position: least relaxation is indicated by muscular tension in the hands and rigidity of posture; moderate relaxation is indicated by a forward lean of about 20 degrees and a sideways lean of less than 10 degrees, a curved back, and, for women, an open arm position; and extreme relaxation is indicated by a reclining angle greater than 20 degrees and a sideways lean greater than 10 degrees (6).

Since a relaxed position can reflect feelings that the other person is in an inferior status, the use of relaxed bodily positions can indicate disdain for the other person.

Generally the more you like a person, the more time you spend looking directly into his eyes as you talk.

Mehrabian suggests that possibly lower-class children are more responsive to facial expressions, posture, and touch, as well as verbal intonation. These speculations have interesting implications for both classroom situations and social settings where communication between different economic levels of society needs to be facilitated.

Birdwhistell (7) is responsible for a comprehensive system of recording behavior. He also has detailed the differences in meanings given to the same behavior in different cultures. As one of the pioneers in the field of recording body movements, he developed a shorthand to record observed movements. Below is one group of such symbols (8).

KINEGRAPHS

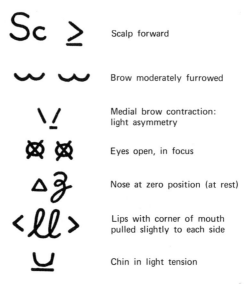

Sc ≥ — Scalp forward

Brow moderately furrowed

Medial brow contraction: light asymmetry

Eyes open, in focus

Nose at zero position (at rest)

Lips with corner of mouth pulled slightly to each side

Chin in light tension

Davis (8) provides some visual cues as to the way people signal feelings and attitudes toward each other.

The woman in the following picture by tightly crossing her arms and legs is indicating she is not open to any approaches. Some researchers have qualified this by indicating that the signal will depend on the circumstances, what the woman is doing with the rest of her body, and to whom she is signalling.

Body cues are culture bound and are learned in early childhood. Some behaviors are specific for each sex. Below the man shows the "broken-four" position (one ankle on the other knee) that American men learn is the masculine way to cross their legs. Readers may remember how Mark Twain used this cue as a way of unmasking Huckleberry Finn. (See Fig. 11.)

Just as birds have courting behavior, so too, do human beings. A male may preen by adjusting his tie, smoothing or straightening his hair. (See Fig. 12.)

A girl shows that she is available for courting by showing the palm of her hand as she grooms her hair. She faces her palm in the direction of the man who attracts her. (See Fig. 13.)

It is interesting to note that those who adopt similar positions also tend to be in agreement in a discussion. Their agreement shows by their forming mirror images of each other. Note in the second picture how the one girl with hand behind her shows clearly her difference from the others. (See Fig. 14, 15.)

Julius Fast's (9) popular book *Body Language* describes in vivid detail the cultural variations involved in "body space" or the meaning attributed to how close the other individual approaches you. Citing research results he demonstrates that in the American culture people who feel good or safe with you sit closest, those who are anxious, farthest away. Because our faces are most revealing of our feelings, many freeze their features into "safe" nonthreatening masks.

One of Fast's more provocative concepts is that by violating the sanctity of a person's territory, and by getting physically close, it is possible to communicate when other techniques fail. It is just this theory which provides the basis for many of the approaches used in sensitivity groups where physical contact becomes the vehicle for communication. As a matter of fact, Dr. Perls (10), a representative of the Gestalt approach, tends to focus almost exclusively on nonverbal communication, since he feels it is more honest and involves less self-deception.

The major problem with using these nonverbal techniques and in reading people's behavior as a precursor to confronting them with it, is that like the other techniques of interpretation, it destroys the person's facade and leaves him naked and defenseless to the world. The ethics, then, of using such "stripping" techniques depend on either the client's request for your help and their trust in your professional skill in dealing with their anxiety or the decision on the part of others that despite the client's awareness or readiness, such experiences are necessary or good for them. Obviously these alternate judgments reflect different philosophical values about the role of the counselor.

Much to William Schutz's (11) credit, in his book *Joy* where he describes in great detail a wide variety of techniques, he takes the time to both demonstrate the appropriateness of a specific approach in a given situation *and* details the cautions one needs to observe before using each approach.

Because these approaches, like games, appear so simple, untrained

64

people can duplicate them. But used in the wrong setting or at the wrong time, the results can be dangerous.

It was my original intention to briefly survey the techniques currently used in group approaches that emphasize the affective physical levels of communication. In Schutz's (11) text, he lists 29 different approaches; Goodwin Watson (12) has a list of 48 exercises and games; and a book recently published by Lewis and Streitfeld (13) includes over 200 "games" you can play alone, with friends or family. Havemann recently speculated that there are now over 200 different group approaches which use over 10,000 specific techniques. Clearly an anthology of these varied techniques would not only be voluminous but of necessity, fairly redundant.

What are the common denominators found in most of these approaches?

1. The removal of one or several sensory sources of information to help people become more finely attuned to the potential communication available in the channel being emphasized, for example, being blindfolded and asked to meet strangers in a room where the use of voice or sight is removed as vehicles for communication.

2. Techniques designed to demonstrate the degree to which we actually trust other people, for instance, using one of the most basic fears, that of falling, having people fall backward to be caught by someone behind them.

3. Techniques designed to show how cooperative group effort makes support of an individual possible, for example, group members lie in a circle on the floor with feet raised high. A person stands in the center, falls back against the feet, and is supported and passed around from foot to foot.

4. Techniques that focus on freeing people to express deep feelings in socially approved ways but with emphasis on purging oneself of the emotion, for instance, beating a pillow representing someone one hates, shouting aloud your hate as you beat the devil out of the pillow.

5. Helping people recognize their strong need to be part of a group, or conversely to be by themselves, for example, group members lock arms and form a circle and a person tries to either break into the circle or to break out.

6. Demonstrating the degree to which specific problems have been transformed into bodily tensions or postures, for instance, the aggressive male may tend to thrust his jaw out and bare his teeth. Through techniques like progressive relaxation (14), his face and mouth are able to relax, and with that relaxation comes a different feeling toward others and himself. In some cases it even becomes possible to recall the incidents or trauma that led toward the development of these feelings.

7. Through a variety of role-playing situations or psychodrama, people have a chance to relive emotionally meaningful incidents and to gain perspective so that their current feelings are changed. The techniques are abreactive in quality, since they assume the need to return to the original emotional trauma for solutions to be possible. A variant designed to increase sensitivity to others involves role reversal so one can feel what the other person experiences in a given situation (15,16).

8. Recognizing that some people have things to say they cannot put into words, people are freed to use song, dance, painting, acting, and so on to convey feelings for which words cannot be found initially.

9. Helping people feel more worthwhile by focusing on a group effort to supply a missing emotion—whether it be love, praise, or close relationships. Many of these techniques are found in the human potential movement, which receives much of its leadership from Herbert Otto (17).

10. Control of others is made explicit by a variety of techniques when people are put into situations where they must react to others. The way they react provides clues to how they feel about and cope with conflict situations, for example, arm wrestling, walking toward each other in a narrow line—who looks away, bumps, or forces the other to move away.

As with all attempts at providing an overview, trying to group thousands of techniques into ten categories is a dangerous process. It is necessary to do, however, if one is not to have a beginning person be unable to see the forest for the trees.

SURVEY OF COUNSELING TECHNIQUES

To insure that this survey of counseling techniques is comprehensive, two other ways of grouping techniques will be reviewed. Some degree of overlap is to be expected.

Geis (16), in an article attempting to develop a comprehensive framework that would embrace all systems of counseling, developed the following list.

· Questioning, drawing the counselee out and evoking problem-related material.

· Identifying, labeling, clarifying and reflecting feeling.

· Summarizing and reviewing important material.

· Restating.

· Establishing connections (referred to elsewhere in this text as the linking function).

- Emphasizing, accenting, or underscoring.
- Interpreting.
- Confronting.
- Reassuring, encouraging, and supporting.
- Creating and maintaining tension.
- Contrasting and showing alternatives.
- Information and advice giving.
- Using ambiguity and "inability to understand."
- Using the counseling relationship as leverage for change.
- Using oneself and others as role models.
- Using hypothetical situations and examples.
- Communicate focus on the counselee's self-interest.
- Using clear, concise, meaningful communications.
- Emotional catharsis and desensitization.
- Psychological homework.
- Persuasion, exhortation, pressure, and coercion.
- Environmental manipulation.
- Simulated experiences.

Fortunately, much of the earlier emotionalism over discreteness of use of such terms as psychotherapy, counseling, and education has diminished. This is partially true because most people today recognize that all three terms require learning or relearning activity.

Before leaving this review of techniques it may be hlpful to see how Louis Raths, one of the early educators to analyze the teaching process, defined teaching-learning operations. Raths (17) has divided teaching into separated operations. We shall specifically examine what he has called the "clarifying operations, the show-how operations, and the security-giving operations." The comments under each heading are my interpretation of the applicability of these operations to the helping process.

Clarifying Operations.

I.1 *Clarifying through reflection.* This has been partially covered by the preceding sections.

I.2 *Clarifying through use of a definition or illustration.* For a person to understand an idea fully he must be able to communicate its meaning to others. Clarification is frequently best achieved by describing an applicable concrete situation. The group seeks to facilitate its understanding by requesting the person to illustrate his idea.

I.3 *Clarifying by pointing up what appear to be apparent inconsistencies.*   Notice the word "apparent." What does not make sense to the hearer initially may be seen as related when the speaker draws up the relationship as he sees it. One good illustration of this comes in the popular refrain, "you always hate the one you love." A moment's thought will reveal the fact that it is hard to feel strongly about someone who is unimportant to you.

I.4 *Clarifying similarities and differences.*   Particularly in a group where there may be a tendency to get support by either forcing a single stand or by the operation of cliques, this approach is very important. Because a pressure group forces opinion by presenting a united front, helping members of this subgroup examine their stand and pointing up areas of hidden disagreement as well as consensus within their group, causes the clique to disintegrate and join the total group. It also points up that the strength of the group can come from difference as well as agreement.

I.5 *Clarifying through questioning underlying assumptions.*   This can be a dangerous tool. If the group by this device rejects all assumptions but those the majority believes in, it can have a threatening and restricting effect. If, however, it is used to help the person or total group define the assumptions they are making so that they can decide if these are beliefs they can really accept, then the approach has positive implications for growth.

I.6 *Clarifying through anticipation of consequences.*   Since the response of others to our actions is a major concern, the degree to which the group helps provide possible results enables the person to determine his course of action. One rather popular way that is used to think through this situation is by having group members act out with a person a scene in which he tries his idea. The other members, by their behavior, give him concrete evidence of what the future effects of his approach might be.

I.7 *Clarifying through questioning meaning.*   Is this what you mean? or, Do I understand you to say . . . ? The latter implies that the bearer could be misperceiving but wants to understand. Thelen (20) has pointed out that children are so imbued with the teacher's role as an authority that they may begin to believe that truth is the opinion of someone on whom you are dependent. Teaching people to question may be the first step toward helping them understand their right to their individual belief. The questioning process may also help them realize that as they question the ideas of a person in an authority role, their questions may cause the authority to modify and change his ideas, too.

I.8 *Clarifying by examining points of difficulty.* This could apply not only to an idea but also to helping the group examine their own group process. For example, sometimes a group seems at a loss as to what they want to do. Helping them examine the feelings or ideas that seem to be causing trouble is the first step in removing this road block. What's getting in our way? Why are we so upset?

I.9 *Clarifying if a personal statement was meant to show a personal feeling or one that the individual feels all people must hold.* This is one way of helping the group see demands that individual members are making on them. It also points up to the individual demands he is making on others.

I.10 *Clarifying by relating feelings to behavior.* By calling attention to the feelings which others are getting from a person's behavior, it helps the person accept responsibility for the way he expresses his emotion. "We all seem to be so angry at each other that we seem unable to let the other person talk."

I.11 *Clarifying through a review of the steps in a person's logic.* This concept is somewhat like I.5. Implicit is the idea that a review of the steps will help a person see the fallacy of the logic involved. Although this approach can sometimes work, it cannot help failing unless the motivation for his reasoning will be more effectively met by an alternative logic which is presently in the client's available repertoire of responses. For example, the group points out to a client that he is tired when he stays out late with the boys and that his health and school work are suffering. The client recognizes the truth of the group's statement, but the logic does not meet his need for peer group approval or the satisfactions he gets when he is out with the fellows.

I.12 *Raising questions of purpose.* What are you trying to prove? This is an attempt to help the person search for and recognize the underlying motivation for his activity. To the degree that he is secure in the group and has a motivation to get an answer, this approach may be helpful. Also, the question must reflect an attempt to help the person rather than be a belligerent challenge of his rights or goals.

I.13 *Seeking origins of an expression or idea.* Since nothing we think or do is unrelated to our past experiences, to the degree that we can integrate a present idea with the concepts that led to its creation, we achieve a fuller realization of the meaning of the idea to us.

The Show-How Operations

II.1 *Through demonstrations.* Although copying another's movements can be a helpful way of learning skills, the motivation to succeed through being like someone else is really a double-edged sword. The more the individual sees happiness as being achieved by emulating someone else, the more he will try to be like the other person. In the process he will tend to overlook the things that make him different from his idol. He will assume an equivalence in their interests, skills, personality, and goals. Since he can never be the other person, he never achieves a sense of accomplishment that he feels really reflects what he could achieve on his own two feet. Especially in a democracy, we seek to preserve the individual's right to his own life. The issue therefore really is: How do we help people incorporate into their own lives the values *we* feel are important? The answer to this is not a simple one. The author takes the stand that society has the responsibility of providing young people with many samples of roles to examine and try. It must then provide a setting in which each person can examine how the parts of each role will be consistent with his unique abilities and goals. The group, with its different members and opportunities for trial behavior, is particularly suited for this job.

II.2 *Use of resource persons and teaching aids.*   The use of resource people and materials is closely tied to the meaningfulness of these sources of help to the goals of the group. The resource person who comes in to tell others what they should be doing will be useful only to the extent that he is supplying information that the group needs, wants, and is ready to use. The fundamental concept here is the difference between *information* and *advice*. Although many people ask for advice as one way of avoiding responsibility ("He told me to do it, it wasn't really my idea"), advice rarely works. If the adviser tells people exactly what they want to hear, it is experienced as reassuring. At the same time, people react with the feeling that they already knew the answer and that the resource person has added nothing. If, however, the adviser suggests ideas that clients cannot accept, a dilemma arises. In the event that they take advice that they basically cannot go along with, they experience the feeling that they are not very worthwhile people if anyone can persuade them to actions that violate their own beliefs. There is then a resulting decrease in feelings of personal worth and in ability to be responsible for their own behavior. On the other hand, if the group decides to ignore the advice of the resource person it is difficult for them to seek his help again, since by their actions they have demonstrated a lack of faith in the correctness of his advice.

Information, as contrasted from advice, then, is provided only when the people seeking a solution which clarifies their problem see need for knowing alternative ways to reach their goal and are willing to accept responsibility both for implementing their decisions and for accepting the fruits of their action.

The timing, then, when information is sought by the group, is vitally dependent on what has preceded their request and on their security in accepting responsibility for their behavior. Information volunteered before a group perceives a need for it actually works as advice, since it implies the direction in which the adviser thinks they ought to be going and his feeling that they ought to be ready to accept responsibility.

II.3 *Exploring alternative methods or ways to solve the problem.* Our security in feeling able to cope with our environment certainly is a function of the range of techniques we have learned to use in coping with a variety of situations. We facilitate security and growth of the individual when we provide both a secure setting and opportunity for trial behavior. In this type of group setting the client can dare to experiment with new methods since the price of failure is not the same as that which society imposes.

An example here might be helpful: Little Billy Smith comes home from school crying. He has been beaten up by another youngster. We could solve (?) the problem by taking action against the other child, but Billy will not have learned how he can cope with the next bully. He will have learned that if you go to someone else he will solve your problem for you. Suppose, as an alternative solution, that Billy had discussed this with the coach, and that the coach had offered to teach Billy to use judo. Let's imagine that Billy receives one lesson, and on his way home he again meets the bully. How will he fight? The way he did in the past. He will use his judo lessons only when he feels he can get results that are equal to or better than what he already knew. Incidentally, Billy was willing to try to develop his skills with the coach because he knew that while he was learning the coach would not hurt him. In his lessons he could make mistakes without suffering irreparable damage. The role of the school or therapeutic group is to offer the same opportunities to make mistakes without irreparable damage to the person.

Also involved in this area is the concept of failure. Typically, failure has come to mean that the person has not measured up to a preconceived standard. This is but one way of looking at the inability to achieve beyond a certain point. A more helpful way is to conceive of the point of failure as a concrete measure of all the person has achieved to that point. For example, how can a person discover how high he is able to jump? He keeps raising the cross bar until he reaches the point where he can no longer clear it. This point of failure is both the measure of how high he *can* jump and a concrete point against which to compare his hoped-for goal. Too often in our competitive society, we spend so much time in measuring the distance between where we are and where we feel we must go, that we lose sight of what we have already accomplished. If our goal in society is to help people feel a sense of personal worth, at some point they need to be helped to examine where they are, where they have been, and where they feel they need to go. It is in helping a person reconcile what he is and the bases he has used to decide where he must go that we are simultaneously providing motivation for learning and are improving his mental health.

Actually, in a true learning situation the goal of the people or person providing help is to help the individual discover which personal tools he possesses which he can use to solve problems. The ultimate goal of any therapeutic situation is *not* the resolution of the problem. Rather it is an attempt to teach problem-solving techniques.

Security-Giving Operations

III.1 *Meeting the need for belonging.*   It has been said that all of us determine our personal worth through the eyes of others. Essentially we recognize that since each person wants to feel worthwhile, to the degree that we share things in common, we are sure of mutual acceptance. The fly in the ointment is, however, that while we can achieve acceptance by being a carbon copy of the stereotype, this role does not enable us to be recognized as a unique person. This need for group acceptance is strongest in the adolescent. Picture the typical high school girl of our day dressed in the uniform of the day. It may be jeans, panty hose, or whatever the group has decided. Suppose this young lady should overhear two boys trying to decide whom to take to a dance. "I don't see what the problem is, Tom, these gals spend so much time together you can't tell one from the other." Young Miss walks away in confusion. What does she have to do and be, not to be considered a square? How different does she dare let herself be without risking group rejection as a queer? Although the example chosen was that of an adolescent, these questions are common to people at all age levels. What are the limits of our society? How can we meet our needs within these limits? And for the mature adult there is added the more difficult question; how can we help others see that the status quo needs changing without losing our group membership?

III.2 *Meeting the need for achievement and personal growth.*   One way we prove to ourselves that we are worthwhile is by examining our day-to-day accomplishments. If we keep repeating what we could do yesterday, the glow of accomplishment fades. Personal growth involves a constant reassessment of the reality of the new goals we are setting up for tomorrow. Since we do not achieve in a vacuum, part and parcel of this assessment process is the support we get from the reactions of others. One of the rather unique characteristics of the group setting is that, as we observe other people solve problems and grow, it gives us courage to try to solve problems ourselves. Part of it might be caused by the feeling that if the other person, whom we feel is weaker, can achieve—we can, too. Along with this is the support that comes from knowing that other people are facing similar problems and that we are not alone.

III.3 *The need for economic security.* Although a group does not meet this specific need it can be very helpful in assisting the person in sharpening his skills in achieving economic self-sufficiency. Job security in our society involves more than just having needed skills. One of the major reasons people lose jobs is their inability to get along with fellow workers and to accept responsibility. Job security rests also on the degree to which the job gratifies basic needs. For some, job satisfaction depends purely on the money they earn. This is not only a status symbol but also a means to gratify needs that cannot be met through their jobs. For other people, the conditions under which they work are more vital. A group can be helpful in assisting a person in defining what he seeks from a job so he can decide if the job he wants will meet these needs. For many, the group can provide a setting in which to practice job-getting or interpersonal skills. The group frequently can help a person think through more effective ways of solving problems on the job. Not least of all, it can help a person examine what he needs in the way of economic security to meet his present needs for effective living in his society.

III.4 *The need to be free from fear.* Although the group can, within its own limits, set up rules that will protect the individual from physical and other threats, there is a real question as to whether freedom from fear itself is a good thing. Fear can be a motivating force to solve a problem. It can also be the basis for avoiding situations which realistically are dangerous and beyond the control of an individual. Rather than freedom from fear there ought to be substituted the ability to face fear. For example, many of us are aware of the fact that any day some trigger-happy person could fire a bomb that might precipitate the end of the world as we know it. This is a very real possibility. There are many things an individual can do to attempt to modify society so that this no longer will be possible. Immediate solutions are not likely. Living in daily fear could make a person unable to do even those small things which on a combined group basis might solve the problem. In other words, at some point we need to help people live in a society where security and the absence of fear can become a possibility. We need to build up individual security that comes from knowing that each person has used the full extent of his capacity. No more can be demanded of any man.

III.5 *The need for love and affection.* Raths has described this as showing others you are hurt when they are hurt. There is a real question if this is a helpful thing. To the extent that you are truly hurt each time another suffers, the trials and tribulations of the world can soon overwhelm you. As an alternative, the development of an empathic attitude might be considered. Instead of sympathizing and identifying with each pain of the other person, you attempt to let him know that you understand how he feels and that you want to help. In your own mind you recognize that *he* is feeling the pain, not you. Unless you are free of the pain, you cannot be objective enough to help him to look at his feelings. When the counselor identifies with his client, we have two clients instead of one. This augments the problem rather than lessens it.

There are many kinds of love. Many of you are familiar with what has been termed "sMother Love," or the possessive kind of attention that robs the person of his rights and personality. All of us tend to be suspicious of other people. A rather frequent question is "Why are you being so nice to me?" People basically recognize that all behavior is motivated by some need of the individual. Understanding the needs the "loving" person is trying to meet helps the recipient decide if this is helping or hindering his own desires. The more honestly we express our motivations for being concerned about others, the more secure both they and we will feel. In the group this problem is somewhat simplified. Very quickly groups come to realize that they will sink or swim together. The growing awareness of how interdependent they are on each other makes very clear that from what may appear as a selfish basis, each person wants the others well and happy so that the other people can meet his needs, which they couldn't do if their abilities were impaired.

Feeling important to others in and of itself demonstrates your value. The security of love works two ways. It proves that there are others who care while at the same time increasing your esteem in your own eyes.

III.6 *The need to be free from guilt.* Feelings of guilt can so immobilize a person that any positive action is impossible. Guilt feelings can be alleviated in several ways. One common method is for an authority to remove guilt by providing punishment that will pay for the action that is causing guilt feelings. A common example of this is the little boy who confesses to misbehavior and feels relief when he is spanked, since he then considers the score has been settled. A group sometimes acts this way, but generally they do not want to sit in judgment. In the group setting there is a more effective method to deal with guilt feelings. As members of the group feel able to share their feelings with each other, they frequently discover that they are not alone in their perceived misbehavior or guilty thoughts. Part of the weight of guilt feelings comes from the sense of being different in one's behavior or problems. Each person feels alone. As he discovers that others face the same situation, although his feelings haven't changed, each person feels better able to cope with his problem. Realizing that others have faced and solved the problem gives support. Knowing that there are others with whom you can feel free to discuss the situation also is a source of security. You are free to talk with them because you feel they are no better than you, and you do not lose group acceptance by admitting your feelings.

III.7 *The need for acceptance of the other person.* A group soon learns that each person in his turn will ask questions that are very naive in the eyes of others. Accepting the "naive" person's need for information and his right to use the group to clarify his own thinking causes the group members to examine questions, not in terms of their sophistication, but rather in terms of what it means to the person who is asking.

III.8 *Ways of controlling conflict situations.* Groups develop a sixth sense in judging when a group member is being pressed beyond his ability to cope with the situation. Since taking a problem out of someone else's hands implies a lack of faith in their capacity to handle the problem, group members hesitate to take overt action. Rather than have the person retreat from danger, or remove the danger, group members provide support to the person under attack so that he has additional strength to face the situation. It is not uncommon for the group to take overt action toward a member who seems to be unfairly treating another. Learning that the way that he treats other group members will affect how the rest of the group will treat him causes each person to carefully consider his effect on others.

These are a few of the characteristics that Raths covers in his article. Although there are many other aspects of teaching, those presented here should demonstrate the communal focus of teaching and therapy.

Teaching vs. Learning.

Recently (21) evaluations of education and its failure to help the disadvantaged have focused on the goals, techniques, and skills needed to be really helpful. At least four tasks have been selected as basic to survival in a free society. Students need to be able to:

Choose, perform, and enjoy a viable vocation.
Exercise the complicated task of democratic citizenship.
Engage in culture-carrying activities.
Engage in satisfactory inter- and intrapersonal relationships.

In defining the characteristics of the teacher needed to meet these objectives, Smith emphasizes the humanness of the teacher and the need for the teacher to get involved in open interpersonal contacts. To function, the teacher needs both knowledge and experience. Most basic of all, to effectively communicate he must know the child's world as seen from the child's cultural frame of reference. The teacher must also be able to communicate in terms the child can understand.

Chapter 2 made the point that each helping person knowingly or unconsciously adopts a philosophy and value system that guide his behavior. The techniques available are selected and used according to their congruence with the needs and purpose of the counselor. Rogers (22), in his recent text relating his philosophy to helping people learn, takes an extreme position as contrasted with Smith. He believes neither he nor others can "teach" people. One can only facilitate the learning of others. Real learning is self-discovery, it is learning which will significantly affect one's own behavior. Rogers goes on to state that learning occurs best when one does not need to be defensive and, at least from time to time, one needs to be able to see himself through the eyes of other people. It is a sort of reverse empathy.

The helping person, then, becomes preoccupied with the ways in which he can use himself so as to free or facilitate movement in the client he is trying to help. Let us return to the saying by Gibran at the beginning of this chapter. "No man can reveal to you aught but that which already lies half asleep in the dawning of your knowledge."

The reader completing this chapter, especially the beginner, must experience concern and wonder as to when to use what technique and for how long. It is at this point that any textbook fails. The intuitive sense the mature counselor and group develops as to what is just right is very much a matter of sensitivity that arises from the use of experience to shape intuition.

The frustration of the beginner brings back to my mind an experience early in my marriage. My wife wanting to bake a cake she knew I liked which my grandmother always made for me, went to visit her, pad in hand, prepared to write down ingredients and amounts.

My grandmother threw up her hands in defeat. She said, "I use a little of this, a pinch of that, and sometimes if it doesn't quite look right I add more flour." Cautioning my wife to watch her, she proceeded to make a cake. Her hands flew, she would taste, make a face, and throw in some more of something. It was only by watching carefully and knowing the possible ingredients that my wife had any idea of what was going through my grandmother's head.

To help develop some of the art that goes along with the knowledge needed to lead groups the next chapter will present portions of group protocols. By reading the running commentary on the right-hand side of the page, the reader may begin to experience the unconscious thoughts going through a leader's mind as he shifts and sorts among the alternative things he could do to find the behavior that might best facilitate the group's having a setting or situation that could produce meaningful experiences in the lives of each of the group members.

Bibliography

1. Thelen, H. A. *Education and the Human Quest*, New York: Harper, 1960, Chapter 3.
2. Bordin, E. Psychological Counseling (chapters dealing with the concept of the role of ambiguity in counseling), New York: Appleton-Century-Crofts, 2nd ed., 1968.
3. Brammer, L., and Shostram, E. *Therapeutic Psychology*, 2nd ed., New York: Prentice-Hall, 1968, p. 281.
4. Lifton, W. *How the Silent Client Communicates*, Symposium on Nonverbal Communication in Group Counseling, APGA Convention, Washington, D. C., April 1966.
5. Ruesch, J., and Kees, W. *Nonverbal Communication*, Berkeley, Calif.: University of California Press, 1956. As reported in *Research and the Classroom Teacher*, March 1970 issue. Published by the Genesee Valley School Development Association.
6. Mehrabian, A. "Communication Without Words," *Psychology Today*, September 1968, pp. 53–55.
7. Birdwhistell, R. *Expression of the Emotions in Man*, New York: International University Press, 1963.
8. Davis, F. "The Way We Speak: Body Language," *New York Times Magazine*, May 31, 1970, pp. 8, 9.
9. Fast, J. *Body Language*, New York: Evans, 1970.
10. Perls, F., Hefferline, R., and Goodman, P. *Gestalt Therapy*, New York: Dell, 1964.
11. Schutz, W. C. *Joy*, New York: Grove Press, 1967.
12. Watson, G. "48 Exercises and Games," Laboratory of Applied Behavioral Sciences, Newark State College, Union, New Jersey.
13. Lewis, H. R., and Streitfeld, H. *Growth Games*, New York: Harcourt, Brace & Jovanovich, 1971.
14. Rolf, I. "Structural Integration," *Systematics*, Vol. I, No. 1, June 1963.
15. Corsini, R. *Roleplaying in Psychotherapy*, Chicago: Aldine, 1966.
16. Del Torto, J., and Cornyetz, P. Psychodrama as an Expressive and Projection Technique. In J. L. Moreno (Ed.), *Psychodrama Monograph* 14, New York: Beacon, 1945.

17. Otto, H. *Exploration in Human Potentialities,* Springfield, Ill.: Charles C Thomas, 1966.

18. Geis, J. H. "Toward a Comprehensive Framework Unifying All Systems of Counseling," *Educational Technology,* March 1969, Vol. IX, No. 3, p. 19–28.

19. Raths, L. "What Is Teaching?" *Sociatry,* **II**, Nos. 3, 4, 197–206, 1948.

20. Thelen, H. A., *Education and the Human Quest,* New York: Harper, 1960, Chapter 4, p. 71.

21. Smith, B. O. *Teachers for the Real World,* Washington, D.C.: American Association of Colleges for Teacher Education, 1968.

22. Rogers, C. R. *Freedom to Learn,* Ohio: Charles E. Merrill, 1969.

4 The Use of Protocols as a Means of Learning About Group Process

"All the world's a stage,
And all the men and women merely players;
They have their exits and their entrances;
And one man in his time plays many parts. . . ."
FROM AS YOU LIKE IT BY WILLIAM SHAKESPEARE

The future group leader needs to establish his philosophy, values, and style. He needs also to be able to identify what is happening in a group so that he can decide how best to facilitate its process. While a member of a group, the neophyte leader finds himself so involved in the interactions that he has neither the time nor skill to both participate and observe at the same time. For that reason I have found it helpful to ask students to reduce their audio tapes to typescripts because it enables a different type of learning to take place. Since the reader's eye can either scan quickly and thereby spot repeated themes or if desired go back over a specific segment repeatedly until it is understood, typescripts provide a basis for analysis not only of intragroup movement but also of the techniques used by the leader. These techniques ultimately define his value system and style.

This chapter contains three different segments in the life of three different groups, all led by the author, but convened for different purposes. The protocols selected illustrate my belief that self-actualization, task orientation, feeling clarification, and personal growth are possible in almost all group settings.

The first protocol illustrates a type of theater-in-the-round used for training purposes. A small group works together to form a meaningful relationship while observed by a large audience. At the close of the session it is then possible to use the personally meaningful material produced by the small group to examine what goes on in a group. The group interaction is experienced at both the intellectual and deep feeling level.

81

It is suggested you read the left-hand side of the pages first. When you finish go back and assume you are the leader. Decide what you feel was going on in the group and the steps you would have taken. As you read, ask yourself what you think you might have done at each point. Consider the issues the group raises and reraises, and decide what themes seem to be dominant in the life of the group. If you find yourself bored or angry, ask yourself what needs of yours would help or hinder your activities in the group.

USING GROUPS FOR DIDACTIC INSTRUCTION[1]

This section includes part of a protocol of a group going through the first stages of defining their societally approved reasons for the group's existence, their own hidden agenda and their need to test other group members to see how much personal acceptance of their ideas exists. The protocol is a transcript of a tape recording made during an institute held at Utah State University, designed to train state employment service counselors in the use of group techniques. The participants came from states west of the Mississippi, were from different levels of administrative responsibility and were all involved in the operation of Youth Opportunity Centers. Their selection to participate in the training program did not always represent their own choice.

During the first few hours of the program, time was spent on administrative details and some lecturing. The cues the group received suggested a passive role, rather than the introspective group concern that was desired by the leaders of the Institute. Accordingly, six participants were asked to volunteer for a session in which they would try to explore how the group might use this setting more effectively. It was also suggested that the larger group, serving as observers, needed also to consider problems of group process being faced in the smaller group. We therefore had a dual purpose: first, to give meaning on a personal level to our institute activities; second, to provide didactic material to which all could relate on a feeling level.

Since it is now possible to evaluate the protocol in retrospect, it is fascinating to see how group members provided clues to their own personal concerns in the first session, which did not become clearly apparent until many sessions later. Note that the leader focused his activities on providing group support through linking group members together, by clarifying problems the group needed to solve, by playing different roles

---

[1] This protocol comes from a chapter by the author on "Group Centered Leadership," in G. Gazda's (Ed.) *Basic Approaches to Group Psychotherapy and Group Counseling,* Springfield: Charles C Thomas, 1968.

and by reflecting the feelings of participants, feelings which provided the keys to their major concerns. It is these concerns, of course, which are the primary source for motivating each individual's participation in the group.

Protocol	*Underlying Dynamics*
General buzzing.	
MAN 1: Do we all get an "A"?	
LADY 1: There are too many men.	
LEADER: There are too many men?	Reflection of content as a way of encouraging further definition of meaning.
MAN 1: Women can outtalk men anyway.	
LEADER: You think the composition of the 'sexes is relevant?	Seeking to determine if group composition itself was a source of threat.
LADY 1: No.	
MAN 1: It doesn't make any difference.	
LEADER: Part of the reason for wanting to get us together in this group, and it's obviously an artificial group, is that as I listened to you this morning your major concern was how you could help people "stick" in your YOC groups. It's true that Logan is pretty far from home for many of you, but you can escape in many ways. You don't have to escape physically. You can escape in other ways too. I think if this session and this	Verbal structuring. Attempts to relate present group to reasons for their selection and participation in the current setting. Leader points up idea that verbal participation does not equate to involvement and that talk can also be used to avoid issues. Indicates group's responsibility for what occurs and their need to take action to set limits.

Protocol   *Underlying Dynamics*

Institute are to be of value, we need to take a look together, from the very beginning, about how you feel about the whole setting and some of the things you'd like to have happen, and the ways in which you feel we can get moving more effectively.

LADY 1:   Well, it seems to me that the thing of "sticking" is basic particularly with the clients we deal with, because most of them haven't stuck to anything and if you can get them to stick to a group counseling session, well then maybe it will rub off on something else too.

Talks about "clients" as a way of maintaining distance. Actually suggests her awareness that content is the vehicle for more significant interaction.

LEADER: So you see their behavior *here* as symptomatic of their behavior in all other settings.

Leader relates feeling to the current setting. By this approach, suggests this group shares common concerns with their clients in other settings.

MAN 2:   I see it in the same way, but when the kids come in they want something and I've been talking with some of the counselors on what is called the carrot theory of group counseling. You've got to dangle something or give them some specific meaning or reason

He seems to be asking, "What do we want?" "What's in it for us?" He also is seeking to define the limits of rewards or punishment present in the current group. He is also asking if motivation will come from leader activity, or is it the responsibility of the group.

Protocol

Underlying Dynamics

of why they are in that group ... and to dangle this in front of them to get people together to discuss specifically how to get a job for themselves and for the rest of the people in the group. Try to get them to work together so if one can't get a job he may find prospects for another. In other words, the group is a resource for each other person in the group.

Maybe one source of support can come from intragroup interaction.

LEADER: If I'm hearing you correctly, I think you are saying quite different things. (Lady 1) seems to be saying that people's departure from a group is because they don't know how to stick to a task, and I think I'm hearing you say that they don't stick to it because the carrot isn't good enough. It's a little different.

Shows the difference in ideas of two group members, focusing on their interrelationship. Also pinpointing different rewards obtainable from a group.

MAN 2: Well, first of all I think you've got to make them want the carrot. I've run into this problem and I assume all the others have too, There's the kid who doesn't want to work and before you can really accomplish anything, you've got to

Member shows awareness of a basis for group common concern. He also pinpoints his own problems as a group leader. He tends to require a status role where he controls others.

Protocol   *Underlying Dynamics*

make him really want
the carrot and then you
go about finding how
you can accomplish this.

MAN 3:   And also what kind of   "Do we all need to get the same
          a carrot will entice him,   reward from the group?"
          because we're all moti-
          vated by different things.
          But I've wondered from
          my own experience if
          we've found the carrot
          which will really have
          value for him.

LADY 2:   I've found that in some   "Just being recognized as a person
          groups that if the people   is important enough."
          come once or twice,
          they'll probably come
          back after that and
          they'll find the motiva-
          tion in simply just hav-
          ing a forum, you know,
          in that here they are
          treated with respect, and
          they can speak out, and
          it's kind of a fun ex-
          perience that they enjoy.
          So that the problem of
          getting them to stick
          can be worked out if
          you can just get them to
          come just the first few
          times, then it's no longer
          a problem.

MAN 1:   Well, in your group   "How compatible are we? Can we
          they have some particu-   get along together? If we aren't
          lar reason, some partic-   similar, can we get along?"
          ular subject that means
          something to everyone
          there. Ah, this is where
          I think that in groups,

Protocol	*Underlying Dynamics*
at least in the vocational aspect of it, part of what we have to learn to do is to select individuals for a group rather than just tossing in anyone at any time.	
LADY 1: Isn't that what you do in group counseling, that you get people who have a common problem, I mean you just can't throw in just this one or that one or the other one in, can you?	"Don't we need to find a common basis on which we can all interact?"
LEADER: There is something I find a little bothersome here. Are you saying that people having a common problem see the problem the same way?	Tries to pinpoint the group's concern over a commonly shared goal versus individual agendas.
CHORUS: No, not necessarily.	
LEADER: Maybe you can help me. I guess I didn't understand you. What do you mean by a common problem?	"You aren't getting through. I need help to help you."
MAN 1: Maybe I can clarify what I was thinking of. This might be a group of people interested in one specific vocation. How do you go about getting into it? What's necessary for each one of them?	
LEADER: May I interrupt for just a moment? How do you know that this is what they are interested in?	Leader goofed! Attempt to move group too rapidly away from facade. Also interruption violates right of group member.

Protocol

Underlying Dynamics

MAN 1:   Well, possibly from a verbal expression or they may have said this before they came in, ah, expressing an interest in a particular field. After involvement in a group, they may find this isn't it and they may branch off into other things.

"Are we committed to what we say now or can we change direction?"

LEADER: Are you saying then that your group is comprised of people who in individual interviews said to you, "I want to find out how to be a plumber," and you said, "I've got five other people who are interested in this. Would you like to talk this over with others who have the same kind of interest?" Is that it?

MAN 1:   Yup.

MAN 3:   I think a more illustrative problem is a person who is an older person. They all have the problem of going to an employer, and they're fifty years of age, and they can't get employed because it's against company rules. Now then, they *have* a common problem. You bet they do! How do they overcome this problem?

"What forms the basis for common concern? How general does it have to be?"

Protocol	*Underlying Dynamics*
LADY 1: What about kids in the Job Corps? They want to, for some reason, get away from their home environment so you would think	
MAN 3: . . . a common problem.	"I'm with you."
LEADER: So from one point of view these people ought to feel the same way about these problems, or at least a common kinship with others.	
MAN 3: Right.	
LEADER: From one point of view.	Attempts to help group see if this is the only answer.
MAN 3: From one point of view, yes!	
LEADER: So we think *this* ought to make a group because they seem to be people who are similar, but somehow when we get them together they don't click, and you sometimes wonder why.	
MAN 4: I wonder if we set them up for the group properly. In other words, do we just get a group together and do they fully understand why they are there? It's my feeling that it takes a certain amount of individual counseling prior to a group session in most cases.	"If a group fails, it's because the counselor hasn't done his job well." "All of us aren't convinced this is the place we want to be."
MAN 3: And I think that's what we should be learning	Returns group to the fact that they are really talking about themselves.

Protocol		*Underlying Dynamics*
	in this Institute, the techniques for determining which ones will make up the best groups.	
LEADER:	And yet Lady 2 said something quite different. She seems to be taking a position which is quite different from any of the rest of you. She said that if I have people in a group, *people,* not necessarily a problem-centered group that has been organized that way, but people, that in this meeting I give them some sense of acceptance as a person, then their original reason for coming into the group may have less meaning. Am I picking up what you are saying correctly? (to Lady 2)	Attempt to support individual perceptions while pointing up problems to be worked on by the group. Tries to help group see that all group members have hidden agendas that may need to be recognized and met before they become task-oriented.
LADY 2:	M-hm!	
MAN 3:	Fundamental.	
MAN 2:	It appears from what I'm hearing as if people who are trying to get a group together may be trying to be too specific on a problem; like, for example, wanting to be a plumber. You have to have your problem more general. If you get too specific you can get the answers out of a book,	Picks up cue from leader and directs comments to group concern. Sees maybe the focus isn't just information giving that applies to all, but rather that some kind of personal feedback that must come from others may be the real purpose.

Protocol   *Underlying Dynamics*

or you can ditto it on
a sheet and hand it to
them.

LADY 1:   Then you would say
that they are youth and
out of a job, and that
is enough.

MAN 2:   And can't find work.

LADY 1:   Yup.

MAN 3:   You say that's too specific?

MAN 2:   No, no, that would be
a good example.

MAN 3:   All right.

LEADER: With one other ingredi-   Introduces another possible way to
ent that I think we've   use the group. Also, attempts to
suggested, but haven't   verbalize the idea that was implied
stated, that they are also   but not stated.
ready to come to a group
because here's a place
they think that maybe
they can get some an-
swers they haven't got-
ten before.

MAN 4:   This seems the most   "Can we offer anything to non-
serious because if you   verbal, shy people?"
haven't got the group
to start, holding them
isn't a problem. Orient-
ing them, or in a sense
selling them, holding a
carrot out to them, try-
ing to get them to feel
that this kind of meet-
ing has a value . . . .
Most of them shy away
from group activity and
they don't verbalize very
well.

Protocol		*Underlying Dynamics*
LADY 1:	But they verbalize better with their peers than they do with us. I think if the group gets off to a real swinging start, that then they'll probably be back.	"Is the nature of the relationship affecting ability to communicate?"
LEADER:	So, maybe we're getting in the way?	
LADY 1:	Could be.	
MAN 3:	Yes.	
MAN 2:	This is a real good point because there are times when you as a counselor in this group are an authority figure or whatever it is. This is some of my anxiety in a group situation. Ah, trying to act as a group leader; ah, what do I say; what do I do to get started; and when do I get started? Do I interrupt or do I interject at the wrong times; do I stick my snout in and cut things off?	Note repeat of content in thirteenth response in group. Man 2 again brings up his own cause for concern. In later sessions group pinpointed this, saying he always needed to be a leader, and couldn't treat them as peers.
LEADER:	So, maybe some of our own decisions or some of our own anxieties about what the carrot is, reflects some of our own feelings about people feeling they got something out of it and that what they got is something that has to make sense to us.	Tries reflecting content to clarify group's concerns and their need, here and now, to apply the relevance of the current situations to their needs.

Protocol   *Underlying Dynamics*

MAN 3: It may not make any
        sense to us whatsoever.

MAN 5: Or to them.

MAN 3: It may be to them or
        not. I don't know.

LEADER: And yet, isn't this the   Again leader tries to help the group
        very purpose for which   see that content is related to them
        we, as a group, are con-   and their current needs.
        vened right now—how
        to make an experience
        make sense? Are we talk-
        ing about two separate
        things, or isn't this our
        problem too?

LADY 1: First of all, you've got
        to get involved.

MAN 4: Got to get an under-
        standing of the group.

LADY 1: Not necessarily an un-
        derstanding. You've got
        to get involved in a
        group.

LADY 2: I think you've got to
        . . . .

LADY 1: . . . Got to get involved
        to get understanding.

LADY 2: . . . Walk in and do it,   Be spontaneous. Be honest. Let
        you know. Don't know   others provide feedback.
        what you're doing, just
        do it. Evaluate it later
        by sharing.

End of segment of session one.

In some ways the preceding protocol is like a play within a play because while the people talk about outside groups they themselves are
going through the same security-providing, limit-testing behavior they
will face with their own groups. As was pointed out earlier, many of
the cues the group members responded to are nonverbal. This protocol

therefore gives no evidence of intragroup interaction seen through head shaking, smiles, closed eyes, or agitated movement. Hopefully, this protocol demonstrates that even in groups convened without prior notice, in what might be considered a minimal therapeutic setting, the actions and feelings of participants permit the group to move from a superficial discussion of conventional topics to those loaded with personal meaning and dealing with intragroup relationships.

However, this protocol was selected for inclusion in this text for another reason beyond those cited. Although the participants in the protocol were participating voluntarily, and despite the inclusion of minority group members, they were typically middle-class in values and in verbal skills. They, therefore, wondered if when operating on an outreach basis with alienated youth they could expect similar responses. In a later chapter there is a discussion of minority group problems, but it should be stated at this time that Maslow's need theory is basic to the use of this type of verbal group. The client who says "I want Bread, man, not talk," is sometimes saying he cannot afford to look at himself until his belly is fed, his children are clothed, and he has a place to sleep. It may also suggest that the client's style of life is action-oriented not verbal-oriented. It may also focus on the present rather than the future, and be impulsive rather than planfully directed.

This protocol should also demonstrate that a group does not just happen. There are things you have to do, overtly do, to help people learn how to provide support to each other. This is one of the reasons why when earlier publications described client-centered therapy as extremely permissive, they were right in one way and wrong in another. They were correct in assuming that the individual had the freedom to make decisions about his own behavior, but were wrong in suggesting that there are no limits. There *are* limits.

The limits most immediately imposed are the limits that come from what fellow group members will permit an individual group member to do. When he acts, he is doing something to them, and they may respond with the feeling that it is an act they will not let anyone get away with One of the things that people learn in a group where open communica tion is possible is that their freedom ends where the rights of others begin. They learn this very overtly through the process of confrontation. But, encounter groups, sensitivity groups, etc., notwithstanding, the ability of a person to hear what others are saying is a function of his security in the group. It is my feeling that it is far better to help people lower their own defenses than to strip them of their protection before alternate ways of coping with stress have been learned.

ANOTHER DEMONSTRATION OF A DIDACTIC
TEACHING APPROACH TO GROUP SKILLS[2]

The following material represents a demonstration given at an American Personnel and Guidance Association Convention. Although it is dated, it is included because readers rated it as one of the more helpful sections of an earlier textbook by the author.

We will try here to have what is rather a typical session for us. How typical is may be of the usual classroom is something we would like to discuss with you later. There is just one other thing I'd like to mention to you: I tried to point out that the goal of the course is indicated to the students at registration and at the initial class session. There are only two other limits imposed in the course. One is that every session, like this one, is to be tape recorded; after every session students are required to listen to the recording so they can have a chance to hear what went on in the group that they didn't hear, because they were so personally involved. We have one other gimmick. Right after each session the students write logs on their impression of what's been going on in the group. They then have a chance when they listen back to the recording to discover what they failed to perceive in their initial impressions.

Generally, when we listen back to a tape, we do it in a group so that we can all share our perceptions of what's going on. It gives us a chance to compare what one person is seeing and the other is not. At this point I'm just going to leave it to the group to carry on. I might tell you that we did not plan this session before and so have no idea of what's coming up. (To the group)[3]

---

[2] The following segment has appeared in *Working With Groups: Group Process and Individual Growth*, by Walter M. Lifton, N.Y.: Wiley, 1966.

[3] In the original session group members were introduced to the audience. Because years have passed, participants are listed below in terms of their present location and status. Curt Stafford, Professor at San Jose State College; Elizabeth Mullins, Southern Illinois University; Mary Ann (Pelican) Milligan, married and living in Canada; Bill Lewis, Professor at University of Missouri, Kansas City; Dorothy (Farris) Rae, married and living in Champaign, Illinois; Bill Carlson, Professor at Western Michigan University; Rita Newton, deceased; Dominick Mazzitelli, Chief Psychologist at Bergen Pines Hospital, New Jersey. Dean Sharpe who served as group recorder has retired from Central Michigan State Teachers College.

Protocol	*Comments*
1. Where do you want to start?	1. An open-ended question indicating immediately to the group that the responsibility is theirs.
2. CURT: Well, we noticed one thing right off, Walt; as soon as you stood up, way back, you notice how the group kind of quieted down. Boy, they perceive you as an authority figure. Well that's your last chance.	2. Continuing of structuring by group redefining initial leader's role.
3. LIZ: I, uh, I don't like the recorder (pointing to Louise Sharpe) down there at the end of the group.	3–17. Group sets about task of developing security with each other. The presence of a nonparticipating and nonvulnerable observer has to be resolved. The group recognizes that Dean Sharpe's presence has both positive and negative effects. They examine ways to incorporate this person so she will not be a source of threat.
4. DOM: If she was not down there then I'll have to be down there, and I don't like being at the end of the group.	
5. CURT: You mean this is something different from what we've had before?	
6. LIZ: We've never had a member in the group before that wasn't a part of the group.	
7. DEAN SHARPE: Well, the recorder doesn't write legibly, so maybe that will help.	
8. WALT: Dorothy. Are you trying to say something?	
9. DOROTHY: I was uh, well, when you were talking about the recorder down here, I thought that maybe we could pull her in and make her be a part of us. Or did you mean that you just don't, you don't	

like anyone writing stuff as we . . .

10. LIZ: Oh no, it's not the writing, 'cause we write ourselves.

11. SHARPE: This is something personal, between you and me. (*Laughter*)

12. DOM: The role, huh?

13. LIZ: I'll see you after class . . .

14. DOM: You leave her here 'cause I need some support on this.

15. BILL L: I think it's the role that she's not comfortable with, not the personality.

16. BILL C: Is it a matter of her being up here with us physically, but not being with us as part of the group?

17. LIZ: That's right.

18. DOM: I have a different idea on this. I think we're going to take out on Dean Sharpe what we would like to take out on the rest of the group watching because we're scared, 'specially the ones behind me. Real paranoid. (*Laughter*) (To Dean Sharpe) So don't take it personally. (*Laughter*)

18. An interpretation of underlying hostility coming from being in a threatening situation. Attempt to help Dean Sharpe see the hostility is not directed toward her, but rather what she represents.

19. CURT: This is certainly something unique from the way we've been used to functioning in class. We haven't had all these externals to try to get over with. . . . I hope we get over them in a little bit. (*Laughter*)

19. Having faced the underlying feeling, the desire is expressed to move on.

Protocol

20. MARY ANN: Have you noticed how we are deferring getting started?

21. BILL: Yeah!

22. CURT: Yeah, we're very much aware of their presence.

23. WALT: We haven't gotten started?

24. LIZ: We've started, but we're ahead of ourselves. (*Laughter*)

25. BILL L: All this laughing shows some tension.

26. DOM: That's an understatement!

27. MARY ANN: (*Jumble of voices*) We got started awfully quickly for a beginning session. It usually takes us quite some time. I think one of the reasons is that I don't think I could stand much silence with so many people around, where I would be comfortable with about 30 seconds of silence in the classroom. No more than 30 seconds.

28. WALT: Then it's not only the person who is using writing differently, but also silence has taken on a different meaning for us in *this* group.

29. MARY ANN: The thing is that I've often found silence to be a very comfortable thing . . .

Comments

20–22. Awareness of the fact that this topic is also serving the purpose of delaying the group from having to face the threats from within the group.

23. Question designed to point up that (20–22) are really subterfuges since they, too, are part and parcel of the steps a a group goes through to achieve security.

24–26. Another reflection of the underlying anxiety and tension.

27. After recognizing feeling, group is again able to examine reasons for tension. Definition of how silence in this context is a source of threat.

28. Reflection of two feelings recognized as sources of threat.

29–34. With acceptance of feeling, they move on to see

Protocol

and here, all of a sudden, it scares me to death!

30. BILL C: I wonder if we had only the people at the table we could comfortably be silent, but we feel some other pressures.

31. BILL L: Well, we're supposed to be up here to show something, to prove something, and we feel that the silence won't prove anything.

32. RITA: In radio the worst crime is over 5 seconds of silence.

33. DOROTHY: Yeah, and we also realize that we won't have too much time to do it in, so we try to make the best use of the time that we do have.

34. MARY ANN: I feel a terrific pressure to perform . . . and say something.

35. CURT: And we've all gone through the experience in the actual class setting. You can't hurry the thing along. That's what really makes it bad.

36. WALT: Sort of a conflict for us. On the one hand we see that we can't speed it up . . . and yet we feel that we've got to put across a point.

37. DOM: What are we trying to put across? We're trying to condense in a half hour the experiences we've felt, and I believe it's very close to all of us, a whole term's work or a whole year's work in a half hour and

Comments

what these feelings really represent.

35. Recognition of the limits of time along with an acceptance of limits of human abilities.

36. Reflects ambivalent needs that are in conflict.

37–38. Sees a need to define problem prior to an attempt at resolution.

show these people that we've got something *good* here! How can we do this in a half hour? I feel defeated before I start.

38. LIZ: Dom, that's a big problem I've run into in my work . . . I want to convince them that here's something good . . . and words can't describe it. You almost have to go through the session to do it, but if you have to go to Illinois and take this course to start using it, it's not going to go very far, very fast.

39. LIZ: It's a frustrating situation!

39. Reflects tension and frustration in problem solving.

40. DOM: Yeah, this is something similar to this meeting I was sitting in on yesterday . . . where we were talking about something, and the thing that they seemed to be talking about was: how do you convey, or how do you describe, how do you *tell* a person about what he feels in a client-counselor relationship? No one seemed to know how to say it. This is the problem we have now, how do we show what we're feeling? How could we describe this? How can we tell them that when we were in this particular class—and I'm using this because there was security there—how can we tell them that this was a good thing? You just don't describe

40. Sees problem as difficulty in communication of personal feelings, along with a recognition that the content of the words used may be very foreign to the feelings they are communicating.

Protocol

Comments

it . . . the words that we use, I forgot the topics we talked about, except the sex life of the Eskimo. (*Laughter*)

41. MARY ANN: That was a good discussion!

42. CURT: You're excluding me from the group now. (*Mixed voices*)

43. CURT: How many different classes do we have represented here now?

44. WALT: Yeah, I think that's one point that we might clarify and that is that the people here were not all in a group together and that we have several groups represented. The people at the table to-day represent a new group that has never really worked together. We are going through some of the growing pains of being a group even at this time.

41–44. Awareness that content cannot serve as easily as feelings as a basis for providing a common denominator. Also present is the right of the individual to help the group see the effect of its behavior on him.

45. LIZ: Wait a minute Walt, hold on.

45. Leader made the mistake of trying to speak for the group without either being so delegated or being sure he represented their position.

46. BILL C: I think we are simply saying that the security we get can be gotten from the groups that we were once in, but we have to get it from the group we have here.

47. DOM: Until I get it here, I'm going to use my other group as a basis. (*Laughter*)

46–56. Group recognizes need to find security. Initially they seek security in past experiences. From this grows the recognition that whatever the basis of past security, to be really useful it must be used to help develop a new basis

Protocol

48. MARY ANN: The only thing is, though, that the support that we once had . . . for example, the four of us . . . pardon me, Walt, the five of us . . . (*laughter*) and the security that we had together, can be a basis to begin reaching out to these folks that we don't know as well.

49. BILL L: Yeah, but why can't . . .

50. LIZ: If they feel left out, what then? How do you pull them in?

51. DOM: What you're saying is that we should pull them into our group. Why shouldn't they pull us into their group?

52. BILL L: Why don't we just realize this is a different group?

53. DOROTHY: Yes!

54. DOM: O.K.

55. BILL C: But it's this group here that we're working with now.

56. DOROTHY: Uh huh.

57. WALT: This is kind of hard for us to face at this time.

58. BILL C: It's nice to look back, but our problem isn't in looking back . . . it's looking here.

59. DOM: I think one thing we can do, though, although they are different groups . . . there were similar types of experiences in the sense that the structures

Comments

for security in this new setting.

57. Reflection of difficulty in facing present threat rather than past security.

58. Acceptance of these feelings.

59. Having faced threat, the group now tries to seek a solution. The idea being confused, the words reflect ambiguity. A good

Protocol

were similar, and we are trying to understand each other
and ourselves through this
structure, and I think one of
the ways in both groups or the
three groups that are represented here, is that we are
looking for some kind of support so that we could feel less
threatened and talk about
ourselves. I think we could
start in terms of that. If I
know what I'm talking about.
(*Laughter*) I'm not sure.

60. MARY ANN: It's hard to talk.
Will you try again?

61. DOM: Yeah, I think that one
thing we've experienced, is
that when we did get a group
going . . . ah . . . we had
enough support from each
other so that we could deal
with problems that we wanted
to deal with, that were pressing, whether they were . . . ah
. . . manifested in the group.
Or . . . ah . . . seemed peculiar
to the group, or they were
really something we brought
in from outside. We had something we wanted to talk about
to somebody. Ah . . . however
we did this didn't make any
difference to me. I got a good

Comments

example of an attempt
through words to search
for the idea.

60. First overt effort of a
group member to provide
specific support to an-
other person. Support is
offered through accep-
tance of the feeling plus
an offer of continued ac-
ceptance.

61. Recognition of effect of
group support on en-
abling a person to think
through an idea.

Protocol	**Comments**
feeling going . . . I felt that somebody was understanding what I was saying.	
62. CURT: The thing that still bothers me about this, Dom, is the thing that was brought up a little earlier, this time pressure. Ah . . . I'm in the class right now . . . and uh . . . we've had something like 12 sessions, 12 2-hour sessions, and just *now* we're getting around to the point where we're dealing with some things that have really been bothering a lot of people. Well that's 24 hours of work. Here we are pushing on this 15 minutes to $\frac{1}{2}$ hour and it still bothers me.	62. A return to a previous strong feeling which, at least for this person has not been resolved. Group, however, accepts the right of the person to return to an idea he has not worked out for himself.
63. RITA: But some of it transfers from one of the 427 (number of group guidance course) groups to another, because one of the people in your group happens to be the minister at our church; and he thinks . . . because he knows I took the course, he's able to say . . . just one sentence . . . "Rita, we've become a group!" (*Laughter*)	63–67. The group returns to an issue which will be a major issue for some time. The question of whether transfer of experiences to new situations is possible. This ability to see the abstract ideas which are common to both old and new situations is the height of mature understanding and learning.
64. LIZ: You understand what he means . . .	
65. RITA: Yeah, and so he singles me out to tell this to. So that in a way, if you were in 427, there are a lot of things like that I could say to you, and I'd know you'd understand.	

Protocol

Comments

66. Dom: I have the same experience with one of the girls . . .
this girl in your class now . . .
she looked at me and said she
was taking 427 . . . and I said
"Uh huh" . . . (*Laughter*) I
didn't have to say a word.

67. Dorothy: But you know, on
the other hand, uh . . . there
can also be some people who
maybe . . . haven't had 427 . . .
that you can be talking about
some of these things to, and
they, too, can understand.
And they can know the thing
you're trying to do and even
be helpful.

68. Mary Ann: I think the thing
that's so hard to in any way
demonstrate to people is the
kind of relationships we establish with each other, that are
so abnormal . . . in the college
community, in the graduate
school . . .

68–69. Beginning of acceptance
of underlying sex compo-
nents of feelings and the
difference between the appropriateness of express-
ing these feelings in different settings.

69. Rita: 427 makes us abnormal?
(*Laughter*)

70. Mary Ann: No, I mean the
ways we acted toward each
other were different in the
ways we could talk and feel
. . .

70–77. An exploration of the
limits and relationships
which distinguish this
type of group from others.

71. Bill L: Such an in-group feeling.

72. Liz: But is this necessarily the
result of the college community . . . or can you do this
anytime you put a collection
of people together in the

Protocol   *Comments*

proper atmosphere and create a group?

73. DOROTHY: We are trying to understand something together.

74. LIZ: That's right, you can do this anywhere, whether it's on a college campus or (*group adds names of other settings*).

75. MARY ANN: What I mean though, Liz, let me try to clarify this, is . . . in the business world, or in the academic world, people *don't* act toward each other the way you and I act toward each other in our groups. It's a stripping of a lot of things.

76. DOM: It's a real different structure.

77. MARY ANN: That we carry around all the time.

78. DOM: When we walk into an ordinary classroom we usually have someone standing up at the front of the room. We don't look at each other, but we look at someone standing there who is going to give.

78–85. Examination of differences between past group experiences and present. Group looks at physical organization, role of initial status leader, security needs, and problems of communication.

79. CURT: Even if it isn't this situation, Dom, even if you've got a group sitting around a circle in the classroom, you don't necessarily have the kind of thing we have here. You're not baring your soul to your neighbor, necessarily.

Protocol	*Comments*
80. MARY ANN: Let me throw this in, if I may, if it means anything. I was talking to an advertising executive the other day. He was . . . Oh, all interested in this kind of attitude . . . and he said, "Well, of *course* we have people seated around in a circle!" As if this was the thing that made for the kind of attitude to relate one person to the other. You can set up the vehicle but . . .	
81. LIZ: You mean the physical setup without the feeling?	
82. MARY ANN: He was still "Boss," and people were still cautious about what they were saying.	
83. LIZ: Are you saying that what we've got here is an unreal situation, as far as reality goes, with the barriers down and security present?	
84. MARY ANN: It's real, very much real.	
85. LIZ: For us . . . but I mean . . . take it up to the Wrigley Building, if you will. (*Laughter*) Then what you get from the group we can carry with us, but you can't go up there and have the same thing talking to "Joe Blow" in the advertising game.	
86. DOM: Oh let me get a word in. (*Laughter*)	86. Upset, needs to verbalize his feelings.
87. WALT: You're real upset about this.	87. Acceptance of feelings as reflected in his behavior rather than words.

Protocol

Comments

88. DOM: Ah . . . ah . . . what I hear you saying is that first of all we had a completely different structure. One of the things that's very important is that when you're not set for this kind of structure, it's hard to see it. How long did it take us to realize what this guy's role was? (*Pointing to Walt Lifton*)

88. As before with Dom, idea presented by person who provided help is incorporated in Dom's thinking. Specifically he focuses on the differences in perception that are gained through words versus behavior. Emphasis is on importance of behavior.

89. MARY ANN: A long time.

90. DOM: He told us point-blank we could take care of the marks, the grades, important. Every class we go for grades. They go up to the Teacher Placement Office and they are on our records, and if we're looking for jobs someone's going to look at them. We think. Sometimes they don't. How long did it take us to work out the idea that he wasn't suddenly going to snatch away this function that he was handing us, and leave us high and dry?

91. MARY ANN: What I'm *trying* to say is that in a normal situation in business or somewhere else people don't have the security to do the things that we do here.

91. Recognition that ability to perceive is a function of perceptual defense. Concept of perceptual defense (you see what you can stand seeing) with increased security people see more of the world around them.

92. BILL L: That's right. It takes so long to get the feeling for the group. . . . Like we were

92. Again a repeat of an earlier theme of the inability of society to recognize the

Protocol

Comments

talking about "we've got a group now." It took how many weeks to understand what it meant? Whereas, in the business world if things don't go like that (*snapping his fingers*) or in the classroom if things don't move right along, well generally the instructor or the students are so insecure they can't stand it.

93. Liz: Didn't we become a group after we hit the wall, and when we hit it and fell, they picked us back up and that's when we became a group?

94. Dom: I still have the scars.

95. Dorothy: Mary Ann, are you really trying to say that in groups outside of this class this thing can't happen?

96. Mary Ann: No, I don't mean that at all . . .

97. Rita: No, but you can't expect it. Sometimes you leave the classroom with a sense of expectancy. I would leave 427 and dash down to a very small seminar group, and we all sat around a table just the same size and boy did I get into trouble day after day!

98. Mary Ann: What I mean is this . . . I'm not saying it's not

realities of both time and human ability.

93. This comment points up the fact that the height of group security is achieved when the person falls in his own eyes, yet continues to be accepted by others. It is the beginning of the feeling that they are accepted as people, not just because of their ideas or behavior.

95–100. Recapitulation of transferability concept now combined with the role security plays in understanding.

Protocol

Comments

possible; as a matter of fact it would be fine if it were able to be put into use. I'm saying that people, in business or somewhere else, can't say kind or nasty things to each other, without having a reaction that is negative. Here we can do both of those things.

99. Liz: Well, isn't that why you created this kind of group for teaching purposes?

100. Bill L: Well, it really doesn't become a group until the anxiety gets so high about this sort of thing and then there has to be cohesiveness.

101. Walt: You mean we became a group because we were so afraid of something else?

101. Reflection that group is perceived as a means of dealing with threat.

102. Bill L: We were so threatened if nothing was going on, we'd have to get together.

103. Dom: I think what we're saying here . . .

104. Liz: Dom!

105. Dom: Wait a minute Liz—(*laughter*). I think what we're saying here is that people are not used to perceiving each other this way or reacting to each other this way and what it takes is a complete reorientation. Ordinarily, when anyone walks into a classroom, he's set, he's been trained, I remember when I sat in elementary school, this way, (*showed his hands clasped in*

103–105. Resurgence of former relationship where these two people competed for leadership. Although Dom cuts Liz off, he indicates his awareness of what he has done, and his feelings of responsibility to her.

Protocol

front of him) everytime the teacher walked down the aisle, it was hard for me to *un*seat myself this way . . . and . . . outside of groups that are planned this way . . . it's a difficult thing to set up. It takes time for people to realize and to become comfortable. They're comfortable in a role where someone gets up and tells them something. They're used to this, and it's very threatening to take on the responsibility of a group member and to be responsible for the other person sitting on the other side of the desk or the chair . . . desk or the chair, I'm confused! (*Laughter*) . . . The table, I'll get to it, Liz. Ah . . . it takes a lot of time to take on this responsibility of somone else's needs and to say if I'm going to get my own needs satisfied, I'm going to have to help someone else! We just don't work that way ordinarily . . . it's hard to shift!

106. MARY ANN: But . . .

107. RITA: Wait! Liz, you had one oar in, this is the supreme sacrifice for me. (*Laughter*)

108. LIZ: I know! The thing that threw me now was when people use the word "group" they generally mean something entirely different from what we have here. And the same

Comments

107–108. Very interesting by-play. Rita is indicating to the group not only how she has changed but is also demonstrating how "time" —time to talk or think— is now seen as "giving" rather than just submission. Liz is re-raising

Protocol

Comments

word being used on two things, and the only way I could differentiate was the way I felt in the two places, and this I couldn't explain. It was terrible.

problems of semantics and communication.

109. CURT: This is what I was wondering about your group, Mary Ann, are you thinking of a group as setting out to do something . . . say get a certain job lined up in business?

110. MARY ANN: Well . . . I . . . certainly . . . people aren't going to group around nothing but, still, does that mean that there doesn't have to be some sort of relationship established?

111. WALT: There's something here that bothers me, as it must. Are you saying that when we are related on a feeling level, we got no tasks done?

109–111. Exploration of concept that goals of groups whether they be work or "people" oriented would effect group relationships. Raises the basic philosophical issue as to the reason for the existence of groups. As a means toward an end or as an end in itself.

112. MARY ANN: Thank you.

112. Support obtained through identification.

113. CURT: No, there's a difference between going specifically at a task as, say, the stereotype which I have, in which you might be doing something in business, as opposed to the way we approach it here.

114. LIZ: I think we ought to let Rita come in with what she has . . .

114. Having been helped Liz now wants to help Rita use the group, too.

115. RITA: You know, this is a real change for me from last year.

Protocol

And it operated back in New York two weeks ago when I gave up the floor in the midst of twenty-five people, when I'd been trying to get in all morning! Ah . . . now I forgot what I was going to say! (*Laughter*)

116. CURT: You lose your thought when you wait.

117. RITA: If you've got the ability to structure this kind of thing in other groups, it can be done in other groups. It doesn't have to be a counseling department of a college for it to work. It can work in other groups but it has to be planned for, and worked for, and wanted. The limits have to be set; it has to be explained. I lived with a minister for awhile. two years ago; this always floors people! She was a *girl* minister. (*Laughter*) . . . and she had a youth group, and it was in a church that was fairly authoritarian about its other relationships . . . at least didn't have this kind of orientation, and she was able to set up a group, of people which included me . . . and it was a church with which I had very little sympathy for. She included me as sort of "Devil's Advocate," and I got the warmest, most wonderful, se-

Comments

116. Support through reflection of feeling while also indicating an interest in what she is trying to say.

117. People can be accepted for themselves not just their beliefs.

Protocol

Comments

cure feeling from that group! And they were people whose ideas I ordinarily could not tolerate.

118. MARY ANN: I wanted to tell an experience. I didn't think I'd get a chance to say anything beyond the Wrigley Building. We designed study groups to work in different geographical and political areas. My pride and joy is the Latin American group, who wanted to study like crazy for weeks. We started in September. We are just getting to the point now, when one of the ladies in particular, who is only there not to learn about Latin America, but to have some *friends,* is making her friends. The group leader is just becoming aware of this. We've begun doing work, and we're learning about *Latin America.* She's not worrying about her friends anymore, 'cause she has them. She's gotten away from all this other junk, which is no longer important. And . . . what I'm saying is . . . it took me from September to April to get this idea across. 'Cause this was a man who's in the insurance business who *told people what to do!* (*Laughter*) And no one seemed to realize . . .

118. Mary Ann returns to her attempts to reconcile work groups and therapeutic groups.

119. DOM: You know, the funniest thing just happened . . . I

119. Indicates support from relationships and strong

Protocol

didn't hear a word you said. I was just so pleased to hear your voice again. (*Laughter*)

Comments

feelings of affection that develop in groups. It was remarks like these that caused some members of the audience to be concerned about the possibility that group members would "act out" their needs with each other, in out-of-group sessions. Briefly, this problem was faced by the group in class and techniques developed to deal with it. Actually it has never represented a problem since basically a respect for the other person's need led group members to be very careful about the effect of their behavior on others. Dom's comment also demonstrates that the relationships are effected by more than just the words used. Mannerisms and physical gestures became a language in themselves.

120. MARY ANN: You see this is what you can't explain to people.

121. LIZ: Aren't we trying to describe what exists here that doesn't exist many places, a climate that permits you to use this kind of group in any way you want to?

122. MARY ANN: Yes.

123. LIZ: We can use it to learn group dynamics, or counsel-

Protocol   **Comments**

ing, or "basket weaving," or
. . .

124. DOROTHY: (*Jumble of voices*)
That we can take it out into
groups that possibly are in
situations or places where people have never heard of this
type of thing before, and apply some of the principles
that ah . . . that we have
gained, that we have experienced eh . . . as you were
talking a little while ago, Dom
. . . we actually experience
these things in this group.
Well, all right, we've experienced them, so we can go out
in situations and . . . begin
making these things *work*.

125. CURT: That was what was get-   125. Picks up idea of learning
ting me. You were mentioning   problem solving rather
things like "basket weaving,"   than the solution in a
and I got to thinking of that,   specific situation.
and I didn't hear all of what
you said Dorothy, so I had to
pick up the tail end. It's more
than what you learn about
Latin America. It's well,
"here's me," "here's how I
function," "I'm learning some
new things about how I function." "It gives me this greater
freedom."

126. RITA: Here's something I   126. Understanding the con-
thought about when you were   cept frees the person to
saying "Go forth and do like-   express his idea in his
wise." The thing I found in   own way.
my sort of work was that I
couldn't go forth and do likewise. And I'm still not cap-

Protocol   *Comments*

able of working with my Art
Ed classes in the way that this
group works . . . but I'm a
different person, so I'm working differently with the classes.

127. CURT: Are you different, Rita,
or are you seeing yourself differently?

128. RITA: Oh well, let's not go
into that!

129. BILL C: Are we saying that we   129–132. Here we have one of the
can't possibly jump from what   major problems in a de-
we have in the security of a   mocracy. Having solved
group like this immediately   a problem once, it's hard
to other groups, but that we   to accept that each new
have to work for some kind   group demands the right
of security with them? Some-   to develop in its own way,
times we have to start quite   even if it involves making
a ways down the "totem pole"   mistakes others have made
to work on up towards the top.   before them. This is the
                                          eternal cry of the adoles-
130. BILL L: It seems like you're   cent who resents parental
expecting too *much,* if you're   domination and wants
expecting every group to have   the right to shape his own
this sort of feeling about it.   life. As the group ma-
                                          tures they are better able
131. LIZ: It takes a long time to   to use other's past experi-
get it, but I think the big   ence as a basis for making
problem, at least I found it   their decisions. They can-
was going as a member of this   not accept this informa-
group to a leader of another   tion until they feel sure
group. The thing that made   they are secure enough
us a group actually was get-   to not let the data itself
ting rid of Walt as a leader   guide them in directions
and pulling him in as a mem-   they may not wish to go.
ber.

132. DOM: It's an interesting thing
we are saying . . . how do we
tell people about this? Do we
go in as a leader and try to
describe this and yet when we

Protocol

Comments

came into the group and Walt described it to us, I thought he was talking Chinese! The conclusion I come to is wherever the specific places that we want to initiate this type of relationship, and you can't do it everywhere . . . it's not the panacea for relationships, it's specific. . . . The only way we can do it is by going out and living it, because you can't do it just by saying it. You have to go out and instead of explaining it, just like we didn't understand it, how do we expect them to understand it? It's a feeling, thing, it's a . . .

133. Liz: A big problem I ran into was . . . here I'm accustomed to saying what I'm feeling. You've clobbered me back down whenever I've gone too high, and I have . . . and I got into a group this year that when I *did* it, I scared some of the people and they backed away. And it really frustrated me because I wanted to say what I was feeling, but if I did it, I destroyed what grouping they had to begin with.

133. Just expressing feelings isn't enough. The setting where it is done, and the way it is done both will effect a person's relationship to a group.

134. Bill C: The group didn't have enough security to accept what you were doing.

135. Mary Ann: For the first time I found the tricky problem Walt probably had, because first of all, here I am . . . I am the leader, and there

135–136. Being a leader may put you in a conflict situation where what you want to be does not always coincide with a group's per-

Protocol

were people there that were 30 years my senior! And yet they referred to me as an authority figure, and this isn't what I wanted! And then, I tried to "group it up" and be a member (*laughter*) . . . and I felt rejected and I drove home with my "tail between my legs" feeling "nobody likes me!" (*Laughter*) You suddenly have to try to find out where you *do* fit in this group.

136. LIZ: I think part of the problem is, we expect the other members of the group to perceive what we're doing, and to see what we're doing as we are just expressing ourselves. They take the common, ordinary way of perceiving it. "They're directing this at me personally."

137. BILL L: Well, one of the big things that Mary Ann was talking about, seems to me, is that when you're taking the course, it's not until we're really *into* the course that we really understand. We get real threatened in the middle, and that's probably what's happened to you . . . now . . . you're right in the middle of it and it's pretty hard.

138. LIZ: But we held together so we could get to the end.

139. MARY ANN: Yeah!

140. BILL L: Yeah.

Comments

ception of your role. It's not comfortable to be misperceived.

137–143. Part of the group process includes periods of threat. The group can face the threat only as they provide support to one another. During threat people regress to a more dependent kind of role.

Protocol

Comments

141. Liz: Sometimes they collapse around you when the first threatening occurs. And then they escape into an authoritarian setup.

142. Mary Ann: That's what they did.

143. Liz: That's exactly what they escape into . . . because it holds security for them.

144. Bill L: Well, Mary Ann's going to have to have a pat on the back once in awhile. (*Laughter*)

145. Mary Ann: Who's gonna give *me* security?

146. Liz: You're kind of by yourself on it because you're the only one that's there!

147. Walt: Aren't we saying that a part of the problem of the leader's role is to help the group cope with him and give him the support to do the role that he wants to have?

148. Dorothy: Yeah.

149. Mary Ann: Uh huh.

150. Liz: That's the problem we keep having trouble with.

151. Mary Ann: Now the point is, how are we going to implement this? Solve my problem please! (*Laughter*) I can't stand another one of these Latin American sessions. (*Laughter*)

152. Rita: Well, you'd have to solve mine, too.

144–147. Until the group develops an acceptance of the leader, he needs a basic personal security to accept the hostility and rejection he may experience. Leader's role may be to help group learn how to deal with the leader.

148–153. In facing this problem group is providing each other support as they identify with each other. Feelings of guilt based on fear of personal inadequacy are alleviated as they are shared.

Protocol

153. LIZ: Mine, too.

154. RITA: I have one group that just doesn't want to be a group. (*Laughter*) And uh . . . I am learning how to use myself in a different way from what I used to be. I think 427 didn't teach me how to use myself as a group leader the way 427 used a group leader. I have become a different kind of group leader, and it fits me, and I can do it that way.

155. BILL L: What . . . what's your concept of a group leader?

156. RITA: In one group I don't . . . this didn't work either and I haven't got any technique for it.

157. LIZ: What's a group leader?

158. BILL L: Look at the way Walt's leading this group. (*Laughter*)

159. LIZ: Yeah . . . but he's not leading it.

160. BILL L: That's what I'm trying to say.

161. RITA: Can you picture me leading a group this way? (*Laughter*)

162. DOM: I think it is a bad comparison because Walt isn't leading this group and . . .

163. BILL L: Well, that's what I mean, she's saying . . .

164. DOM: We have already had other experiences with Walt.

Comments

154–166. With an acceptance of problem, group now is free to examine different ways members could solve problems.

Protocol

We have him sort of controlled in our own minds. (*Laughter*) However we did it, we did it, but Rita is talking about going in with a new group, and I think this is a different situation. I don't know . . .

165. WALT: Are we saying that there is no leadership in this group?

166. BILL L: No.

167. LIZ: No, we're saying no one person holds the role of leadership.

168. BILL L: But . . . apparently . . . it seems to me that she is perceiving it differently.

169. DOM: (*Everybody said no*) Why not . . .

170. LIZ: Because leadership is a quality of the group, and we shift it back and forth as we go. You had it a minute ago; I've got it now. Bill's gonna get it.

171. CURT: I think one thing we can . . . (*Jumble of voices*) (*laughter*)

172. CURT: Uh . . . this business of leadership I think it's been a group leadership on this one point. Now compare our group here. We're a first . . . an initial group here. This is

Comments

167–170. Group explores idea that leadership doesn't need to be the prerogative of only one person. Concept that leadership can include verbal passivity is examined.

171. Play on words "who's going to get it" reflects anxiety over hostility expressed by group members when a leadership role is assumed by a person.

172. Facing anxiety, group examines how with less tension their behavior is changing.

Protocol

Comments

our first session, and you compare it with the first sessions
you remember from 427 and
. . . uh . . . boy! We went
through a period here where
everyone was trying to get
into it so (*gesturing cutting
each other off*). In the beginning it was fast and furious
. . . but we have slowed down
a little now. I am starting to
recognize some of you as I
normally know you outside
. . . I . . . (*laughter*) I . . .
we're talking a little more
slowly and also we've moved
off . . . uh . . . uh . . .

173. Dom: A good indicator of this
is that we haven't bothered
Dr. Sharpe here. (*Laughter*)

174. Bill L: Let Curt finish.

175. Liz: Yes . . .

176. Mary Ann: Let's let Curt finish.

177. Dom: Well, I . . . if you insist . . . (*Laughter*)

178. Curt: The things we have
been getting into here at the
end of examining these things
that have been happening to
us since then. We have moved
a good bit from the opening.
I . . . I think we've grown.

179. Dom: I see what you're saying, what you are saying is
that we have reached the level
where people don't bother us
as much as they did, and one
of the indicators is that we

174–178. Almost because of 170
and 171 group fights to
protect the rights of the
individual.

Protocol	*Comments*
didn't bother Mrs. Sharpe. She's sort of faded in the background.	
180. MARY ANN: I only want to say one thing . . . uh . . . and that was what Rita said. I want to try to figure it out, if I can . . . uh . . . she was giggling when she said, "Try to imagine me being as quiet as Walt has been." Try to imagine *me* being quiet as Walt has been, but I have done it. And it's completely amazed me. I mean . . . under particular circumstances where the only thing you could do was to shut up, you shut up.	180–188. Growing awareness that new roles are possible, and that new behavior in some situations is valuable. Also present is the realization that real growth comes not from identifying with and copying someone else, but in developing one's own way of doing things.
181. CURT: You know, we're . . . we're loaded here in one thing. Now . . . looking around at the table. I don't know Dorothy and Bill too well from seeing them in class, but the rest of you I have seen in action. There isn't anyone here who is noted for his silence.	
182. BILL L: Well, we can't all be talkers. (*Laughter*) We can't imitate Walt. We have to relate in the way we feel most comfortable.	
183. MARY ANN: It depends on what at that point is the thing one must do.	
184. LIZ: But . . .	
185. BILL L: Uh hum.	
186. RITA: Mary Ann, I can do	

Protocol

Comments

what he does by being quiet, and I can do it by talking, too. I found this out just a few weeks ago. I was leading a group and uh . . . uh . . . I got the same kind of results, I think, in terms of people being able to come out with highly unacceptable opinions in a group that had never seen each other before and never would again.

187. DOROTHY: Are we saying in a sense that . . . .

188. RITA: Uh . . . but I did it by doing more talking than he would do. I did it Newtonian instead of Liftonian, I guess. (*Laughter*)

189. LIZ: Yes . . . but . . . no . . . there were times in our classes when Walt carried a large verbal part of the 2-hour session.

190. MARY ANN: Yes, but what always happened? He'd get slugged at the end.

191. CURT: Wait, wait, I'll tell you.

192. DOROTHY: Just a minute. I . . . I was wanting to say . . .

193. DOM: Bang the table, kids. (*Laughter*)

194. DOROTHY: Maybe there are many, many ways of being a group leader.

195. GROUP: Yes . . . sure.

196. BILL C: For example, uh . . . if we could go on long enough,

189–198. Repeat on theme that leadership carries with it possible group hostility and rejection. 196 may be in response to Dom's statement that to be recognized one needs to bang the table. The idea here is that the group has a mellowing effect. It subdues the too aggressive while encouraging the more subdued.

we might guess that people who had been most aggressive here might find themselves in rather . . . find themselves in certain leader roles . . . that the group would react to. I remember this happening in our own group that uh . . . uh . . . after the group settled down after some of the beginning sessions, and then some of the individuals in the group began . . . began to pick up bumps because Walt . . . the group had . . . well, I guess Walt took it first, didn't you?

197. WALT: Uh huh . . .

198. BILL C: And then . . . then it got passed around to some of the others.

199. CURT: Walt, do you mind if I mention a little bit about . . . about the way you were using the group . . . uh . . . as a member yourself?

199–202. Reflects concern for concept of confidentiality.

200. WALT: Uh huh.

201. CURT: You *would* mind?

202. WALT: No. (*Laughter*)

203. CURT: Something that pointed out a lot to us . . . uh . . . Walt's wife has been sick, for those of you who have been away . . . she's been sick for 3–4 weeks in the hospital now and boy! We could . . . we could just see his behavior in class. He wasn't a leader at all. I mean, he was in there.

Protocol

. . . "I've got some problems."
Boy, "my home is all shook
up and all." I think everyone
in the group was aware of
this after a very short time.
He was . . . he was just using
the group to help himself out.
And uh . . . this I think,
above all is the thing that . . .
oh . . . which destroyed any
ideas that anyone may have
had that he was still an authority. He was just using us
for himself.

204. WALT: It is a real question,
now, Curt, as to whether that's
a good thing. Certainly people differ on this.

205. LIZ: Isn't that the . . .

206. CURT: Well, I know that . . .
oh . . . the way . . . we had
been discussing his role so
much, trying to find his role
and all. Not the fact that it
came out and here it was . . .
uh . . . we were doing his role,
I mean. It was defined by his
actions.

207. BILL C: Is this suggesting that
to the extent that the leader
can himself get help from the
group, he can then help other
people?

208. LIZ: I think it's also saying
that to the extent that the
leader is seen as an authoritarian . . . uh . . . it's related
to how much the group will
become a group as we speak
of it here.

Comments

204–217. Controversial issue as to
whether initial group
leader ought to allow personal needs to enter into
group situation. The con-
cept present here is
that since initial leader
provides, through group
identification with him,
clues as to ways to be-
have in a group, the
more roles he is able to
play with honesty, the
larger the range of pos-
sibilities of behaviors are
made available to the
group. Group seems to
react to behavior as de-
scribed in 203 with the
feeling "If it's all right for
him to admit these feel-
ings and weaknesses it
surely ought to be O.K.
for me to do the same."
Along with this is the
idea that if a group can

Protocol

209. MARY ANN: Well . . .

210. BILL C: I think you are turning it upside down. To the extent that he's *not* an authority, he can be helpful.

211. LIZ: That's right.

212. MARY ANN: Yeah, the point is that . . . that he is not the only therapist, that each one of us, in our turn, we are equal to serve when we are able to be a therapist.

213. LIZ: But it is terrifically frustrating to people, and I know 'cause I was one of them . . . that have relied on an authority for security.

214. CURT: Uh hum.

215. LIZ: And to have it pulled away . . . why you hit hard. I bounced back up, though, fortunately.

216. DOM: That's an understatement.

217. BILL L: That's where the (*laughter*) where the group leader, the one who is initially the group leader, has to be very secure because the group members when they first start out say "where's the authority; where's the security," and they all start griping and complaining.

218. LIZ: And if you can't find it in him, you turn and look to each other for it, and the minute you get it or get a taste of it,

Comments

accept a leader as having human weaknesses, rather than being perfect, they change their concept of what to expect from a leader. It also changes their concept of the ways in which they should relate to him. Concurrent with this changing concept which permits the leader to be imperfect, is the growing willingness on the part of group members to assume a role they feel they now can measure up to.

218. Awareness that group members, too, have potentiality for giving leadership and support pro-

Protocol

why that's when the group rolls.

219. MARY ANN: Yeah.

220. BILL L: Yeah, that's when it's worth all the anxiety and frustration.

221. WALT: I have a problem at this point . . . I wonder how we want to solve it. We didn't set any finite limits on this group. Do we want to keep rolling, or should we let the other people have a chance?

222. LIZ: Let's let them have a chance.

223. BILL C: Yeah.

224. WALT: How about it?

225. CURT: I think so . . . because there's only so much that they can get from listening.

226. DOM: I would like to let the rest of the people in on it.

227. WALT: O.K.

228. DOM: They have been so *quiet. (Laughter)*

229. WALT: Well, I am going to stand up so at least I can see people. Also, with the session over, my authority role won't get at me so badly. Thanks a lot. I would welcome any questions or comments that any of you (to audience) would like to raise. We would feel, I am sure, much more comfortable if we could have a chance to explain what we . . . yes?

Comments

vides . the security that promotes group growth.

221. Setting of limits is a group function. Time is a major limit. In deciding on limit, group, as usual, examines its own needs as the basis for making a decision.

End of demonstration.

Protocol   *Comments*

From audience:

230. DR. MARGARET BENNETT: The
young lady directly across from
you . . .

231. WALT: Rita Newton.

232. BENNETT: A moment ago . . .   232. Question   of   nonjudg-
uh . . . made some statement   mental nature of a thera-
about a person expressing a   peutic group.
highly unacceptable opinion,
and I'd like to raise a question
and hear the group discuss
. . . uh . . . whether in a real
group therapy class you can
ever say anything that is highly
unacceptable or whether what
you say may not be a means of
your helping to understand
yourself.

233. RITA: What . . . what . . .
what . . .

234. BENNETT: Or . . .

235. RITA: I'd like to answer.

236. BENNETT: Or allowing the
group to help you understand
yourself. I wasn't quite sure
what she meant.

237. WALT: Rita.

238. RITA: When I said unacceptable I meant . . . this was a
human relations conference,
and people went with the expectation that they would talk
in favor of brotherhood. People . . .

239. BENNETT: Oh, I see, you were
speaking about . . .

240. RITA: People came out saying   240. Focus on acceptance of
things that sounded very . . .   person rather than his
unorthodox as far as what one   idea or behavior.

Protocol   *Comments*

is supposed to believe about
brotherhood if one comes
to a brotherhood conference.
(*Laughter*) There was a great
deal of hostile feeling; there
was a great deal of chauvinistic type feeling, and it was getting expressed by people. People were saying . . . I noticed
that the leader of the entire
convention was sitting facing
me and they had asked me to
lead this particular small
group. And when anyone said
anything which was not part
of the brotherhood party line,
uh . . . uh . . . a frown would
come over her face, whereas I
was sort of saying, "No, keep
going . . . I see what you
mean. I see the frame of reference, I think, in which
you're saying this. And even
if you say it and no one agrees
with you . . . they at least now
know that there are people
who think this." So that's what
I meant when I . . .

241. BENNETT: Yes, but in a real
group therapy class I wonder
if you can ever say anything
that is highly unacceptable.

242. WALT: Not in a value sense   242. Attempt to distinguish
or judgmental sense. What-   between role of group in
ever you say hasn't a value of   helping others see what
being acceptable or unaccept-   "society" would reject, as
able, but rather in societal   contrasted with what the
terms, these are some of the   group will permit to be
things we don't usually talk   expressed.
about because they're threat-
ening.

Protocol

Comments

243. WALT: Dr. Wrenn?

244. DR. WRENN: What is the so-called leader's role? Now, I grant you that this is a leaderless group (*laughter*) . . . leaderless group in the sense . . . in the fact that the leadership shifts . . . uh . . . as a teacher in a situation like this for instance . . . when somebody sticks their neck way out . . . and says something that others resent. Maybe it's a statement of hostility toward the so-called leader, you see. Then is it possible that it is the leader's role to try to relieve a little of this hostility against the one person or rather should we leave it to the group to take care of that over a period of time?

245. WALT: I think I can answer that. It's a function of the leader's own security and his feelings of confidence in the group. But . . . uh . . . for myself, I think that at the beginning I tend to be more anxious, wondering whether this group is really going to jell. And . . . I don't always have the confidence I ought to have. But my role then becomes not pulling the pressure off a person, but trying to help clarify the feeling that we're facing. "We seem to be pretty mad about something here. I wonder whether we can take a look

244. Therapist has responsibility for welfare of group members. Question raised if this does not include controlling experiences and threats the person faces in the group.

Protocol   *Comments*

at what's happening and what
we can do about it." Uh . . .
as a matter of fact, I had another kind of role that sometimes the group found helpful
and sometimes not. It almost
might be called didactic.
"What's going on now?" I
would say. "What are we doing?" "Do we like it?" So
that we could all not only
label what was going on and
see it for what it was, but possibly begin to take a look at
the way we wanted to deal
with it. And this I did fairly
actively. But, as I say, this is
me and some other person
might . . .

246. WRENN: In a well-jelled group
somebody else might take over
and try to fix the situation.

247. WALT: I think that there is
something that's very important here . . . that uh . . .
might be clarified. My role
as a leader . . . uh . . . as
I perceived it anyhow, was
to help the group set up a
structure with me in which
they could work. It was not
in terms of the *way* they would
work. I would try to help
them. But because folks like
Liz and others had feelings
about authority figures, I had
to be destroyed as an authority
figure before there *could* be
other leaders in the group.
That's what happened in the

Protocol

Comments

group that Dom was in . . .
that after I was . . . chopped
off . . . Dom was next. And
after Dom, Liz was next. You
see, we were all three authority figures, and we had things
in our personalities that made
us this. And when the group
disposed of some of our needs
that were getting in their way
and they learned how to cope
with them, then things really
rolled. I think there is one
concept here I'd like to make
clear. Uh . . . there are many
weaknesses as a person that I
am sure that I have. Uh . . .
I'd like to live with them. I'd
like to be aware of them. But
I think that my ability to work
with a group depends not
upon being a perfect person,
but trying to set up a setting
where my weaknesses won't get
in the group's way. And I
recognize that I have some of
these needs that aren't always
helpful to the group. It, therefore, to me appears more important that I give the group
a device to get me out of their
way when I am not being
helpful. But . . . just . . .

248. UNKNOWN MALE VOICE: Walt,
I would like to get some ideas
about the original problem
that was brought up by the
group here. That is, this business of getting some identification since they were more
or less strangers from the

248. Focuses on importance of
group cohesiveness as re-
lating to the degree mem-
bers relate with one an-
other. Demonstrates the
way the physical setting
can effect the nature of
the relationships.

three different groups. And I
noticed some cohesion and
some division here, one particular physical one which
seems to be . . . uh . . . uh . . .
by chance. That is, there is a
brief case between two people,
and they are seated apart . . .
(*Laughter*) This man here has
had his back turned practically
the whole time on one group
member.

249. WALT: Uh hum.

250. (As in 248): She, in turn, has
been sitting on the opposite
side of her chair. Could we
get a poll of the people around
here to see how they feel identified with each other in this
group relationship between
each other?

251. WALT: How about it? Do you
want to speak to it?

252. GROUP: Yes! It's all right with
me. I . . .

253. LIZ: I . . . I feel quite well
identified with everybody. I
completely forgot the recorder.
(*Laughter*) Umm . . .

254. SHARPE: Is that a compliment?

255. LIZ: I have become identified
with Miss Farris (Dorothy)
and Bill on the end I have less
identity with. Now, I've never
met these two people before
10:30 today. Uh . . . I didn't
. . . I feel quite well identified
with both of these people, and
then the others I have known
from the group I was in and

251. Group is still given responsibility of making
decisions.

Protocol

so I automatically picked that up, I think.

256. WALT: I think there is one point I'd like to raise. I . . . I feel a certain mission involved in this session. The things that you are describing are the things that came out in the logs. These are the things that people began to perceive and recorded in their written impressions of each class.

257. WALT (*to Mary Ann*): I . . . do you remember one of the things that you did? May I tell about it?

258. MARY ANN: Sure, I don't care. (*Laughter*)

259. WALT: In one session, Mary Ann . . . for whatever her reason was . . . (*laughter*) . . . made a wall chart of how many times people participated. Boy, did the group clobber her with that. She was raising the question as to whether or not we were worthwhile people. If we weren't . . .

260. LIZ: It was how she presented it.

261. DOM: Yeah.

262. MARY ANN: Yeah! It was the manner in which I did it.

263. WALT: You carry on . . . (*Laughter*)

264. MARY ANN: Well, it was . . . uh . . . (*laughter*) . . . and . . .

Comments

257. Vital that confidentiality be preserved. It is the member's right to decide what can be shared with people outside the group.

260–264. Demonstrates again effect of "consultant" or information giver who volunteers data group has not sought. It was not the data itself that was rejected, but rather what the presenting of the data implied about the group members' capabilities of

Protocol

the tapes, and I took down the number of responses of each party in the group. And . . . uh . . . *(laughter)* . . . and . . . uh . . . as I did this . . . uh . . . I found . . . uh . . . to some extent, the people who I thought were not talking were actually responding. Well, I came into class on my white horse *(laughter)* . . . and uh . . . instead of . . . I certainly learned a lesson. *(Laughter)* Uh . . . I put it on the blackboard without saying anything to anyone in the class. And 15 minutes of the session went by and somebody, I guess it was Liz, made some crack about "What is this baloney on the blackboard?" And then they all climbed down my throat, and I had to try to explain what it meant and I also . . . the thing that was most important in my regard is that I realized the personal, emotional reason why I had done it. And uh . . . it was a matter of terrific antagonism toward me. And yet it was followed up by *so* much security and support afterwards that I was able to face it, and . . . uh . . . personally was almost raised rather than diminished.

265. WALT: What we're suggesting here is that through this action which threatened the group, the group became responsible

Comments

recognizing problems on their own.

265. Despite hostile nature of the act, group accepts the person while rejecting the act.

Protocol

for helping an individual see what it meant to them. And in doing this, the person who had been threatened got support.

266. MARY ANN: Uh huh.

267. WOMAN'S VOICE IN AUDIENCE: I'm interested in the language used here . . . and I would guess that perhaps you found this in the beginning sessions . . . uh . . . perhaps that such words as "threatened," "external security," or "insecurity" were quite frequently used in class discussion, and then began to drop out. Do you find this in the regular class session as a kind of barrier? How is that handled in your group?

268. WALT: Dom, I wonder if you want to talk on the question of jargon and what happens in the group when you do use jargon? (*Laughter*)

269. DOM: Uh . . . the question of jargon came up quite abruptly with me. I had a lot of clinical background, and in the class I used quite a bit of the specific terminology of the clinician. And . . . uh . . . for a while I threatened the group with this because they felt . . . first of all, they didn't understand, and second of all, they . . . uh hum . . . it sounded like I knew so much more than everyone else until finally when they got a little

Comments

267. Communication being a vital issue, part of a group's growth comes in developing a "language" which is commonly understood. Part of the role of slang in the adolescent is that this is a clearly understood language.

Protocol   *Comments*

security, I started getting my
head banged in. Until . . . I
had to leave this realm, otherwise leave class bloody every
day. Uh . . . but . . . the jargon comes up not in terms of
this internal and external security and threat, it wasn't, I
would say, part of the vocabulary of the class . . . until we
would have sessions, part of
the sessions in which we would
try to find out . . . just as we
did here toward the end, we
were trying to say where have
we gone; what have we done.
And uh . . . these were the
best words we could find to
. . . uh . . . describe the process that had gone on previously, if someone said, "I
didn't like what so-and-so
said." Well, in this session
where we were trying to pull
things together and understand what went on, some-
one said, "You might have
felt threatened." And this was
a good word to express the
feeling. And this is how the
words developed, because actually when you come into the
class with jargon you have
such a diversified group, you
tend to run into the "wall." I
developed the word "wall" because I felt I was running up
against it quite a bit. I kept
bouncing off it for a while until the group felt secure with
me. And I was insecure with

the group, and this is why I
was using it, let's face it!

270. CURT: Uh . . . I would like
to speak on two points, one
right along with this and another that is somewhat new
here. We haven't brought it
in yet. I can't describe too
much about a similar instance
going on in the class now, because there's a problem of confidence in this group and . . .
uh . . . this is one of the
things that you don't come out
with in one session . . . about
how sacred are the things that
we say in here? How far
should they be carried? One
of the persons in the present
group is sitting out in the audience now. And so . . . uh
. . . I can be reported back on
this by this other one in class.
(*Laughter*) I'll be very careful about what I say, but I
would say almost 100% the
same problem has come up in
the present class now, Dom.
We have a person who is being accused of being a Freud-
ian, and throwing his Freud-
ian terms around. And . . . uh
. . . boy, it wasn't about two
sessions ago it happened.

271. DOM: I'd like to add another
thing, by the way . . . that
when the group felt secure
with me and I felt secure with
the group, they didn't hesitate
to ask me when I did use a
word that I was using as part

270. Demonstrates that this is
a common problem.

271–277. The group language is a
growing thing. They will
tend to try to share each
person's unique language
as long as they feel it
will help both the person
and the group.

Protocol   *Comments*

of my ordinary vocabulary because of the setup I was in. It
didn't . . . they didn't hesitate to ask me what I meant.
They allowed me to use it
after they understood what I
was . . . my own problem,
and they accepted me this way.

272. WALT: One of . . . I'm sorry.
Go ahead.

273. DOM: Don't interrupt me!
(*Laughter*) In fact, in fact,
there were times when they
asked me about different
things that I have had in my
own experience, which was related to this, which they had
clobbered me for previous to
this. So that it was strictly a
matter of relationship and
counter threat . . . and threat.
That once we worked this out,
it . . . this didn't constitute a
threat any longer, so it was
all right to do this.

274. CURT: There's something else
that bothers me, Dom, this
word clobber that you use. I
think this is part of our jargon.

275. RITA: We made a new jargon.

276. DOM: Very descriptive term.
I'll show you the bumps.
(*Laughter*)

277. CURT: Clobbered is more than
getting hit over the head with
a baseball bat, but it is with
soft pine because, after you
have been hit over the head,
there's security in this group

so that you can take a hit over the head and you can grow from it.

278. WALT: Well, I think the thing we learned from it was that we get hit because people care enough about you to try to do something about it.

279. MARY ANN: Let me, let me say something about what Dom said in his use of jargon in our group. And that was . . . we certainly clobbered Dom, but good! And then he found out that he could be a man that could explain things to us. After the threat was gone to both Dom and to us, he could explain his words to us and help us understand. I think part of this was in my counting responses, this same thing happened to me. I found I could help people if we both felt well enough about it.

280. WALT: Part of what we're saying here is an important concept. "How can the group learn to use people as resource people, but not as advisors who will tell them what to do?" And I think that when anyone came in with jargon or anything similar to that which by implication said to the group "This is right, this is the way it is, this is your label," the group resented it. But when a person came in and provided something that

278. Repetition of theme that honest feeling reactions from group, rather than being seen as source of threat, provide comfort since they not only let person know where he really stands but also show others' concern about him.

Protocol

Comments

the group needed and he had, the group was very, very accepting of him. And that was a hard lesson for us to learn.

281. RITA: I'd like to say something about the value of learning your vocabulary this way. If you . . . if you learn what the words mean by feeling them first, and then maybe using words like "clobber," "the wall," and all the slang we put into it, it isn't awfully hard to pick up the technical jargon when you start reading. Because when you read all of the technical words, you know how they feel inside. And somebody else could have been taught the vocabulary in a straight academic class and never know what the words really mean.

281. Words to be truly meaningful need to be incorporated into each person's personal frame of reference.

282. WALT: Yes? (*to woman seeking question*)

283. WOMAN'S VOICE: I noticed that these two people were sort of left out of the group (*referring to Bill C. and Dorothy F.*) What would you as a leader do about this?

284. WALT: Nothing, absolutely nothing. I want to explain something about that, because I think that's kind of interesting, too. In several groups now, I have had members who have said almost nothing, and as the group continues one of the things they discover is that

284–286. Role of isolate is a common source of concern. Idea is presented that this is both a problem for the person and for the group, rather than being solely the responsibility of the leader.

Protocol   *Comments*

their security with each other depends on knowing what the other person is feeling. Communication, incidentally, I might indicate, goes on in other than just a verbal level. People who are indicating their feeling by their affect, by their faces, by their movements or in any way, are accepted by the group, but the individual who seems to be isolated forms a threat to the group and the group takes it up as a problem. And then the individual who doesn't talk becomes quite anxious because his status in the group depends upon his . . . and his acceptance . . . depends upon his giving to the members what the group needs for security. And so the pressure is not my asking them to talk, but the person's seeing that they'd better talk if they want to use the setup.

285. WOMAN'S VOICE: Dorothy seemed to have a lot of the answers in her mind so she gave out this feeling to the rest of them so that's probably the reason she was accepted more by the others than he was and yet she didn't ever say very much. She perhaps could be frustrated in the group. Would you as a leader have shown this?

286. CURT: Walt, you wanna . . . (*Laughter*)

Protocol   *Comments*

287. DOM: Wait a minute. I think one of the things that will explain this is a question that was raised by this gentleman here. We only have met for a half hour. I am very close to the girls because . . . (*Laughter*)

288. DOM: Good enough, maybe I shouldn't say more. I have been in class with them in particular situations. I could sit here and I know what they're talking about. Dorothy has the same experience because she's been in with this group. Now Carlson . . . I don't know whether Carlson . . . I met Carlson here yesterday. I don't know if Carlson has been in a class with any one of us here, you see. Curt I know from around the campus, but I haven't been in classes with him so I didn't feel as close or as understanding because I hadn't shared this experience with either Bill Lewis or Curt.

289. CURT: One of the problems here is the fact that I was blocking you (to Mary Ann) out because I was concerned. I was picking this up. Most of your talk was directed down in this corner and Bill off in this corner was getting sort of shut out.

289. Indicates some of the motivations for physical "blocking behavior."

290. MARY ANN: Let me . . .

291. CURT: It was kind of hard to get around to see him, so in

Protocol   *Comments*

trying to pull him in I was
shutting Mary Ann off.

292. MARY ANN: Well, let me just   292–293. Comment provides illus-
try and answer this lady's   trations of how people
question. We had this occur   learn to be responsible
in our group . . . uh . . . and   for own behavior. On a
it was a matter of sometimes   symbolic level it also
there would be a daddy who   shows how a single person
would say, "All right now,   can be perceived as rep-
Mary Ann wants to talk." So I   resenting to others, a vari-
would always depend on Dom   ety of important figures
making room for me to talk.   in their life. To the de-
I took no responsibility on   gree that one group mem-
my own. But he mothered me   ber can use another to
along the path.   work out significant rela-

293. WALT: (*to Dom*) Now you are   tionships, and to the
a mother too. We seem to   degree these relationships
play many different roles for   are perceived as being
each other.   common to other situa-
                                          tions, to that degree, inci-
                                          dents in the group, have
                                          a major effect on the
                                          person's total life.

End of tape.

As all beginning groups this group starts out by trying to answer
several basic questions. What are the limits within which we are allowed
to function? What do we have in common that can serve as a basis for
providing group cohesion? What needs do we have which are pressing
and must be dealt with immediately?

The group resembles a mature group in that they are less concerned
over the role of the initial group leader, they are ready and willing to
express their feelings to each other, and they are ready and able to accept their responsibility to the group.

As all groups, this one actually moved on three planes simultaneously.
One level represents the actual manifest content of the topics they explored. The second level comes from the feelings being expressed through
a diversity of content. The last level is represented by the learnings which
occur through the actual relationships they establish with each other.

In some ways a group may be likened to a symphony. There are several basic themes that keep winding their way in and out of the fabric of the total piece. Separate instruments try out the theme for themselves. The theme is changed and modified and sounds different as either instruments are combined or two themes are joined together. When we listen to a symphony we enjoy the repetition and embellishments. Unfortunately, in most groups, progress is judged by the newness of the content and the lack of repetition. If the group worker could accept group process in terms of an ever-tightening spiral, he can then begin to perceive how during the repetition of the content new individuals join the chorus, and how associated ideas are integrated with one another.

Topics will not become the focus of the group's attention if they are not meeting the needs of several members of the group at the same time. The topics themselves tend to be less important than the way they are used. To some degree the extent to which a topic is continually prolonged may provide a clue as to the degree to which the conversation is being used as a way of delaying facing something else (1).

When topics appear loosely related to the objective of the group it is more helpful for the leader to help the group explore what it is doing, rather than switch topics or inhibit discussion (2).

Just as the content repeats, so too do the underlying feelings crop up again and again. The idea that a person's ability to perceive is a function of his security is the basis for this phenomenon. Members of the group move at different rates. They require different relationships to provide security for them. As each person reaches the threshold of security he needs, he suddenly perceives what others may have already understood. Not only is this new insight something he wishes to share with others, but he needs the chance to concretize his insight by testing out if he can use words to communicate his idea to others. The acceptance of individual differences in growth and insights is vital to the atmosphere in a group.

Typical themes in groups include feelings of hostility or warmth toward authority figures or peers, fear of personal inadequacy and the threat of admitting the need for help, confusion over responsibility for self or others, ambivalent feelings of dependency vs. autonomy, and confusion over what constitutes reality.

An illustration of the relationship of content to movement on a feeling level may be useful. In the group session there is reference to a class session where the group explored the sex life of the Eskimo. One could wonder, and appropriately, what relationship this has to a course on groups. The actual discussion evolved in the following way. A member of the group commented that she felt the group was getting very close to home because they had begun to discuss their feelings about the difficulty in expressing their anxieties over death, birth, and other phenomena that could not be easily explained. At this point several members of the group related incidents in their lives that were important to them. One told of her concern with a practice near her home in North Dakota. It seems there were times during the winter when the ground was too hard to be able to dig a grave. Bodies were, therefore, stored until the first warm day and a mass burial was held. Another person expressed his attitude toward the loud wailing of his relatives at a funeral. The overt expression of emotion by the Italians led the group to think about the part culture plays in determining how feelings are expressed. Basically, several things were happening. Not only was the group broadening its acceptance of cultural differences, but as each person revealed his own cultural heritage, and found the group able to accept him and his heritage, a more basic security within the group developed. It was after this session, which included the discussion of peoples as culturally distant as the Eskimo, that a silent member of the group participated for the first time. She was a Black who had migrated from the South. She had learned not to express her feelings and to avoid Black labels as they led to rejection. In this group she, for the first time, began to feel that maybe she could be accepted as a person. When she began to talk the group became very quiet. They recognized how difficult this was for her. After she finished speaking, person after person told her how much they appreciated her confidence in *them*, by being willing to share her feelings with them. This floored her. She had never believed she had anything of worth to others (3,4).

One way in which the group succeeded in relating content to feelings was through the use of its daily written logs. Since the log was essentially a personal document it provided each person a chance to record feelings he was secure enough to see in black and white but feelings he may not yet have been ready to share with others. In a sense the writing of these logs formed a kind of rehearsal that enabled group members to discover a way of expressing feelings in a manner they could accept yet in a form others could perceive. Frequently the ideas written in a log one day were expressed verbally or physically in the group the next session.

Because the logs were available over a period of time, it was possible for each person to see how his feelings in relation to specific content shifted. He could also see different types of content discussions that evoked similar feelings in him.

The third level, represented by the relationships in the group, is illustrated by the members' references to each other as sister, mother, or daddy. It also can be seen during the group's exploration of the leader's role and how identification with the leader was only a first step in developing their own leadership pattern. This level suggests the value of understanding the theory and operation of transference and countertransference.

In many philosophies the use of time is an essential part of the therapeutic process. The protocol provides several examples of concepts related to time: time as giving, time as a limit on doing, time as representative of something you cannot change (a minute is 60 seconds, no more no less), and the use of time as a way of accepting responsibility for oneself.

There is an interesting concept demonstrated by members' reaction to others' use of time. The counting of frequency with which members participate occurs commonly in groups where I am involved. Typically the person who decides to do this is an individual who feels he has been too verbal and resents the fact that others do not talk more, since that would free him from feeling he is being unfair to the group. As the group deals with this situation several insights usually develop. The group tends to agree that to use the group a person must share his thoughts with others. Identifying with verbal members is seen as only one part of a total process. The group then becomes aware of a peculiar phenomenon. Although measuring a person's increasing use of group time may provide a measure of behavior, since the total amount of time available in any one session is limited, the theoretically optimal share for each person is obtainable by dividing the total time by the number of group members. It is at this point that the group discovers that the instrument not only has theoretical weaknesses but also it postulates that in a democracy everyone *must* have an equal share of everything. Desiring to preserve the right of the individual to talk or to be silent, the group reaches the understanding that although the person has a theoretical right to equal time *he also has the responsibility of asking for this time if he wants it.* In other words, where freedom of choice is present, silence can be interpreted as assent. This brings home an associated important lesson. *If you do not exercise your rights you cannot be resentful of others who meet their own needs.* Responsibility to others is predicated on knowing the needs of others. Since we have no right to assume their needs, it remains the responsibility of each individual to make his needs known to the group.

An examination of the way group members were interrupted or supported will provide an example of how a group tends to limit a person they may feel is monopolizing the discussion, while encouraging the less verbal person.

Basic to the use of any group is the feeling on the part of the group members that what they say in the group will not be used against them in outside settings (5). To insure this security every group rapidly develops ground rules covering the confidential nature of the sessions. This is not as simple a problem as it would appear. Group members are very anxious to use their newfound insights in other settings. Typically, groups decide that concepts or feelings can be shared with outsiders, *if* the specific content is not divulged nor the people involved identified. An associated issue is the right of group members to meet together in subgroups outside the group sessions. Although no breach of confidence is involved here, the group discovers that any insights they develop outside the group are not useful in the group, if the group does not understand these ideas. Many groups therefore suggest that, where appropriate, outside discussions of group members be reported in the group so all can share in the thinking process. It is this attitude, among others, which makes it difficult for group members to act out their needs outside the group, rather than in the group session. It is also this attitude which inhibits the development of cliques (6).

One of the most important aspects of group therapy is the tendency of the group to strive together to solve a problem. They seek to become more self-reliant and less lonesome (7).

Foulkes (8) has presented an interesting rationale as to why group therapy works. He points out that although group members reinforce each other's normal and neurotic reactions, collectively they represent the very norm from which individually they deviate. Redl (9) has pointed out that group therapy, unlike individual therapy, includes elements of societal reality, not the least of which is societal retaliation for perceived misdeeds. Probably one of the most comprehensive descriptions of group life can be found in a series of articles by W. R. Bion (10). His analysis and presentation has stood the test of time. It is well worth exploration by the reader.

Of all the issues raised by this demonstration, the question of the role played by the leader has major significance. It is within the leader's role that one can find evidence of the psychological theory that a group is using as a basis for operation and evaluation, and within an examination of the leader's behavior lie basic clues as to the skills and personality characteristics found most useful by a group.

I have taken the position that for a variety of reasons it is helpful for the initial leader to lose his position of authority as soon as possible. As he seeks membership status by changing roles in the group, he is then in a position where he must contend with others on the basis of equality. Such a role serves well, after the group has learned to cope with its leadership needs, in preventing the initial leader from using the group to meet his own personal needs in a fashion detrimental to the group.

Acceptance of the group of a leader on a membership basis carries with it loss of any right to maintain special privileges. Readers will note that members of the group refer to the author by his first name. Early in the relationship the question of how to address the author provided the basis around which the group could express its feelings toward authority figures. The way group members fluctuated in using Professor, Doctor, Mister, or Walt provided a sensitive barometer as to how that person perceived the author at that moment.

The protocol should certainly demonstrate the vicarious thrill members seemed to get in controlling an authority figure, at the same time they express concern for the individual in the role.

Basic to the security of any group leader must be the recognition that much of the hostility the group directs toward him is not meant for him personally but rather what he represents. Knowing that all groups go through common stages helps the group leader recognize when the group process he observes is a normal development or is a function of something he is doing.

"SELLING" A GROUP–A PROTOCOL INVOLVING RESISTANT CLIENTS

Every school has a group of youngsters they have labeled under-achievers. Sometimes they function at such a low level that they fail class after class. Many become convinced that they cannot achieve and fear to try, desiring to avoid another unpleasant experience.

One summer, while serving as Coordinator of Pupil Personnel Services in Rochester, I was talking with the principal of a high school about his plans for summer session. He expressed deep concern over a group of boys and girls who planned to attend summer school, but who he felt were doomed to fail unless something different was tried. Recognizing that changing teachers or the curriculum did not appear likely *in the immediate future,* the question was whether anything could be done to help this group of students develop attitudes and skills that would improve their chances of success in that setting. The school counselors saw each student and offered him or her a chance to join a group, prior to summer session, which might help them in school. It is hard to know how much arm twisting occurred, but on a hot summer day, I met a group of 6 students, in a dingy school basement, to see if somehow I could help them (1) feel someone cared, (2) express their feelings so they could deal with their anger and permit themselves to recognize their positive strengths and (3) provide study skills, if or when the group saw a need for them.

The reader will note that as leader, I played an active role. It is of interest to read that Rogers (11) in his book "Freedom to Learn" (p. 73) now feels that in school settings, providing initial limits or requirements may supply the group with enough structure for them to feel secure enough to start work. It is then possible to help the group face the freedom the leader would have preferred to offer initially.

Unlike the other two protocols, no running commentary will be included. It is suggested, instead, that the reader try to identify with the leader. Place yourself in a small dark room with six scared and angry students. Second guess what you might have done during the segment of the first session recorded below.

The session started with an introduction of myself and a request for each student to identify himself. We then moved off almost immediately into their feelings about how teachers rejected them. Notice the leader's attempt to help the group discover the many answers and resources they already possessed.

Lifton: Teachers are more comfortable with people who can understand what they're saying than with those that don't. Is that what you're trying to say?

Girl: Yeah, and they more or less, I mean, don't ignore, but they don't really pay too much attention to people who don't.

Lifton: So you kind of feel that if you don't master the stuff, they don't give you the attention. You don't feel that they care and you don't care. And so it sort of goes on like that.

Same Girl: I guess so.

Lifton: Well, we're saying some things about teachers that are very real, and I'm sure you have some teachers that click and others that don't. The chances are that you're going to have some more teachers that you're not going to click with. What then? Are you doomed? (pause) How do you cope with it? Suppose you have a teacher who doesn't seem to really act toward you the way you'd like her to act toward you. She really isn't warm, interested. Is there anything you can do about it?

Karen: Pay attention.

Lifton: Paying attention will change her attitude?

Karen: Well, if you just work up to your ability and show her what you can do.

Lifton: Yes, but you know, Karen, it's kind of a booby trap. If I understand what Gail is saying, she is saying "If you don't care about me, I say 'the hell with you'." And so it's sort of, you know, a cycle, and I'm not sure that I'm on the track.

Boy: If you don't like the teacher, you're not going to be able to do very well in the work.

Lifton: Bill's saying something interesting. He's saying if you don't like the teacher, why should you try.

Girl: (Inaudible comment.)

Boy: Well, the teacher's not the one who's got to get along.

Lifton: (Noticing a boy's attempt to contribute, but his hesitancy to talk) What do you think, Bill?

Bill: I don't know.

Boy: The teacher's got to be interested in the class. . . .

Boy: If the teacher don't like you, he's going to make it hard for you.

Girl: Not always.

Boy: But one of my teachers did.

Girl: Who are you referring to?

(Giggling)

Lifton: (Recognizing concern over confidentiality) Don't worry about mentioning names. We can wipe this tape. So don't worry about it. But I think the question is an important one because no matter who the person is, you're likely from here on in to get other teachers, or bosses, that you may not like and so the real question is what do you do about these characters? Are you just stuck or, of course, one way of doing it, is to do as Bill suggested, to say "Go peddle your papers. I don't want anything to do with you." But you can't; you can't always do that.

Boy: Try to get them to like you. Show interest.

Karen: It happened to my brother last year. He just worked up to his ability to show the teacher what he could do. And that helped.

Lifton: So this would be one way to prove the teacher was wrong, by being something different than what he thought. Suppose you had a friend that you'd like to have like you. How would you get this person to see you in a way that she would want to be your friend? What would you do about it?

(Pause)

Girl: Nothing.

Gail: If a person doesn't like you, you can't make them.

Lifton: There's no way of helping people see you differently than they see you at first? Are you stuck with the first impression?

Girl: Oh, no.

Lifton: How do you change people's ideas about you?

Gail: Well, you can't just be perfect when you're near them, be different. You are what you are. You can't put on fronts in front of people because I think that would make them like you least.

Lifton: So you've got to be true; you can't be false to them. But do we act the same—are you the same person to Diane as you are to your mother or as you might be to Tom?

Girl: No.

Lifton: So that there's more than one "you" too. (Laughter) That's kind of a funny idea, isn't it—that there really isn't one you. There are several different "yous."

Girl: Well, I think people are like her, she . . . I mean I'd show my personality to her. When I'm home, I'd be showing my—there's a word for it but I can't think of it . . . .

Lifton: Just try.

Girl: Myself.

Boy: Another character. In other words you have a different front.

Girl: Yes, everybody does. I mean you're different when you're home. You're more relaxed and . . .

Boy: You wouldn't treat your mother like a girl friend, in other words.

Girl: That's right—I'd be uncomfortable.

(Laughter)

Lifton: We're also saying that the people that we feel very comfortable with, we're able to let them see more of us than others; that the more we feel comfortable in letting a person know who we really are, the easier it is for us to talk to them and to begin to work with them.

Girl: That's why you really never know a person until you see them in their home. . . .

Lifton: You see, that's one of the problems that we've really got to understand. For this group to be most helpful, we have to find a place where we can be comfortable with each other because until we feel able to say what we really feel, we're just playing games. We have to begin to say under what conditions would we be willing to share things with each other. How can we help each other feel that the other guy cares, or that he won't misuse what we're saying, or won't think less of us. That's the real problem that we've got to face. If we could have with this group, what you have with some of your girl friends, except that here you have different kinds of people, you might have a chance to think through some ideas that you wished you had a chance to talk to somebody about, but don't know if they could manage it. This is really what the problem of this group is. This is why I was trying to have us see ways in which we could get comfortable with one another.

(Long pause)

Lifton: Kind of scares you, huh? Not always sure that you do want to share things with other people. Some things that maybe you don't feel you want to talk about.

(Long pause)

Gail: We all don't want to talk. When we do, we get in trouble.

Lifton: Interesting, isn't it, Gail? Have you any idea why we got caught up? I have an idea. I said something that I think some people didn't like and they pulled away in a hurry. They're letting me know that they're not sure that they like this and so the best way of getting away from me is just being quiet because that's safest. Isn't that somewhat like the classroom then? I don't like the teacher; so I'm just going to keep my mouth shut and then she can't know what I'm thinking and I can't get into trouble. That doesn't quite solve it though does it?

Tom: (inaudible reply)

Lifton: Can't hear you, Tom.

Tom: Keep your mouth shut and they give you a bad mark because you don't do anything in class.

Lifton: It's a funny thing, isn't it? If you do something, then they hear what you're saying. If you don't say something, then you're in trouble anyway. So that it sort of says that (interruption by boy)

Boy: That you're doing something.

Lifton: For the public?

Boy: Yeah.

Lifton: Kind of odd though, isn't it? No matter what we do—if we keep our mouth shut or if we open it, we still are doing something. Gail pointed this out very nicely. You're bound to do something. (long pause)

Lifton: You know it's an interesting thing. Part of what we're saying is that sometimes the exams don't measure what we study. We're saying some of the teachers don't teach what we're being tested on. We're saying some of the teachers don't like us—what's the use of trying? We're saying some of the courses, we wish we weren't in them in the first place. And all these answers are real, and there's no question that for many of you this is one of the problems involved. But is this going to solve it for you if we come up with this as answers? Is it going to solve it? Is this going to make it easier? For example, this summer, is this going to make it easier for you this summer when you go to school if we come up with these answers?

Girl: Yes, I believe so.

Boy: Maybe.

Girl: Because if you walk into a room with the right attitude, then . . . I don't know.

Girl: Then you can do better. If you walk in with the wrong attitude, then you hate it.

(Pause)

Karen: Oh, I know why I worked the way I work in school, I mean, why I'm working for a goal. Well, I'm planning to go to college. I think if you have a goal set, I think you work harder.

Lifton: I'm wondering, would any of the rest of you be willing to share with us what it is you see as your purpose in school. Karen has suggested that she sees a goal that seems to be very clear to her. What about some of the rest of you? Can you see any purpose in returning.

Gail: We have no choice.

Lifton: Beg your pardon.

Gail: We haven't got any choice.

Lifton: You have no choice?

Gail: You have to go to school. It's compulsory. I think if you didn't have to, I think more people would take an interest in it. There might not be as many going to school but there would be a better attitude in school.

Lifton: In a sense, I think what you're saying is that you're kind of not liking it because you have to.

Girl: It's true.

Lifton: So you'll prove to them they can't make you do something, huh?

(Pause)

Boy: If you could pick your own subjects, that would be better.

Lifton: Just for kicks, what would you take if you had your own way?

Boy: Math.

Lifton: You would take only math?

(Inaudible comments and laughter)

Lifton: Do you want to tell us about it? Why math?

Boy: I just like math. I don't know why. It just came to me easy. I like numbers better than I do words.

(Pause)

Girl: I'd take all English.

Lifton: You'd take all English.

Boy: Science.

Lifton: You'd take all science.

Girl/Boy: Science.

Lifton: You'd take science too.

End of segment of session one

There is a particularly interesting sequel to this group. Gail, over time, began to try to accept more and more responsibility for finding ways to improve not only her appearance but also some of her academic skills. She chose to explore the help she could get in reading, and asked for the address of a reading clinic. During an orientation visit there she saw a reading accelerator. That is a machine which covers a page with a bar that can be regulated to move down the page at varying speeds. Learning how to figure her own reading speed, she was fascinated to discover that on her second trial her speed had improved by several words. Here was actual proof she not only could find a way to help herself but also concrete and immediate reinforcement of her ability to learn.

Readers who are particularly impressed with operant conditioning will see in this illustration evidence of its value. They may in the process be overlooking several important differences. Gail was given group support to face threat. She selected the behavior she wanted to change. She chose the technique that was most rewarding, and she was free to terminate at any time she chose.

SUMMARY

This chapter has provided three sample protocols which although they occurred in different settings do represent a consistent philosophy, the author's. It is not the intent of this textbook to survey all the different approaches possible. Readers are encouraged, instead, to read presentations by authors championing the different points of view.

Gazda (12,13,14,15) has edited several books that include chapters written by representatives of different points of view. Other sample protocol can be found in Bion (16), Otto (17), Dinkmeyer (18), Perls (19), Schutz

(20), Slavson (21), Yalom (22), Golembiewski (23), Burton (24), and in addition, although of older vintage, in Corsini (25), Bach (26), Hinkley and Hermann (27), Gordon (28), and Moreno (29).

If you wish to use audio-visual aids refer to the April 1971 issue of the *Personnel and Guidance Journal*, "Audio-Visual Materials for Group Workers" by H. L. Stevens, J. J. Doen, and R. Chatten. This source, although recent, is biased in its listing in favor of encounter-type groups. Some earlier films not included in their list still remain useful.

Role Playing in Human Relations (30)
Activity Group Therapy (31)
Meeting in Session (32)
Belonging to the Group (33)

The next chapter focuses on some specific problems in group counseling.

Bibliography

1. Talland, G. A., and Clark, D. H. "Evaluation of Topics in Therapy Group Discussion," *Journal of Clinical Psychology,* 10, 131–137, 1954.
2. Thelen, H. *Dynamics of Groups at Work,* Chicago: University of Chicago Press, 1954, p. 57.
3. Slavson, S. R. "Racial and Cultural Factors in Group Therapy," *International Journal of Group Psychotherapy,* VI, No. 2, 152–165, April 1956.
4. Wittenberg, R. M., and Berg, J. "The Stranger in the Group," *American Journal Orthopsychiatry,* 22, 89–97, 1952.
5. Lindt, H., and Sherman, M. A. "Social Incognito in Analytically Oriented Group Psychotherapy," *International Journal of Group Psychotherapy,* II, 209–220, July 1952.
6. Slavson, S. R. "The Nature and Treatment of Acting Out in Group Psychotherapy," *International Journal of Group Psychotherapy,* VI, No. 1, 3–27, January 1956.
7. Frank, J. "Some Determinants, Manifestations and Effects of Cohesiveness in Therapy Groups," *International Journal of Group Psychotherapy,* 53–63, 1957.
8. Foulkes, S. H. *Introduction to Group Analytic Psychotherapy,* London: W. Heinemann, 1948, p. 29.
9. Redl, F. "Group Emotion and Leadership," *Psychiatry,* 5, 573–596, 1942.
10. Bion, W. R. "Experiences in Groups," *Human Relations,* 1, 314–320, 1948; 1, 487–496, 1948; 2, 13–22, 1949; 2, 295–303, 1949; 3, 3–14, 1950; 3, 395–402, 1950; 4, 221–227, 1951.
11. Rogers, C. *Freedom to Learn,* Ohio: Charles Merrill, 1969, p. 73.
12. Gazda, G. M. *Group Counseling: A Developmental Approach,* Boston: Allyn and Bacon, 1971.
13. Gazda, G. M. (Ed.). *Basic Approaches to Group Psychotherapy and Group Counseling,* 1968.
14. Gazda, G. M. (Ed.). *Innovations to Group Psychotherapy,* 1968.
15. Gazda, G. M. (Ed.). *Theories and Methods of Group Counseling in the Schools,* 1969.
16. Bion, W. R. *Experience in Groups.* New York: Basic Books, 1959.
17. Otto, H. *Group Methods to Actualize Human Potential: A Handbook,* Beverly Hills, California: Holistic Press, 1970.

159

18. Dinkmeyer, D. C., and Muro, J. J. *Group Counseling Theory and Practice,* Illinois: F. E. Peacock, 1971.

19. Perls, F. S. *Gestalt Therapy Verbatim,* California: Real People Press, 1969.

20. Schutz, W. C. *Joy: Expanding Human Awareness,* New York: Grove Press, 1967.

21. Slavson, S. R. *A Textbook in Analytic Group Psychotherapy,* New York: International Universities Press, 1964.

22. Yalom, I. *The Theory and Practice of Group Psychotherapy,* New York: Basic Books, 1970.

23. Golembiewski, R. T., and Blumberg, A. *Sensitivity Training and The Laboratory Approach: Readings About Concepts and Application,* Illinois: Peacock, 1970.

24. Burton, A. (Ed.). *Encounter: Theory and Practice in Encounter Groups,* San Francisco: Jossey-Bass, 1969.

25. Corsini, R. *Methods of Group Psychotherapy,* New York: McGraw-Hill, 1957.

26. Bach, G. R. *Intensive Group Psychotherapy,* New York: Ronald, 1954.

27. Hinkley, R. G., and Hermann, L. *Group Treatment in Psychotherapy,* Minneapolis: University of Minnesota Press, 1951.

28. Gordon, T. *Group Centered Leadership,* Boston: Houghton Mifflin, 1955.

29. Moreno, J. L., and Moreno, Z. *Psychodrama,* New York: Beacon House, 1959.

30. Film: "Role Playing in Human Relations," Washington, D.C.: National Education Association.

31. Film: "Activity Group Therapy," New York: Columbia University Press.

32. Film: "Meeting in Session," New York: Bureau of Publications, Teachers College, Columbia University.

33. Film: "Belonging to the Group," Collaborator R. Havighurst, Encyclopaedia Britannica Films.

5 Problems in Group Counseling

I believe that unarmed truth and unconditional love will have the final word in reality. This way Right temporarily defeated is stronger than evil triumphant.

REV. MARTIN LUTHER KING, JR.

The point has been made repeatedly that each group leader needs to develop his own philosophy and to clarify his own values. These then provide the yardstick by which the leader can evaluate his own performance and the progress of the group.

I believe the following concepts guide my behavior as a group leader.[1]

1. Individuals and groups, when freed of threat, strive toward healthier, more adaptive kinds of behavior. There is a drive in everyone toward homeostasis.

2. Each individual lives in a world of his own, bound by the uniqueness of his perceptions and past experiences. No one can share past experiences or perceptions with another. We can only help people experience and clarify their own perceptions. Each group member checks his perceptions of reality by comparing them with significant "others." The most important "others" tend to be the member's peers.

3. Even when the individual is convinced of the correctness of his perceptions, if his behavior, based on these perceptions, does not cause others to respond to him in the desired fashion, from a purely pragmatic point of view, he will have to revise his behavior if he seeks a different response from others.

4. Because everyone needs ways of defending himself and avoiding unacceptable pressures, everyone has defenses which may cause behavior

[1] These concepts, as listed, appeared in a chapter on Group Centered Leadership by the author, in Gazda (Ed.) *Basic Approaches to Group Psychotherapy and Group Counseling*, Ill: Charles C Thomas, 1968.

161

that is inconsistent with the verbalized goals he states to others. These defenses are necessary to existence and cannot be removed until a substitute is found.

5. People react to each other based on what they feel the other person's behavior implies. Because of the incongruity between a person's communications to others (on a feeling versus a content level), breakdown in communication occurs. We assume people respond to what we say rather than the feelings our words convey.

6. By providing acceptance and support to individuals and groups, they may be less constricted in their perceptions of their behavior, feeling safe enough to let themselves face feelings they know exist but could not before afford to acknowledge.

7. Since most people tend to move in their thinking from the concrete to the abstract, members dealing with their here-and-now problems in the group are more likely to see the relevance of the group's activity and, given the security of the group, are likely to be able to generalize from their current experiences to past ones, which then have new meaning. Put in another way, by dealing with the here-and-now we also alter the meaning and import of the past.

8. The group leader to be effective must be able either to live out a variety of group roles or, at the very least, to ensure that other group members can serve as role models. Members then learn not only the many types of roles needed in our society but they also can learn to emulate these roles and thereby increase their ability to cope with society.

9. Society is not something external to the lives of the group members. The group members by their behavior have a vital role in setting the limits and mores that individual members learn to understand and live with.

10. In a democratic society the ultimate source of authority is not vested in a single individual, but remains the responsibility of the entire group.

11. The group provides almost all of the elements needed to assist change. It offers support, feedback of perceived behavior, information about alternatives that could be considered, reinforcement of positive behavior and rejection of unacceptable behavior, and new experiences designed to broaden the repertoire of experiences and skills needed to cope with society (the group). The one missing ingredient, supplied by the initial leader, is how to make the group a helpful setting.

A simple summing up of these assumptions would suggest that this approach is a humanistic, existential one, where the source of support for the individual rests on each person's perceived dependence on his fellowman and his willingness to help others, since in the process he helps himself. The leader's role is basically one of facilitating group interaction so that the group develops ways of functioning that will increase communication between group members, while providing a setting for ongoing reality testing.

The point has been made that there is eclecticism of use of techniques, but not of values. Having set that as a value, I am then faced with the question as to how one can use techniques that demand counselor control and manipulation of the client's environment, and yet remain consistent with the concepts listed above.

I finally found the answer to this ethical question in an article by Gilbert Wrenn (1) in *Revolution in Counseling,* edited by John D. Krumboltz. He states (p. 104):

> If it is clear that the *client* is to select his own ends, that it is his life, not the counselor's, then the client is safe in agreeing that the counselor is to use his professional judgment and skill in selecting and using the means that will help him, the client, reach those ends. He does not need to know what is happening to make the relationship productive if he trusts the judgment and integrity of the counselor. (Nor, incidentally, does this seem too necessary in straight perceptual psychotherapy.) There is nothing ethically awry about counselor choice and operation of means if there is equal adherence to the inherent right of the client to decide *what* he wants to change—or to be.

The client has the right to select his goals, to understand the approach that will be used to help him, and to accept limitations on his (the client's) freedom when he feels that it will provide a return he desires. I disagree with Wrenn that the client does not need to know what is happening. I do not foresee the need for a running commentary on process, but instead a prior general description of the way the group counselor will function and why.

Few professions contain the degree of trust required in a good doctor-patient relationship. Yet few doctors will operate on a patient without his permission and without describing ahead of time why the doctor feels the procedure is needed, the risks involved, and in broad terms, what the operation will entail. As a matter of fact it has been found that patients who understand the process are more cooperative, have less anxiety over the process, and make a faster recovery.

In counseling, the client's motivation to deal with a problem stems from the discomfort it causes. This discomfort (anxiety?) is not a bad thing if it moves a person to seek a better solution to his problems. But the ability of a client to face anxiety about his problem is reduced if he needs to use his psychic energy to cope with the threat faced in the problem-solving setting itself. We therefore seek to develop security in the counseling setting, but to accept the need for anxiety about the problem.

As will be discussed in Chapter 6, which follows, not all groups provide optimal settings for therapeutic growth. The characteristics needed in groups that will be helpful to their membership do not just happen. The role of the initial leader in helping the group develop the climate needed for growth is crucial.

THE INITIAL LEADER

All groups depend on a catalyst to merge the individuals into a cohesive unit. The steps involved in achieving cohesion are very much a function of how the initial leadership in the group develops. Studies in leadership (2,3,4,5,6) have demonstrated that no one can become a leader if he represents ideas or behaviors that are beyond the group's present knowledge or acceptance. The best leader is the one who helps the group achieve their desired goal. To do this, he needs to help the group examine each of the following ideas:

1. What common goal exists among group members (7)?
2. What can they expect from him as a leader?
3. What group roles does the group need? In many groups these roles are defined and acted out on an unconscious basis. Generally all groups seem to need people who seek help, those who are willing to provide help, and those who represent societal reality. In the previous chapter, the group labeled these roles as those of client, therapist, and "wall" respectively. Other groups have had their moralists, seducers, advisors, etc.
4. What can the group members expect from each other?
5. What limits does the group wish to set on their own behavior?
6. What limits exist which set boundaries on group actions or goals?

It would be relatively simple if all the leader had to do was to raise each of the questions above for discussion, have members vote, and record the group's decisions. Unfortunately, for those seeking simple solutions, groups get the answers to the above questions through observing each other's actual behavior rather than the words being spoken. This means that what the leader does from the very first moment describes to the group the leader's actual desired role in the group. He must be willing to let the group make their own mistakes. Benne (8) describes it as follows:

He must be willing to let them try and fail as well as succeed. He can-not protect them from reality if his goal is to support them in facing the reality of self and others in all of its complexity and in handling such reality more rationally than before. What he can insist on is that realities be recognized, named, and analyzed, rather than ignored, de-nied, or oversimplified. But his version of reality is not reality, and he must be strong enough to have his version of reality challenged and changed if he is to be permitted to challenge the versions of others.

LEADER'S ROLE IN STRUCTURING

Schwartz (9) emphasized that a group has an organic life of its own, which the counselor needs to recognize and respect if the group is to be able to use him. It is not the counselor's role to manipulate the group in accordance with his goals for the individual members.

Schwartz, Benne, and Klein (10) all indicate that this does not mean a laissez-faire type of leadership. Natural groups will incorporate all the pathology of their society. It is the group counselor or leader's job to help the group see the problems so the group can recognize the need to face and resolve them.

One way for the leader to demonstrate his concern for the group is by providing them with an immediate opportunity to express their feelings and problems. Typically, groups start by expressing their insecurity over unclear boundaries. (Are we supposed to . . . ?) From the very beginning, groups will need to test out the leader's reaction to their needs. The earliest needs to appear in the group will be those of dependency-inde-pendency, love-hostility, and the need for acceptance by both the leader and the group.

It has been pointed out that a group seeks security by discovering the societal limits within which they must function. This question of society versus the group, with the group seen as a subculture, has been described very ably by Beck (11). For readers interested in the sociological impli-cations of group psychotherapy, her article will be of particular interest.

COHESIVENESS AND THE LINKING FUNCTION

Each person will try to cope with the group situation by using his existing repertoire of defenses. If he can get others to respond to him in the expected customary fashion, he has no need to consider change or to examine himself. Since change is threatening, part of the leader's initial job will be to develop in the group sources of security to meet these threats.

The major role of the initial leader is to be able to recognize the needs expressed by group members as being a function of both the person and the group setting rather than merely a reaction to the leader personally. The leader not only tries to reflect the feelings being discussed, but also, probably of greater importance, helps point out the similarity and differences in feelings among group members. By showing how different members using different content are expressing similar feelings, he helps the members see their common concerns and facilitates identification between members.

Gordon (12) has clearly articulated the functions of the leader in providing links between the thoughts and comments of different group members:

> Another important function which the group-centered leader serves in the group is the "linking" function. In face-to-face discussion groups, it often happens that one person will say something, then a second person will add a new idea but without conveying the relationship of his idea to the first contribution. The thought of each member remains independent or unlinked to other thoughts. Occasionally, someone may enter in and relate his thought to that of another, but usually we can observe several currents of thought in a group, each going its own way. If, however, the group-centered leader makes an effort to perceive the linkage between the separate comments and then conveys this relationship to the group, the discussion then seems to flow in one current, building up force as each new contribution is linked to it.
>
> The "linking" function of the group-centered leader is related closely to his function of reflecting the meanings of members' statements. This is because the meaning of a member's comment often *is* the link to the main stream of thought or to the previous comments. Its actual linkage is frequently hidden by the content of the comment. Thus, by clarifying the meaning of a comment, the group-centered leader makes clear to the group how the new contribution is related to the previous discussion.

Basically, the leader's initial job is to help the members of the group learn to direct their attention on each other rather than on a leader. He achieves this by continually focusing on:

1. The meaning of an idea to the group.
2. The issues that the group seems to be in disagreement over and that they feel a need to resolve.
3. The feelings they are expressing through their behavior rather than their spoken words.

4. The ways they are forcing others into roles or behaviors.

5. The actions or problems which the group raises and needs to solve.

6. The continuity between group sessions and themes raised.

Although all groups do not develop in the same way, after the first period spent in orientation and testing limits, there usually will be a sharp rise in tension and hostility. It is almost as if the group must discover if members will accept each other at their most obnoxious levels. It is helpful to realize that groups tend to permit well-liked members to deviate from group norms while they demand exact obedience to limits from members they tend to reject. Where this behavior occurs, it is sometimes helpful for the group leader to report factually the differences in the group's treatment of members.

The following two excerpts demonstrate rising tension and hostility while the group members are attempting to discover ways to relate to each other.

M: I wonder—are we picking at each other intellectually or not?

Do: What?

M: Are we picking at each other intellectually?

Do: Well . . .

E: Yeah, I kinda get the feeling that we are not doing anything. We are just talking to pass time.

M: Using big words—that's about it—or not—I don't know.

W: Talk accomplishes nothing?

E: Well it all depends—I just don't feel that we have a goal. I think that everybody is just saying something to get the tension out, and doing a very good job of it.

Ro: I think it's increasing rather than decreasing.

Ri: I was just putting down (in her notes) that every time somebody says something, someone interrupts and that this isn't going to get us anywhere.

Do: I didn't feel that we were picking at each other, I feel that we are getting tense and anxious because we can't solve our problem.

E: Well, what is the problem? I don't even know what the problem is!

Do: The problem is what are we going to do . . . what . . . we found that . . . I hate to use the word define—we're trying to define what this group is going to be—trying to come to some kind of a conclusion. A. has given his conception of what he thinks it should be. I gave mine, ah,

. . . we are throwing out things actually to try to get some kind of problem solving here, and we seem to be complicating it more than anything else.

W: At this point we are pretty clear on what everybody else doesn't see *our* way, but we are not quite sure what we see together.

L: And I think, even in this group, when somebody takes the role where they become a professional analyzing the core group feeling in the group, even we resent this.

A: Because we realize that they're just as involved as the other members.

L: It's just that we don't like someone putting themselves in a position to say "Well Daddy will look at you and decide what he thinks is wrong with you."

In groups meeting two hours weekly, I usually find this happening after 10–16 hours. If, at this point, the leader remains calm and helps the group face its anxiety, the group rather rapidly breaks loose and begins to define problems to be solved. It then continues on to seek causes and possible solutions.

In the following protocol, group members were using an attempt to define what constitutes a group to achieve several goals at once. They were forcing other members to define their ideas so they could see if their own ideas would be acceptable. At the same time they were testing the limits *this* group would impose on group membership. (Do I have to talk to be considered a participating member?) Less obvious, but also present, is the group's concern over the possibility that group membership in some unclear way may have effects on them in other situations. At one point, the leader appears to have the need to point out the importance of members identifying with each other. Since it is his need and not the group's, they ignore him and continue on.

(A few minutes chatter and discussion about the tape recorder.)

W: Where would you like to go today?

Laughter

Di: What did we do yesterday? Somebody take a quick five minutes to summarize.

L: I nominate you.

M: ———— didn't take part too much yesterday so he should do it.

Di: The person who didn't take part yesterday summarize.

Do: Who's going to volunteer for that?

Di: Who's going to volunteer?

Short Silence

Do: Sort of putting someone on the spot.

Laughter

Do: I felt like I didn't take much part yesterday.

Ro: Don't forget the difference between oral and mental participation.

W: This is a point—can we be part of a group and yet not have the group feel that we are sharing? (*Short silence*) Putting it another way—can you have a group on a purely mental participation basis?

Ri: The Quakers seem to be able to feel that. And I feel it when I'm among the Quakers.

M.L.: Sure, deaf people have groups.

W: We are raising the question, really now, as to what is a group.

E: I think even more basic than that is the idea of whether you can participate in anything without actively participating. You can listen to a record and participate, some can participate and listen, and some can just shut up for a minute.

W: You have a full house of people at the Virginia Theater all participating in watching the movie—do you have a group?

L: Yeah—the environment is the same and the goal is the same—it's an awfully loosely knit group though.

E: And yet all their emotions will be tied up in the same thing.

Ri: More so than if they were all sitting listening to a lecture.

Ro: Depends on the movie.

M: Is that spectator kind of thing a group?

Ro: Of course, we are all spectators at some time in the group.

Di: Are they interacting now, or are they only reacting to a common stimulus?

Ro: Well do you have to have interaction for a group?

M: I think so. You could have people writing letters to each other in different parts of the world—they have some commonality but there is no actual change—I think you should have a face-to-face relationship, don't you?—a give and take, if not orally at least gesturewise.

Ro: You think then a group has to have a face-to-face relationship to be a group, M?

M: I think so.

Ro: That would be limiting the group to an awfully small (*interrupted*) . . .

E: Wouldn't you say in regard to religion that everybody in a religion no matter where he is, is more or less a group?

M: Yeah, but sort of secondary—just because people think alike does that make them a group?

E: Well, some people it does—it depends on how strongly they feel about what they are thinking about.

B: Would you say the spectators at a basketball game were a group?

B: They were all actively participating in a certain way not in the actual game; they were all having the same goal.

L: During a period of the game they would be a group.

W: Seems to me we have two or three ideas that have been presented. One is that a group is defined as any, I'm trying to pull out some of the common elements as I think I heard them, ah, any collection of people who have something in common. We have also said that a group is any collection of people who are reacting to a common stimulus. We have also said that a group, and this is somewhat different from the others, is a group only when the people are interacting with each other, and then we further defined that this interaction is predicated on a face-to-face relationship and that they cannot interact unless they can perceive one another. We have had several different ideas expressed here.

E: I would like to carry this religion thing a little farther too. You take the Jewish religion. Some people who feel strongly about their religion will do some things for other people that they have never seen before, so long as they are the same religion, or orphan groups, or clothing for Israel, or whatever else. And there is something there. I don't know if they are really a group; there is something there that a mixture of other people without the same kind of goal wouldn't have.

W: I'm wondering if you are saying this, I'm reading into your remarks now, that isn't exactly what you said—I'm adding something to this— are you saying people feel a group if they identify with the others?

E: Yeah (*hesitatingly*).

W: I wonder whether it is necessary to identify with people in order to have a group?

E: No, it isn't necessary (*interrupted*) . . .

W: But this is one possible way of getting it.

L: I was going to ask, on this interaction with a face-to-face relationship, when the people disband such as when we meet here—then the group no longer exists?

M: No—I say it still does—ideally.

L: Yes, now in a case where it still exists ideally, you would incorporate her idea, ah, whether it be religion or a common goal in a schooling situation.

M: I'm beginning to . . .

L: If it disbands every time—if every time it disbands, it dissolves, then the next time they met face-to-face, would they have to start from rock bottom again to become a group? And how can you ever form a solid group, if when one disbands, the group dissolves? (*Short silence*)

L: Now like the group at the game last night—they dissolved and will never be a group again until there is another athletic situation where there will be stimulation of the formation of another group, which is not the kind of group which we are really interested in. But you take the group like the religious group, or, ah, within a school. If you develop school spirit you are trying to develop a group actually, and you are trying to develop a group that will maintain this group feeling outside of the school building. If that can't be done, I think you are sort of lost before you start in a school situation.

M: I think that my differentiation is that the people in the group not only have to identify with the people in the group and with the group as a whole, but they have to work together to do something.

L: Still that could be incorporated under any collection of people with a common stimulus or something in common—a common goal.

W: Let me ask this question. I don't know whether it will help in the thing we are talking about, but when people form in a group in the sense in which you are talking about it now, does this entity represent something different from the people involved? Is the total more than the sum of the parts?

R: Definitely. I think so.

L: I think it's the melting of the parts rather than the sum of the parts.

W: Is this something we are all in agreement on?

LIMITS, THE THERAPEUTIC CONTRACT, AND THE LEADER'S ROLE

Ohlsen (13), discussing selection of people for group membership, emphasizes his feeling that if group members are to profit from the experience, they must recognize and accept the need for assistance, be committed to talking about their problem, to trying to solve it, and to changing their behavior. He also feels they will profit most if they understand what is expected of them before they join.

One cannot quibble that counselors who function in a controlling way will be most successful if they select clients who will be most comfortable and accepting of their style. Nor can one object to clients who are prepared to use the setting. My concern with this approach is that it is based on several prerequisites.

· That the goals of a group are predetermined before a group is formed. (A group becomes defined in terms of its task instead of its interactional effect. Goals change as groups mature.)

· That verbal facility is a prerequisite to group help. (What about activity groups, nonverbal groups, and so on?)

· That the leader must resemble his clients in order to be helpful. (I can understand you because you are like me.)

· That behavior change is the goal. (This does not suggest that maybe the behavior *is* appropriate but the environment is wrong; it implies counseling is a way to facilitate adjustment to the status quo.)

The concept presented by Ohlsen and many others of a therapeutic contract usually presumes an initial diagnosis of a person's needs by a referring agency, tends to operate from a medical model of presumed pathology, and demands a client's acceptance of the leader's authority to be effective.

Since many people have been helped through just such a model, why do I raise questions about it?

My initial concern comes from the counselor's effect on group members as a role model. This model reinforces the hierarchical concept of the leader who is not to be questioned by his group members and from whom help can be expected only if you follow the rules he sets down. It also limits group counseling to those who clearly recognize their need for help rather than seeing a counselor's responsibility in society to help people be secure enough to recognize why changed behaviors might be worth exploring.

The basic difference is similar to traditional case work versus aggressive out-reach techniques.

Many studies have shown that the bulk of the people receiving group counseling help resemble their counselors by being middle-class, economically affluent, and verbally facile. The lower socioeconomic groups tend to receive less help and tend to be reluctant to seek it. Within these statistics one can see the reasons why there is a growing rejection by have-nots of traditional helping professions. The growth of storefront counseling centers, use of paraprofessionals from the inner city, growth of nonverbal self-actualizing approaches all document the dangers of restricting a group counseling situation to conditions like those set forth by Ohlsen.

The model suggested by this text is that of a counselor who, because of his knowledge, can serve as a consultant to a group to help them identify areas of concern, techniques possible for use in obtaining change, and the group need for established group limits in order for them to be secure enough to work. Since the counselor can afford to serve the group, as needs develop, he may find his role shifting from time to time and, in the process, he may be providing group members with the wide range of social roles possible in a group. His initial group leadership role communicates that the responsibility of the leader is to his constituents, not the other way around.

VOLUNTARY AND INVOLUNTARY GROUPS

One of the first questions one raises in looking at a group is the nature of the group membership. Is this a voluntary or an involuntary group? In other words, although the group members may share a common concern, did they come together of their own volition or were they forced to belong by some societal agency? Although there is little doubt that groups desiring a vehicle to meet a common need have the edge over involuntary groups, since there is no problem of motivating members to cooperate, it is unwise to assume that any other kind of group must of necessity fail.

Frank Field (14) in his book *Freedom and Control in Education and Society* points out that we rarely start from scratch with people. Although he believes that most people are capable of forming democratic values, most have experienced authoritarian training and are extremely unlikely to change patterns on their own. To accomplish this he feels it will be necessary "to employ powerful controls upon individual freedom in order to break existing antisocial 'set,' habitual patterns, value systems, and the beliefs underlying them." He recognizes the inevitable picture of brainwashing this presents so he introduces a series of areas where group controls are possible and where meeting basic individual needs might compensate for some loss of freedom. Unfortunately, he feels people are already so conditioned that he no longer trusts their ability to examine or consider better ways of achieving satisfaction unless present techniques are denied them.

Membership in an involuntary group can be a source of security. A group of men in the stockade at an Air Force base explored their feelings about being in the stockade. Although, to a man, they would have preferred freedom, they admitted some ambivalence. While in the stockade they could not easily get into more trouble. Most of their primary needs were being met. They could allow themselves to be quite dependent people and not have to feel guilt about their lack of responsibility, since they could blame society for their presence in prison. To put it another way, not being secure enough to face their own need for help, the men found it comforting to initially be able to get help while pretending they accepted it only because of outside limits.

The issues described in involuntary groups raise the following general questions:

1. At what point does society have the right to place its demands before those of the individual?

2. When will society's demands serve as a basis for help and not interfere with the helping process?

3. How can a group resolve the confusion arising between their conception of the demands coming from society and the demands which will represent their own needs?

Unfortunately, there are no neat answers to these questions. They do, however, represent the common starting place for groups, regardless of whether the groups initially are composed of voluntary membership or not.

To better understand the problems associated with the character of an involuntary group it might be helpful to examine a group where the initial motivation for membership was not present. During World War II I was assigned to serve as a Psychiatric Social Worker as Welch Convalescent Hospital (15,16). Welch was an Army hospital specifically designed to help rehabilitate patients suffering from combat fatigue. The labels change with time; in World War I the patients would have been called shell-shock cases. Despite labels, these were confused, hostile men with a variety of psychosomatic complaints, with guilt feelings about their inadequacy, and with a common desire to be discharged from the Army. Recovery carried with it the possibility of return to harsh Army discipline, and even more frightening, a return to possible combat and death.

The hospital setting represented the stereotype of the place where rich men go when they wish to retire. Situated in Daytona Beach, Florida, it included several swimming pools, athletic facilities, well-equipped shops and classrooms, and it had access to deep sea fishing and other forms of entertainment. The men were assigned to treatment battalions where a team of psychiatrist, psychologist, and psychiatric social worker tried to provide help. It was the psychiatric social worker's job to help the men plan their day's activities and, in group settings, to examine their problems and to suggest possible solutions. Initially, because the men focused all of the hostility caused by their troubles on the Army, they were freed of as many assigned duties as possible. Given the freedom to use or not use the camp facilities, large numbers of men preferred to lie on their beds, dreaming and isolating themselves from each other. After a period of time, all professional personnel realized that some changes were needed. An order outlining a schedule of activities for a day was issued. Men were forced to go to the activities but were then *free* to decide on the level of their involvement. Some interesting things happened.

The men were lined up in Army style and were marched to the occupational therapy shop. Once inside, they were free to spend the hour as they wished. Initially, they wandered around making hostile remarks to the patients who were busily engaged. Several questioned a man working on a bracelet as to why he bothered. He told them he had been successful in selling the bracelets. It suddenly hit some of the men that if they, too, could sell bracelets they would have money to get liquor. The shop suddenly became active.

What were some of the dynamics beneath the behavior described in the foregoing experience? There seem to be several concepts that emerge:

1. For all groups, but especially for involuntary ones, society's demands must be clear and pressing.

2. Given the freedom to explore ways of relating their needs to society's demands, people will tend to meet their most consciously perceived needs first.

3. In the process of meeting primary needs within a societal framework, clients learn that, at least at that simple level, they have the capacity to help themselves. Their attempt to prove even this level of competence is the first step toward tries at more difficult problems. In other words, people can only develop confidence in themselves by experiencing success that is meaningful in their own eyes. This last idea is frequently misunderstood. The teacher who wishes to provide success to a youngster by giving him honorary jobs or frequent compliments may find his efforts to no avail. The compliments have to be perceived by the youngster as having been merited by his behavior. The jobs have to be ones perceived as desirable by the youngster and not just by the teacher. In other words, manipulating the environment fails when the client does not perceive

the new setting as the manipulator had anticipated he would. Rather than guess at desirable experiences, the helping person should help the client to relate content and meaning within the client's frame of reference.

Supporters of operant conditioning can cite the use of positive reinforcement without the conscious awareness of the subject and of subsequent behavior change. But for the new behavior to persist it must either be continually reinforced or provide secondary gains that *are* perceived as meaningful to the client.

The nature of membership in groups has been presented as but the first step in a client's acceptance of responsibility for his behavior. The nature of his group affiliation also may involve his acceptance of the limits imposed by society and his acceptance of his own limited individual capabilities.

LEADERSHIP AND THE TRANSFERENCE-COUNTERTRANSFERENCE PHENOMENA

People needing help are very responsive to a warm, accepting, helping person. It is not surprising that they feel fondly toward that person, and seeing them as capable, use the helping counselor as a role model. Because they see the counselor as a caring person, and because they use their traditional defense in coping with him and other group members, it comes as somewhat of a shock when the counselor's response to their behavior does not replicate their experiences with other significant important people in their lives. Within this dynamic, clients have a chance to examine their traditional behavior and alternate behaviors that might cause the counselor to respond in ways the client would find rewarding. This type of interaction has been called transference in some philosophies. Because past experience has taught people that past help has almost always come from authority figures who demand specific responses, group members approach the initial leader with the same expectations.

Mahler (17) has listed some of the typical questions group members ask themselves as they check out the initial group leader.

Does this guy know his stuff?
Does he know how far to go and when to stop?
Does he really respect us as individuals, or is he just saying this?
Will he be frank and open with us, or will he hide when we put him on the spot?

Does he detect it when some member is unfairly picking on another?

Can he really accept our strong feelings and handle our hostility?

Does he know where things are going with the group even though it is not clear to us?

Will he analyze some remark of mine and make something real big out of it?

Can I really trust him with my innermost thoughts and feelings?

To the degree that fostering an identification with the counselor is a significant part of the approach being used, the sex of the counselor may initially facilitate or inhibit the desired relationship. But where, as presented in this text, the counselor is seen as more of a group facilitator, his or her sex or age becomes less relevant to his ability to gain group acceptance or to function effectively (18).

At first the leader is treated as an authority figure despite his own desires (19,20). I believe that a verbal structuring by the leader is helpful. As illustrated in the protocols in the preceding chapter, the group members hear the words used in structuring to help them know what is going on and what they can do, but they do not accept the idea until they experience the behavior that goes along with the words. One might ask then, why bother talking? Why not just start right in and let actions speak for themselves? This might work if group members are familiar with the helping process. If, however, a person's behavior does not coincide with the group's past experiences, their ability to recognize what is happening in the group makes the leader's behavior less threatening. Now, having both words and action, the concepts can more easily be integrated into the group's own storehouse of ways to relate to others. Within the context of learning theory, connecting words with behavior develops cue responses which in the future can cause the words to carry new meanings and stimulus value.

The role being suggested for the leader is an active one. To the degree that the leader feels a need to structure every eventuality, he will so limit members' perception of their freedom to act that nothing he does later will convince them that they are free to act. It is here that sensing the feelings of the group provides the leader with clues as to what information the group wants rather than what he feels they eventually might need. If he is to be the leader in the true sense, the people who make up the group will define for him the goal and the needs which must be met.

I find that people look *visually* to the leader for guidance. Therefore, I systematically shift the place where I sit each session. I not only make it difficult for the group to develop a set place to look for help, but by changing my seat I also force group members to shift their seats as well. This brings many members into contact with each other who had not really perceived each other before. Symbolically it also demonstrates the initial leader's desire to be free to become part of the group and his desire to have mobility of thought and action.

Frequently, after helping a member work out a rough problem, the group will appear immobilized. If the leader explores this apparent plateau with the group, it frequently is defined by the group as a sort of breather. During this calm spell the group recoups its strength to face the next issue.

As the group grows with maturity, leadership functions are so consistently carried by group members that an outsider observing the group would be unable to determine who was the initial leader (21). Each person who serves as leader needs to discover ways of communicating to the group his desire to help but not to direct. No one behavior is the answer.

The reader will recognize that it is much harder to listen to a group and try to offer the help they need and seek than it is to come in with a preplanned objective that a leader achieves through group manipulation.

The really difficult part of being "used" by a group is that as a human being the leader's own needs may get in the way of his ability to help. It is these needs that have been labeled as countertransference. Since, to the degree that the leader is trying to make himself comfortable, he may not be able to help the group, it is helpful if the leader can check his own behavior by asking himself the following questions (22–30).

1. Have I defined societal limits to meet my needs, or is greater flexibility possible?

2. Have I used words or behavior which force others to look up to me and accept my knowledge and control?

3. Was I aware of the feelings people were trying to express, or did I become more interested in the content or ultimate goal?

4. How did I respond to hostile, affectionate, or other disturbing needs members expressed toward me?

5. How did I relate to a group member who represented my ideal?

6. Was I more accepting of group members who were helping the group more than I was of those whose needs prevented them from relating to the group as a whole?

7. Have I been hostile or sarcastic or critical toward any group member?

8. Did I have a personal goal I would have liked to see the group accept?

9. Was I reacting to sexual charms of the opposite sex?

10. How did I react to emotional demands of members of my own sex?

11. Did I foster total group decision, or did I support a subgroup?

Since answering these questions demands a level of self-understanding all of us may not have, other cues may be easier to locate. The leader can ask himself:

1. Was there any time when I found myself perspiring? What was the group talking about at that time?

2. Did I ever raise my voice? Why?

3. Were there points at which I was uncomfortable and wished the group would move on?

4. Did my mind ever wander to things outside the group discussion?

5. Are there members of the group I'd like to spend more time with?

6. Are there members of the group whom I wish would drop out of the group?

If any reader's answers to the questions listed above were in the affirmative, he needs to reexamine the needs he has that would be best met in other settings. In the event the initial leader can comfortably handle the problems raised, he will find the group increasingly taking over responsibility for individuals and group process.

Leaders need to learn that, by accepting feelings of hostility directed toward them and by not responding with hostility, the leader helps the group learn how to help others look at their feelings without the need to be defensive.

An interesting study by Thibaut and Coules (31) found that communicating back negative feelings to the source of the feelings reduced interpersonal hostility and overt acts of aggression.

THE MISSING LEADER

Particularly in groups where the leader has been initially active in trying to help the group learn how to use the group setting, there may be a residual dependence on him. Despite the fact that group members may have served as temporary leaders for topics of concern to them, the group has difficulty in forgetting the status of the initial leader. The group seems to experience security in feeling that if any situation that they cannot handle should arise, the leader is present and will bail them out.

If for unavoidable reasons the leader cannot attend a session, the group is faced with proceeding on their own. As was demonstrated in Chapter 4, typically the more active aggressive member tries to step into the status leader role. If, by this time, the group has learned to use its own resources, any attempt by the new leader to direct the action as he thinks it ought to go will precipitate rapid censure of him by the group. With the second leader deposed, another member may try his hand. In this fashion member after member seeking status recognition learns that in this group status comes from helping others, not from controlling them.

LEADERSHIP AND GROUP RESPONSIBILITY

Members also can learn that their skills command group acceptance. Hansen, Niland, and Zani (32) found that models in group counseling who were socially successful appeared to be more effective reinforcers of group learning of social behavior than either the counselor or other low sociometric students.

One of the fundamental assumptions behind the philosophy presented in this book is that individuals, given the freedom to grow *and* help to perceive what they are doing, will accept responsibility for themselves and others. They also will choose healthy and socially acceptable solutions to problems.

This philosophy is one many people find difficult to accept. Not infrequently people respond with the feeling that the idea is all right in the abstract, but would not work in their concrete situation. At times, I too have wondered if I lived in an ivory tower. When such moments have happened typically I have tried to put myself in these "impossible" settings and see what happens. The following illustrations represent some such experiences.

When I worked with a teacher group concerned with discipline, I found that several of the teachers felt that greater controls were necessary because children were not old enough to handle responsibility for their behavior. I suggested that people learn to be responsible only by handling responsibility (along with support to face the anxiety it raises) and that children not only could handle responsibility but that they also might have good solutions to the discipline problems that were worried about (33–35). To test this hypothesis it was decided to secure a group of youngsters and see what happened. One fifth-grade youngster from each of six different schools was purposely chosen to differ as to his race, socio-economic status, intelligence, school adjustment, and verbal ability. None of these youngsters knew each other.

As planned, I met these youngsters for one hour before going with them to a teacher's meeting where they were to conduct a panel discussion. It was explained to the children that the teachers were concerned about discipline and that they felt that the students might have some good ideas which would help.

The youngsters' initial reaction was one of concern. They raised questions like:

"I would like to tell about the troubles in our class, but I wouldn't want to hurt my teacher."

"If I tell about something they will think it's my problem I'm talking about. What will they think of me?"

"How can we say things so they will not laugh at us?"

To summarize, the group was concerned about defining limits and protecting their security and the rights of others, while trying to find ways to be helpful and communicate clearly. The group was helped to see the problems it was raising. It developed several ways of coping with these problems. I was instructed to tell the audience that the things the children said were to represent the thoughts of others who were not present, that they had swapped problems so that the source could not be identified, and that they were interested in solutions rather than criticisms of the status quo. The youngsters did a particularly fine job of proving how able and ready they were to handle responsibility. One problem faced in the panel session might demonstrate this:

One youngster complained about the slow learner in his class who was monopolizing the teacher's attention. Although the youngster did not say so, this was a good example of possible sibling rivalry in a class where a teacher gives different or favored treatment to those she feels may require it. Faced with this problem, the group decided that the brighter youngsters who finished earlier should help the slower ones. They felt that students could explain in a way another student could understand, and that by this help the total group would be speeded up. In other words, they solved the problem by accepting more responsibility themselves (peer counseling).

In a completely different setting, I was asked to help a high school-age church group plan a regional conference. The group came to the planning session loaded with suggestions from adults as to what they thought it would be good for these youngsters to discuss. Idea after idea was rejected. Finally, one boy said "everyone tells us what to do and think, why can't we be free to do as we please?" Because this feeling seemed to be highly popular in the group, I asked the group if this feeling itself might not serve as a theme for their sessions. Rather quickly things fell into place. The group decided that their theme would be "If I could do anything I wanted, as long as the people with me agreed to it, what would I do?" Since they did not want to be told answers to their question, they organized the conference around work groups. Each group had the same problem of answering the idea raised in the theme. Being curious about other groups' decisions, they planned on a general session where ideas from each group could be reported and where they could see what they had in common.

Given the freedom to organize society to meet their needs, the groups happily tackled what they considered failures of our society. The role of the family, sex, money, government, politics, freedom to think, and problems of minority groups all were areas for decision making. The members of some groups, with tongue in cheek (and partially to test adult reaction), suggested organized prostitution, no family life, etc. It was particularly interesting to see the total group reaction to such proposals. They asked which of the girls were willing themselves to serve in degraded roles. They also asked if anyone really did not feel he wanted someone special to share life with. In other words, when faced with living out the ideas that initially seemed to represent freedom, time after time the total group decided on a way of life which was closer to existing society than ideas that meant overthrowing the past. The major result of the sessions was that the youngsters now had reasons that made sense to them for the rules and limits of society. They also saw ways some changes in society could be accomplished. Limits were now seen as desirable instead of as something being imposed on them by others.

As a last example there is the case of the group of residence hall workers who were up in arms over the behavior of their superior. They came to me seeking help in finding ways of coping with the situation.

Each of the women recited grievances and problems she experienced. I clarified feelings, pointed up areas of similarity and disagreement in the perceptions of group members, and helped them feel free to express their negative and hostile feelings. After releasing these feelings, the group began to examine how they might deal more effectively with their superior. Feeling accepted themselves, they began to try to perceive the feelings or needs the superior was having. In the process they found many needs she was expressing to be ones they could meet. They also began to realize that just as they were threatened by her, so too the group was a source of threat to the superior. Ultimately the group began to accept responsibility for their own behavior, for their obligation to provide support to the superior so she could be able better to perceive their needs, and to help her see how she could relate to them in ways that would be mutually more satisfying.

These cases are but a few demonstrations of the fact that groups given the security needed to face themselves react with increased responsibility for themselves and others.

THE LEADER'S DIAGNOSTIC SKILL AND GROUP EFFECTIVENESS

To be helpful to a group, the counselor needs to be able to spot problems arising in groups and to have information he can offer the group, if asked, on ways to deal with these situations.

Presented below is a schema developed by Klein (36) to assist group counselors to spot problem areas in group functioning. He recognizes that symptom pictures can neither be precise nor reflect the many possible variables operating, but he has found the general schema helpful in assisting group leaders seeking to locate the sources of group malfunction.

I. *Where the Problem Lies within the Individuals:*
    A. Where the individuals in the group are so needful that they are unable to function in a group, are injurious to others, are in conflict within themselves:
        1. Individuals cannot communicate or do not respond appropriately.
        2. Individuals act out and their bizarre, seductive ego-alien behavior is frightening to others.
        3. Individuals control the group by virtue of nuisance value, fear, or contagion.
        4. Behavior is withdrawn, apathtic, isolated, or fearful.
        5. Members exacerbate problems of others.
        6. Group support pathology or reinforces symptoms.
    Indications: Acting out, bizarre behavior, extreme provocation, distorted communication, withdrawn behavior, fear, etc.

    B. Where individuals have no interest in the purpose or goal:
        1. There is lack of cohesion.
        2. There is lack of commitment.
        3. There is lack of any group goal, contract, or agreed-upon goal, or where goals of the members are contra-indicated for each other, or for the group goal and purpose.
    Indications: Exploitation, apathy, conflict, scapegoating, do not listen to each other, ideas attacked before they are expressed, intolerance, no movement toward developing or working toward goals, etc.

C. Where the grouping is inappropriate:
1. The role behaviors set up an isolate at either end of the range of accepted behaviors.
2. The individual symptoms cannot be tolerated by the group.
3. The group composition is out of balance with group purposes.
4. The group composition is out of balance, that is, the composition is weighted on the side of negative rather than positive factors and toward pathology instead of health; when taken as a whole its fulcrum is not at a modal point but skewed so that the negatives outweigh the positives.
5. The grouping is not suited to the psycho-social level of tasks, needs, and resources.
6. The members have primary allegiance to reference groups external to this group.

Indications: Reinforcement for existing behavior, anxiety about revealing self or sharing, absence of mutual aid, mistrust, punishing each other, absence of bond, etc.

D. Where individuals have personal value conflicts.
E. Where individuals have excessive superego controls.

II. *Where the Group Is in Conflict with the Environment:*
A. The environment superimposes demands.
B. The demand of the environment is excessive.
C. The structure of the environmental system is inadequate or inappropriate to carry its function, as for example, it is frustrating, rigid, and punitive for the group.
D. The values of the group are in conflict with those of its environment.
E. The group does not understand the demand.
F. The group is unable to fill the demand.
G. The group leadership is anti-social.
H. The group is rejected by the environment.
I. The group is in conflict with authority such as worker, agency, subculture, community, culture of society.
J. The environment is noxious, endangering, seductive, anomic, or contradictory.
K. The environment does not provide access to resources that are needed by the group and its members.

L. The kind, nature, and intensity of the relationship of the group to its environment is inappropriately dependent, non-stimulating, overprotective, seductive, overly stimulating, overly demanding, defiant, exploitive:

1. The agency's values, procedures, and culture are contrary to the group's and the agency superimposes.
2. The neighborhood is hostile to the group and its members.
3. The forces of social control are hostile to the group and its members.
4. The members are impoverished economically and culturally.
5. The social values in the impinging society are inconsistent and rewards are given for deviant behavior.
6. The group leader is from reform school or local gang.
7. Worker is too different from members to be able to accept them, or they him.
8. The group lacks skills necessary to match the environment.
9. The group does not want to match environment and environment does not want to change.

Indications: Group solidarity and hostility to anything that is not of the group, anti-social acting out, low self-image, braggadocio, subvention, arguing inconsequential points, autocratic leadership, bullying, scapegoating, projection, rationalizing, ridicule, sadism, brutality, insecurity, etc.

III. *Where the Internal Structure of the Group Is not Appropriate or Is Inoperative:*

A. The structure is inadequate to meet the needs of the members.
B. The structure is insufficient to carry out tasks.
C. The structure is too formal, too ritualistic, or too much for the purpose, size, and functioning of the group.
D. The formal structure does not function.
E. The structure is in contradiction to the values of the group.
F. The structure is in contradiction to the group goals or there are no goals.
G. The structure blocks interpersonal interaction or group transaction.
H. The structure works against group movement:
1. Leadership is too strong, too weak, inept, inappropri-

ate, absent, centralized, there is conflict for leadership, leadership is inappropriate for stage of group development, leadership denies access to resources and thwarts need-meeting, leadership operates through power, power is not distributed.

Indications: Attendance falls off, dropouts, participation index low, scapegoating, fighting, communication patterns centralized, poor movement toward goals, overstructured rituals and procedures, goal displacement, poor esprit de corps and low hedonic tone, high level of frustration, aggressive behavior, apathy and projection, informal channels wide open and formal channels neglected, taking sides with no compromises, etc.

2. Positions occupied or available do not meet needs of group or group members. Positions do not articulate or fit each other or the group. The formal positions do not match the informal functioning. Positions and status do not match. Status is not given for performing group requirements. Position and status are unfilled or in contention. Positions and status block person-to-person interaction.

Indications: Attendance fluctuates, poor interest in elections, positions unfilled or poorly carried, clique formation, conflict, inability to make group decisions or to keep those made, poor organization, and avoidance of communication channels, etc.

3. Communication is limited to few, or is skewed, is distorted, is lacking, is not heard or decoded, is double-bind, is not responded to, is not appropriate to desired goal, is delusional and not related to reality.

Indications: Poor participation, i.e., many do not talk, cross talk, talking all at once, responses inappropriate to what was said, movement diffuse and in all directions, schizoid behavior, unreal communication, group decisions made too quickly, etc.

4. Role patterns do not meet needs of individuals or of the group. There are role gaps; roles are inappropriate to purposes, task, or stage; are threatening or anxiety-producing to occupant; not complementary or reciprocal; ambiguous; conflicting; overlapping; non-

functional; stereotyped; role patterns block person-to-person interaction.

Indications: Flight, fight, pairing, dependency, acting out, withdrawing, role playing, inappropriate role performance, difficulty in making group decisions, escape to irrelevancies and high-level abstractions, silences, hostility, anxiety, inappropriate reciprocal role relationships, etc.

5. The group procedures are faulty. They are too rigid, inappropriate, ritualistic, not followed, inconsistent, unformed or unknown, unsuited to group purpose or task, inappropriate to group values. Group procedures block person-to-person interaction or consensus. Procedures allow majority to dominate minority.

Indications: Excessive procedures and frustration, insufficient procedures and frustration, wrangling about procedures, undemocratic controls, floundering, impatience, dropping out, poor participation, goal displacement onto procedures and rituals, scapegoating, endless debate with no decision, decisions reached with too little or irrelevant discussion, railroading, etc.

6. Sociometric (affectional) ties are scarce and weak, skewed patterns, subgroup cleavage, few linkages, isolates, rejection.

Indications: Low cohesion, fighting, racial or ethnic intolerance, poor morale, diffusion of group goal, do not listen to each other, ridicule, diversity of interests, difficulty with program, each pushes own plan, idea possessiveness, do not help one another, no hedonic tone, do not share, group breaks under pressure or crisis, denial of access to resources, isolates, no closeness, interpersonal fear, etc.

7. Structure is designed to perpetuate domination, rigid decisions, keep clique in power, monopolize, thwart change, rationalize behaviors.

Indications: "Big Joes" and slaves, nondemocratic decisions, ingroup top clique, communication star pattern, domination, favoritism, power struggles, procedures ignored, punishment and fines, main concern is to gain status, subtle attacks on leadership, obeisance, contagion, physical force, etc.

8. The structure maximizes loyalty to outside reference groups.
9. The structure is a defense against interpersonal confrontation and a response to anxiety.

IV. *Where the Group Was Reasonably Well Grouped but the Group Composition Is out of Balance:*
   A. Because of group stage.
   B. Because the purpose has changed.
   C. Because individual behavior changes.
   D. Because a member is absent, dropped or added.
   Indications: Unusual acting out and withdrawal, reversal of decisions already made, realignments, attacks on leadership, discuss breaking up, unusual scapegoating, etc.

V. *Where the Group Is Reasonably Well Grouped and the Structure Is Adequate for Normal Functioning but there Is a Temporary Loss of Good Group Functioning:*
   A. There is a new, largely externally caused problem which is causing stress.
   B. There is a group crisis.
   Indications: Projection, tight ingroup, exclusion, fighting, delinquency, momentary loss of interest, self-discipline fails, reject limits, regression, etc.

VI. *Where the Group Is Reasonably Well Grouped, the Structure Is Adequate for Normal Functioning, but there Is Regression:*
   A. There is a change in the power structure.
   B. There is a change in the leadership.
   Indications: Conflict and infighting, seek to seduce worker to intervene, suspicion, childish behavior, random behavior, confusion, etc.

VII. *Where the Group Is Reasonably Well Grouped for the Purposes, the Structure Is Adequate, but the Worker Does not Promote Good Group Functioning:*
   A. Worker is not sufficiently skilled.
   B. Worker is not tolerant.
   C. Worker dominates the group.
   D. Worker lacks conviction.
   E. Worker does not listen and cannot understand.
   F. Worker is not responsive and does not enable.
   Indications: Fight authority, neurotic transference, retreat, conformity, gross defiance and discipline problems, hurt each other, submission, no movement, etc.

VIII. *Where the Group Is Reasonably Well Grouped, the Structure Is Adequate but the Program Fails:*
A. Does not meet the interest or needs.
B. Exacerbates problems of individuals or the group.
Indications: Apathy, heightened unrest and disinterest, aggressive behavior, destruction, regression, pathology, scapegoating, chaos, etc.

IX. *Where the Group Is Internally in Conflict over Values, Norms, and Standards, Is Ambivalent, or in Transition:*
Indications: Conflict, infighting, low cohesion, warring subgroups, poor decision-making, derision, low esprit de corps, vacillation, no group goal or commitment, etc.

Some of the behaviors which are listed above may be viewed, if one is judgmental, as deviant. A more useful way of looking at it is to see that behavior is a response and in most instances as such may be rational and appropriate. The behaviors also give a clue to the developmental stage of the group and therefore help the worker to adjust his stance to the immediate needs of the group in its struggle to become a viable group.

TIMING AND CUES

Although Klein's schema can be helpful in spotting possible areas of difficulty, no text can readily set down in cookbook fashion when the group counselor will use his insights or the type of intervention that will be most helpful. Obviously the different frames of reference a leader can use may provide him with different answers to these questions.

The following quote from Revolution in Counseling (37) provides one answer and a fascinating rebuttal, illustrating the paradox of whether our focus should be on changing a person's behavior or changing the environment.

Telling a person what to do may sometimes be effective, but the timing of the remark is often crucial and the importance of this timing is often overlooked. One parent I know consulted a psychologist about how her children were driving her crazy because they constantly forgot to do the things she asked of them. One of the most annoying habits the children had was to run in or out of the house without closing the door. The difficulty was that the mother reminded the children to close the door after they had already passed it. The psychologist pointed out that the most effective cues are those that occur just prior to the behavior, not those that occur afterwards. The mother was told to observe her children and as they approached the door to give the reminder: "Close the door." Just a few days of extra-attentiveness on the part of the mother enabled her to give the reminders to each child just prior to touching the door so that soon thereafter the child needed no further reminders. (One of my graduate students said it would have been easier to put a spring on the door!)

GROUP COMPOSITION AND SIZE

Group Composition. If the group atmosphere is a function of the composition of its membership, the question of who shall be included in the group is of importance (38,39,40,41). Slavson, working from a psychoanalytic point of view, believes a potential group member must be evaluated in terms of (a) having had at least minimal satisfaction in his primary relationships during his childhood, (b) not being too sexually disturbed, (c) needing a quantity of ego strength, and (d) having minimal development of his superego. Bach (42), working from a different orientation, excludes people from the groups he leads if (a) they have insufficient reality contact, (b) have culturally deviant symptomatology, (c) are chronic monopolists, or (d) have psychopathic defenses of an impulsive nature.

Both of these authors, thinking essentially in terms of severely disturbed people, seem to be saying that they are looking for people who can relate to others, who do not have mannerisms others find too disturbing or offensive, and who will not by their aggressive nature present the group with problems of setting and maintaining group limits. Bach and Powdermaker and Powdermaker (43) seem to agree that admitting at least two of any one kind of personality is helpful, since it will prevent the person from feeling isolated. They also seem to agree that when the differences between group members are not too radical, learning tends to be facilitated, since the client is exposed to a wide range of experiences.

A quick rereading of the preceding two paragraphs should demonstrate that the emphasis is not so much on the presence of a characteristic as much as it is one of degree. Unfortunately, I have not been able to locate any dependable device that both calibrates the quantity of the characteristics discussed and suggests the number of adverse traits any specific group can assimilate. In reviewing the literature in this area one always discovers that the ultimate composition of these groups reflects "clinical judgment" and in some cases more likely reflects what the leader believes *he* can tolerate. Studies like the one by Ash (44) certainly raise questions about the reliability and validity of clinical judgment.

Certainly if one is developing a group for therapeutic purposes, he has every right to try to develop a group which he believes will be most effective. Unfortunately, most of us will find ourselves in group situations where membership would not be open to our approval even if we were sure about the criteria we ought to use. Does this mean that groups with an unselected membership are bound to be untherapeutic? In my opinion, nothing could be further from the truth. The degree to which any group can represent society as a whole certainly will affect the usefulness of that group as a testing ground of ideas. The issue then is not so much one of how to limit people from membership as it is how to achieve a heterogeneous group that has the tools to control the elements within it that may lead to disintegration.

It is on this basis that it is felt that the primary basis for membership ought to be common concern over a situation or interest. Cartwright (45) has pointed out that for a group to be effective as a medium for change it must first of all be important to its members. Thelen (46), following up this idea and summarizing research in the area, indicates that groups composed of friends are likely to have more energy to spend in participating. Being initially secure with each other, they are free to use energies in other ways. He also points out that groups composed of friends are more likely to deal with whatever problem they need to, whether it centers around school achievement or another area of concern.

For a group to be therapeutic there must be help given to enable members to discover the need for different roles than those typically played in friendship groups.

It should be noted that some research exists which suggests that the type of group has a selective influence on the people who seek to join. Sensitivity group volunteers tended to be people who emphasize achievement through independent behavior (47).

It has been suggested that specific situations represent a helpful core around which people can learn to relate to each other. Because interests and behavior of people change with age, it is logical that the basis for group formations will differ at varied age levels. It is also to be expected that the manner in which the groups choose to communicate will also change. Little children still accustomed to acting out their needs may find play and activity groups most natural to their typical behavior (48,49). Adolescents form a special problem in group counseling. This is a period of very rapid growth in both their emotional and physical drives (50,51). It is a stage where their speech is highly developed. They have a growing ability to express themselves verbally with less need for physical activity to release their needs. Because adolescence is a period of rapid shift, however, group activities may not remain stable in one mode or the other.

Thelen (52) has suggested that the major need of students is to find their places in the group. They are also concerned about their ability to adjust to authority and to explore and define their assets and limitations. He believes that these needs primarily color what students learn in class and the meaning to them of the material learned.

Certainly parenthood, with its concomitant increased sense of responsibility, forms a ripe basis for group help. As parents see themselves through other parent's eyes they may be able to better evaluate their own behavior. As their own information increases and as they are better able to empathize with their children, their total adjustment improves. To the degree that they discover that other parents share their feelings and anxieties, they feel less guilty and can feel better able to relate more positively to their children and mates.

Although society and peers are important at all ages, the role of group counseling with older people deserves special attention. The growing sense of isolation experienced by people as their families grow up and become self-sufficient, when added to the isolation caused by both the death of friends and the loss of physical contacts, increases the sense of loneliness of the older person. Inability to hear, see, and travel all form special problems to be explored when working with "senior citizens."

There seem to be several yardsticks one can apply in determining members for a group.

1. Does the initally stated purpose of the group provide enough of a common base for initial communication to occur?

2. Does the leader and his way of operating reflect the type of help the group seeks and can use best?

3. Do the members reflect the group best able to achieve the desired goal? [Gilmore's (53) research on underachievers demonstrated better results when he worked with their parents. In times of staff shortage it may pay to work with significant adults rather than with those whom they affect.]

Group Size.   Size has a direct relationship not only with the defined purpose of the group but also with the possible relationships between group members. In a two-person "group" there is no escape from the need to react to each other. With the addition of each member to the group it becomes increasingly possible for a person to diminish his interactions with others. At the very least he can participate by identifying with active members. Since the security of the group depends upon the ability of the members both to communicate and to receive a sense of acceptance, a point is reached where it becomes physically impossible to be aware of all people present. Because visual cues are part of communication, too, the increasing size of the circle needed to accommodate more people creates greater distance; words need to be shouted and too many people lose the chance to express their ideas, since the time available for the total group is limited. Authors differ on when this magical point is reached. The popular upper limits are between 8 and 15. When the group gets beyond this size, the group may find the need to operate in subgroups at critical points in order to reestablish the conditions needed for emotional involvement and release. Under good conditions, where group involvement is high and large numbers of people in the groups tend to identify with each other, it has been possible to have members of groups of as large as 25 work and help each other despite the size. Certainly the larger the group the more difficult it is to achieve the level of group security needed to explore threatening ideas or behavior.

Aggressive, talkative participants should be encouraged to sit next to each other rather than facing each other, since the absence of visual cues may cut down on their need to interact with each other. In contrast to this, shy members may profit through the visual support offered by sensitive group members or by the leader.

Groups using activity techniques obviously will require different size limits depending on the activities involved and the need for active involvement by the group leader (54,55,56).

ADMITTING NEW MEMBERS

The admission of a newcomer to the group after initial organization involves considerable group concern and attention. Each group develops its unique atmosphere. The flavor of the group comes from the rituals, limits, permitted behaviors, and interpersonal relationships they develop. When admitting a new person, the group basically is faced with two alternatives. They can indoctrinate him into the mores of the group so he does not change the status quo or they can allow him to examine present traditions and make recommendations for modifications which would increase his security in the group. The way any group handles this question provides a rapid clue to the security of the membership. The more rigid groups will tend to find their security in form and content rather than personal relationships. Groups that are secure about themselves and the value of their ideas do not feel threatened by competing ideas.

The basic thesis of this book has been that groups serve as a tool to meet individual needs. The termination, continuation, or modification of the group, therefore, becomes an issue that the group itself needs to face, examine, and resolve.

When, because of the setting, a group's purpose and way of functioning have been predetermined by an outside agency, it is the responsibility of that agency to interpret for any prospective member what group membership will demand of him.

In schools, the teacher has the responsibility of interpreting for the student the defined goals of a class, the way the class operates, and the demands that will be made on the student. Similarly, any referral of a client to a group setting carries with it the responsibility of helping the client face and evaluate what potential group membership could mean to him.

It is not wise to place a person in a group at the time of a specific crisis in his life. He will feel the need for immediate help, which the group will share, but which realistically cannot be offered by the group. Feeling inadequate to help in a crisis will precipitate considerable hostility against the referring agency which put them in this spot.

CONFIDENTIALITY

Very early in the life of any group it becomes apparent that exposure of one's private life could increase vulnerability. Although feeling that group members care helps to overcome reluctance to share private material, groups also recognize that if content revealed in the group is made available to nongroup members, it would represent a violation of trust. Confusion over how to preserve the confidential nature of the group, while recognizing that in most societal settings group members will have occasion to meet outside of the group, causes groups to examine early in their life how best to handle the multiplicity of relationships group members may have. This area is one of marked disagreement among writers in the field. Some authors insist that it is necessary that group members do not see each other outside of group sessions. For isolated therapy groups this may be possible, but when groups are formed as part of an existing institution, such a limit is unreal. Although the simpler the relationships are between people, the easier it is to cope with them, it is rare in society for a person to be able to so purify his relationships with others. If, on the other hand, the group can develop clearly defined roles for in-group and out-of-group relationships, group members have a chance to learn the basic idea that different behaviors are appropriate in different settings.

The following protocol illustrates the awareness of the group of their desire to maintain the group atmosphere in other settings, and then their awareness that this may not be possible. Being concerned over the effect of these out-of-group meetings, this group set up a rule that obligated group members to feed into group settings the ideas or relationships developed outside the group between members in order to achieve group security and cohesion.

Ri: I always wanted to be the first one to arrive in our dorm at college and the last one to leave, and I didn't want to miss a thing. (*Laughter*) Even if I had an important committee meeting or class, I would feel threatened if I didn't go out for coffee because I've always been that compulsive about it. I sat at one of these big tables, and at another table a lot of people were talking and I didn't know what was going on . . .

E: I just thought when Ro said that—God, I wish I was that normal!

Do: (*To W*) This is what you meant when you said that your wife wasn't going to see you all semester.

Ro: I also missed E. not being there.

M: We go out for coffee a lot, and I think part of us weren't there.

Ri: I don't think we can stop these between class meetings because we can't stop seeing each other, and if I were to see M. and if you were to see E. and have coffee this would be a subgroup of our group, and we can't make a vow that we don't see each other in between time. It may be we can learn how to deal with it. Personally, I don't know how you felt about it, but when we left yesterday, I said something about, if you want to know what we talked about the other time we had coffee I'd be glad to tell you, although it wasn't particularly related to class.

B: Well that's why I said it, because I was interested in the type of things you talked about.

E: This kinda reminds me of a family now we're getting so close it's kinda like a mother and the mother doesn't want to let go of any of her kids.

Do: Who's the mother? (*Laughter*) The group.

Di: I think one thing we can do to reduce the threat about some of these meetings is geared to what W. said he would like for us to do. We do not discuss class at the luncheon. (*Refers to session where confidential nature of group was explored.*)

L: But, Di, I don't think it's only a matter of discussing class. It's a matter of people liking you and . . .

Ro: A group feeling.

Do: I think we are going to have to live through it a while.

THE SILENT MEMBER

The concern of the group over members' participation is made quite clear. Although group members accept nonverbal signs of participation, a time is reached when the highly verbal members feel guilty and exposed by all they have said. At this time they begin to pressure silent members to talk. Their motivation is complex. Not only do they desire a feedback and reaction to their ideas, but also they wish to make all members equally vulnerable since everyone is treated the same. This pressure, coming from the group, is far preferable to leader-based techniques designed to pull silent members into the group (57). Not only would action by the leader reinforce his authority role, but it would also threaten the group, since each member would wonder when he would be forced into a role he might find uncomfortable.

The protocol which follows demonstrates how a group, while applying pressure, provides support by identifying verbally with *Ir*. This protocol also demonstrates a typical reaction of a silent member. Frequently the silent person says little because she feels inferior to her peers. As the silent person talks, and as others identify with her and accept her feelings, she feels more worthwhile.

Do: I would like to, ah, change the subject a little because I have a little need—I would like to know something about Ir. Ah, we all had our say about our background . . . I don't know anything about her except that she's sitting there. (*Laughter*) I know her name is Ir ——————, and I would like a run down on your background (*to Ir*). I think we should give her the same treatment all of us had.

E: May I pose one thing now? I don't know if anybody else is doing this, but I was upset because Ir hadn't said anything. And I think maybe, I don't know whether . . . I was trying to think up some way that I could get Ir in. I didn't know this was your need too (*to Do*), but this is what you felt too . . . is it that you want to know about *her,* or is it that you want to bring her into the group?

Do: Well . . . well, I think that's up to her—I just wanted to know about her so I could feel more comfortable, and I think we should give her the same treatment in terms of the group. This is one of the ways I feel we could bring her into the group—I mean pretty much the same thing. We are all talking about *our* needs while Ir is sitting there. (*Laughter*)

Ir: I am, ah, getting all my needs satisfied . . . I'm more or less trying to find out where I am 'cause I came in late and, ah, the class had already started . . . but, ah, my background is very slim—I got out of school in June last year and I started last summer doing graduate work and when E. said something about being scared about these people, I had an experience in the summer 'cause I was the only person in any of my classes who had done no work at all—I had no experience and everything was done in terms of experience.

Do: What kind of experience have you had? You were an Illinois grad?

Ir: No, I got my undergraduate degree in Mississippi.

Do: Uh huh.

Ir: And I came to Illinois last summer and started my graduate work.

Do: What did you do your undergraduate work in?

Ir: Social Sciences.

Di: Teaching of Social Sciences or . . .

Ir: Yeah, social science education.

E: And now you are going into guidance work.

Ir: Uh huh—so there. (*General laughter*)

Do: Are you married?

Ir: Yeah.

Ro: She was telling, before class, that she has her husband in the hospital ever since the first of January and she is kept rather busy running back and forth between here and Chicago.

Ir: Oh. Right now he has pneumonia. On the first of January he had a punctured gall bladder.

Do: Got any children?

Ir: I just got married. (*Laughter*)

Do: Well, the only way to find out is to stumble into it.

Ir: I just got married. (*Laughter*)

Do: Oh! I see.

Do: Ir, you and B have a lot in common.

As suggested before, silence usually reflects fear on the part of the silent member. Silence may indicate a desire not to reveal too much or to expose feelings. Sometimes silence represents a fear that no one would listen if he did talk, coupled with anxiety over testing the hypothesis out. It is not unusual for the quiet person to desire strongly to speak but to be genuinely unable to break through his own resistance (58). Since, basically, these people fear that speaking will cause them to be looked down on by the group, there are two avenues open to help the quiet ones. The first and most preferable approach is to help the person feel wanted and secure in the setting so that his fears lose force. The second and less usual approach is to allow the person the security of knowing that he can enter the group when and in the manner he finds most comfortable.

An illustration may help demonstrate this second approach. All patients in the author's battalion at Welch Convalescent Hospital were informed that at a set time all men were expected to attend group therapy sessions. The men would gather around the center of the long barracks and arrange their foot lockers in a circle.

One of the men chose a bed at the far end of the barracks, and to all appearances went to sleep. A few days passed, and instead of sleeping he now read comic books. After a few more days he began to move from bed to bed, getting closer to the circle. The day finally came when he arranged a foot locker in a concentric circle to the group. He listened intently to the men discussing their fears in combat and freely admitting their reactions. He would nod his head in agreement. The next day he further identified with speakers by saying "Me, too," or "I'll say!" Finally the day arrived when, listening to the men, he broke in saying, "You think you guys had it tough, well . . . ," and at last he was a full-fledged participating member.

This man's feelings of inadequacy were such that any presssure from the leader or the group would have forced him to defend himself by building a higher wall so others could not penetrate or reach him. This illustration may sound extreme, but have you ever watched a small timid child in a play area? He may choose a toy which he appears to be using, but which actually permits him to observe others freely. Slowly he moves into the group choosing the children who threaten him least. The shy adolescent at the party who gets busy fixing punch to avoid being forced to cope with the total group is not too different.

SILENCE IN THE GROUP

Just as with the individual, silence in the group can be a sign of resistance, but to interpret it this way all the time would be an error. Silence can also represent the fact that all members need time to digest the ideas that preceded the silence.

In so-called leaderless groups, the start of a session frequently is marked by silence. Group members chat with one another waiting for all to arrive. When everyone is present, the chatter dies down, and the group prepares to shift gears. One sign of the security of a group is their ability to tolerate silence when it represents the need of the members to gather steam or face a block.

Regardless of the cause of the silence, just as in individual counseling, the group learns that the ideas expressed immediately after a silent period tend to be ones loaded with meaning for the speaker.

For many groups in which social convention is strong, lack of talk is felt at first to be rude. Along with this is the feeling that people must constantly interact verbally to be productive. Ultimately the group learns that you can't think and talk at the same time. Neither can you think your own thoughts and listen at the same time. At that stage, silence becomes something precious. It provides a chance to think without pressure from others, but with the security of knowing the group is there if you need them.

TALK AS AN AVOIDANCE TECHNIQUE

The way in which group members persist in discussing a specific topic or introduce apparent irrelevancies can, in and of itself, tell a group leader something about the security level and cohesiveness of the group. As Bradford (59) points out:

> When individuals are feeling their own anxieties and fears most keenly, they seem to conspire to keep the discussion centered on group action or on events unrelated to the present anxiety. Later, when some predictability has developed, some norms for sharing feelings and perceptions have been constructed, and greater understanding of one another has been established, concern centers on the group and its developmental problems. But now there is much more discussion of individual feelings, perceptions, and needs. Indeed, group problems are resolved through open discussion of individual reactions. A problem of group movement is examined not only in terms of suggestions for group action, but also in terms of individual perceptions and individual needs.

The Army expression of doing a "snow job" reflects the way in which a mass of words can cover up feelings or behaviors that the speaker isn't ready to reveal to others. In addition to achieving camouflage through a flurry of words, actively holding the attention of the group by forcing them to listen rather than react enables the speaker to hold off from others comments he would rather not hear or face. Generally, the less a person feels accepted in a group, the more he may feel pushed toward introducing safe and irrelevant material.

CATHARSIS—OR LETTING IT ALL HANG OUT

At the opposite extreme from the nonparticipating member is the person who, while under pressure, bubbles out ideas and feelings to the point that he feels empty and exposed (60). All of us know that being able to blow off steam from time to time makes us feel better. The problem is that a certain amount of steam (anxiety) is needed to motivate a person to solve a problem. Just like the steam engine with a hot fire underneath, letting out steam may relieve the pressure, but as long as the fire is lit pressure will build up again. Letting out the steam, then, is symptom treatment but it doesn't get to the heart of the trouble.

Because losing symptoms gives a feeling of relief, and since the experience of catharsis is part of group members' societal tools, a group needs to learn how to deal with this device to achieve more therapeutic results. The person who is permitted to cathart without group intervention may discover that, while reacting to the pressure, he has verbalized feelings or ideas he is not ready to face. Feeling threatened by what he has exposed, the person grows hostile toward the group. His hostility reflects a feeling that they have no right to know things about him even *he* does not wish to face. His hostility is also defensive, because he anticipates rejection as a result of what he has said or done.

Some authors would feel it was more important that the ideas the member expressed be verbalized and available for inspection, than to be concerned over the period of hostility which may result.

I believe that ultimately the person and the group grow faster if the group setting can maximize rather than minimize security. Accordingly, when a person catharts under pressure, every effort is made to continually reflect to the catharter the feelings he is expressing. By helping the member hear what he is saying as he says it, the group enables the person under pressure to decide if he wants to continue to reveal himself. At the same time, by continuously reflecting feelings, the group provides the person with evidence of their support. They also demonstrate that the ideas being expressed are not effecting the person's acceptability to the group.

THE PROBLEM CHILDREN IN A GROUP

Some leaders will purposely exclude individuals who because of their problems tend to slow up or inhibit group functioning.

Although getting a group to function efficiently is difficult enough, the reality is that these "problem children" are present in our society and the rest of us better learn how to cope with them. Given enough patience, group security, and leader skill, few clients cannot help but benefit from an opportunity to do reality testing in a secure setting. Let us look at the dynamics behind some types of behavior that trouble groups.

The Monopolist.   Many authors have stated that the monopolist inhibits group growth. Although no one can take exception to this idea, the question certainly is raised as to how groups can learn to cope with people like the monopolist if they are not given a chance to learn to do so. In many ways the monopolist resembles the member who seized group leadership described in the preceding section. He tends to be a person with strong status needs and frequently is a rather basically insecure person despite his overt behavior. The monopolist has learned that as long as he controls topics and direction, people cannot raise issues that will threaten him. It is this last dynamic that spells out how a group can both control and help the monopolist.

The monopolist's behavior causes hostility in the group. When the group has learned to express its feelings, these hostile reactions will be verbalized and directed toward the monopolist. When this happens, the monopolist is confused. Why, he wonders, are people acting this way? "I'm trying to help them and they don't appreciate me." As his anxiety grows, he reaches a point where, since he is dependent on group approval, he asks the group to help him understand their reactions. In a way he has learned that the group's attack on him demonstrates that they really care about him (supportive) but that he isn't getting the relationship with them he desires. Since the monopolist tends to have used his aggressive tactics for a long period of time before the group started, these crises in the group may have to occur repeatedly until the monopolist has learned a new mode of relating which will be equally effective as his unwanted controlling tactics.

At all points of hostility between group members, it is the role of the person serving as leader to remain objective and help the participants examine their behavior.

The Group Manipulator. In the next chapter there is a discussion of how group activists can use the traditional rules of group behavior to defeat the will of the majority.

Klein (61) has stated his reaction to parliamentary procedures by indicating that "parliamentary procedure is for parliaments, it is not designed to facilitate communication in small groups." Since tradition about voting, as a democratic process, is so deeply ingrained in our habits, it creates special problems as the group leader tries to help group members examine their feelings about the process.

From the very beginning each group faces the problem of which method to use to achieve group decision. Partially because it is the most familiar technique and partially because it seems most expedient, groups use voting to make decisions. Similar to the experiences reported by Gordon (62), I have found that voting brought with it problems the group was not sure how to solve. Desiring to provide all the needed time for discussion, the group could not decide when to vote. When several members of the group were ready to vote, but the others were not, they found themselves voting about whether to vote. The group perceived how ridiculous this was, but initially knew no other way of solving the dilemma. Robert's *Rules of Order* provides a method, but does not recognize individual needs.

When because of individual pressure a group votes prematurely, they frequently ignore the decision and act out their unmet needs. In one group, based upon discussion by group members it was decided to end each session earlier than originally planned to enable one group member time to get to her next activity. During the following several sessions, the group found itself in animated discussion at the new closing time. Despite the fact that the young lady got up and left, the group continued until their initial time limit. When the young lady pointed out how the group was failing to respect its own limits, the group was forced to examine its behavior. In so doing they discovered that although they desired to help the young lady, they resented losing time they originally had. Seeking ways to solve the problem, they explored with the girl ways she could solve *her* time problem. Several members provided solutions that would involve their help. This they did willingly, in order that the total group could meet as originally planned.

This sensitivity to the needs and rights of the individual makes it difficult for a group to accept the concept of a minority subgroup within the total group. In one group with which I worked, this concept of the rights of the individual met the supreme test. A young man, whom we will call Mr. X, joined a group knowing its purpose and typical method of operating. He reasoned to himself that if this group was truly democratic he had the right, as an individual, to participate or not as he chose, and to vote or not when he chose. Participating or voting when he didn't want to represented coercion of a minority member by the majority.

The total group, desiring to respect his needs, found themselves immobilized because they:

1. Did not want to set up limits he would not respect (confidentiality, time, etc.)
2. Were threatened by his perception of them when the absence of feedback made them unable to know his true thoughts.
3. Felt cheated by not getting a contribution from him that would enrich the group.

In trying to solve this problem the group developed the following concepts:

1. Groups have a responsibility to be aware of minority group needs and the effect of a majority group decision upon the minority.

2. Minority group members have the right, following a group decision, to continue to work toward changing the beliefs of others so that their values might someday represent majority opinion.

3. Minority group members need to be helped to evaluate the price they are paying for their decision *and* to discover other needs the group *is* meeting that makes giving up a specific need worthwhile.

4. The majority group recognized that if it has met the previous criteria by providing opportunity and support to minority members, then when a group decision is being made silence must be construed as consent.

*5. In a democracy people not only have a right to vote but beyond that also have a responsibility to do so. Failure to vote involves more than individual rights; it involves taking from others something they need to be successful. Being interdependent, no man has the right to receive group benefits without accepting his share of responsibility.

It is this last concept that our schools and citizenry have failed to comprehend. Unless youngsters are helped early in group life to learn the lesson of their voting responsibilities, no government that uses votes as a method of group decision can succeed.

As a sidelight to the illustration above, the reactions of the author to this situation might be of interest. Like the group, he was threatened by the man's behavior. Feeling responsibility as the initial leader, it became important to try to understand the needs behind Mr. X's behavior. Because he felt that it might be difficult to be objective about the situation, he asked an outside person to provide answers to his questions. The questions and answers received were:

1. Is Mr. X a psychopath? No.
2. Is Mr. X a monopolist? No.
3. Is Mr. X a cultural deviant? No.
4. Is Mr. X deeply neurotic? No.
5. Does the group appear to be accepting and supporting Mr. X? Partially accepted by three people. Acceptance of his ideas but not his emotions.
6. At what point do you feel this group's demands on the individual are going beyond the rights of the group? Felt group had no right to insist on verbal participation.
7. Is Mr. X a person who cannot be helped in a group? Why? Mr. X

* Major rule in groups' eyes. Clever minority group activists have used this concept shrewdly by delaying group business until most members have left the meeting; then issues are voted on when the minority represents a majority of those present at voting time.

has a real need for help, but at present seems unable to face receiving help from this group.

As the reader can see, the answers suggested a lack of real support for Mr. X and an impatience by the group at the rate of his ability to participate.

There is an interesting sequel to this incident. Several years later I met Mr. X at a professional convention. After being greeted warmly, I was brought up to date on Mr. X's life. With surprise I learned that not only was Mr. X working with groups but that he felt his early experiences in class had been meaningful and helpful. Once again the lesson was brought home that the true meaning of any situation can only be evaluated subjectively. It also demonstrated how time can affect the way an experience is evaluated.

Within these examples, it is felt, lies the whole crux of the democratic philosophy. At some point, a truly democratic group needs to accept the limitation that it can move only as fast as the slowest member. With this concept comes the corollary that the speed of movement of the individual is a function of his security in the group, security which the group has the responsibility of facilitating. Last but not least, the contribution of each individual makes for total group strength, and therefore no person is truly expendable.

In the last analysis then, voting is meaningful and helpful only when the needs of all the members have been evaluated and only when the group is able to accept loss of some freedoms as a price for having others.

RESISTANCE

It has been pointed out above, that readiness is an important concept in groups. Resistance, then, is one sign of lack of readiness.

Looking at one's behavior or feelings creates anxiety. Every member of the group has established some way of coping with his environment. His present method is working sufficiently well for him to get some rewards. Although each person dimly suspects that life could be more rewarding, he is not sure he has the ability to change or that changed behavior will be an improvement. Feeling this way, there is a strong effort on the part of group members to maintain the status quo.(63)

Resistance takes many forms. As with the monopolist it could represent an attempt to control the environment. With the silent person it can be achieved by remaining beyond the reach of the group. These are both direct and clearly observable methods. However, group members employ more devious techniques that are not always easily recognized.

One person in a group the author worked with kept his mouth full of chewing gum until the group observed the repetitious nature of this act. For another person, taking voluminous notes provided a "legitimate" excuse for lack of verbal participation.

ROLE MODELS AND ROLE PLAYING

Role Models. A close inspection of the problem of the role model used by present-day youngsters reveals some interesting facts. Horatio Alger's heroes now tend to be replaced by the most noticeable person with whom the youngster can most easily identify. It is not surprising to discover that adolescents turn to personalities made famous through their activities in space flight, television broadcasts, or because of their unique racial or national characteristics.

One basic requirement of a hero is that he be discoverable. The slum children, the suburban children, the black or brown children, the orphan children, the city and rural children will find him in a dozen different places; for as they grow up they are confronted with slices of society so varied as to be almost from different pies. The same heroes simply are not visible to all groups. If this is a cause for concern, it immediately suggests that group leaders need to take an active role in publicizing desirable role models in populations now using antisocial models.

Let us examine typical pressures exerted by parents on their children. It is truly difficult to find parents who do not want their children to move up the socioeconomic ladder. Even if parental strivings were not enough, the rash of articles on the importance of a college education would create pressure toward high-level occupational goals. Lacking information about the world of work or education beyond his own level, the parent tries to motivate his child by painting the status quo as undesirable. "Do you want to slave like me?" "Don't you want to amount to something?" Unwittingly, by deprecating his own status, the parent is sowing the seeds for later trouble. Youngsters whose motivation is based on an escape from something rather than on an attraction toward a desirable goal tend to use large portions of their potential energy coping with their anxiety about the future. Feeling that they and their parents are worthless in our society, they react with frustration and sometimes with aggression. Ultimately, in order to reach adult status they are forced to dissociate themselves from their parents before they can be free to be themselves. Clearly parents need help in learning new ways to motivate youngsters. Without doubt, they are unaware of the way they are currently laying the foundation for their later rejection by their children.

The basic concept behind group counseling is that in a protected setting people can evaluate themselves and their ways of behaving. This, however, is only the first step. For movement to take place they need to do something about acting in a more effective manner. Some members know few alternative ways of relating. For them seeing the leader and other group members function provides living examples of some alternate behaviors (role models).

Role Playing. To be effective in any new role, as any actor can attest, one needs to get "the feeling" of how this type of behavior affects oneself and others. For this reason, Moreno (64) developed a series of techniques to help people learn skills and new feelings. His approaches include:

1. Technique of self-presentation—group member portrays himself as he would act in relation to a significant other.
2. Technique of self-realization—group member presents his ideas about life—past, present, and future with the aid of others who play roles of auxiliary egos.
3. Direct soliloquy technique—a monologue where person steps outside of a scene and speaks about himself.
4. Therapeutic soliloquy technique—an attempt to portray the hidden feelings and thoughts promoted by the scenes being played.
5. Double technique—entering the inner world of the group member through the use of an auxiliary ego, group member has a chance to view himself as he watches "his other self."
6. Multiple double techniques—use of a wide range of auxiliary egos representing group member at different stages of his life or his different and conflicting feelings.
7. Mirror technique—when group member is unable to play role himself, an auxiliary ego acts for the person and represents him.
8. Role-reversal technique—group member takes part of the significant other with whom he is having problems, tries to put himself in the other person's shoes.
9. Technique of future projection—shows how person views his future.
10. Technique of life rehearsal—a chance to work out problems in advance of being called on to face them.

Because in acting out a situation one behaves as one normally does, not as one wishes he might, role playing provides many opportunities for the group to learn alternate coping skills, to see the distance between idealized goals versus actual behavior, and to develop needed new skills in advance of being asked to use them.

Klein (65,66), has pointed out that these approaches, although effective and powerful, contain some danger. Thrusting people into roles without regard for the compatability of the role expectations and a person's physical and psychological predisposition can cause some very unhappy results. Throwing people into settings where they feel inadequate or degraded can cause them to defend themselves by coping in maladaptive ways.

Readers will find articles by Schwebel (67) and Lippitt and Hubbell (68) helpful if they wish to learn more about ways to help group members use roles to help solve problems.

SUMMARY

This chapter reviewed problems of group leadership, composition, size, membership, and problem-solving techniques. It presented the role of the leader as a facilitator of the group process. It reviewed some problem spots in group life. The emphasis was on the dynamics of group process and although examples were cited from real life, there was little discussion of the role of the larger society as it affects the goal or process to be used in a group.

The next chapter will focus on several groups that exist in real life. Some choose behaviors that are seen as threatening by society. The role of the group in seeking social change instead of just adjustment to the status quo will be explored.

Bibliography

1. Wrenn, G. C. "Two Psychological Worlds: An Attempted Rapprochement." In John D. Krumboltz (Ed.), *Revolution in Counseling*, p. 104, Boston: Houghton Mifflin, 1966.

2. Jennings, H. *Leadership and Isolation*, New York: Longmans, Green, 1950.

3. Haiman, F. S. *Group Leadership and Democratic Action*, Boston: Houghton Mifflin, 1951.

4. Hare, P., Borgatta, E., and Bales, R. *Small Groups*, New York: Knopf, 1955.

5. Kemp, G. C. *Perspectives on the Group Process; A Foundation for Counseling with Groups*, 2nd ed., New York: Houghton Mifflin, 1970.

6. Kemp, G. C. "Bases of Group Leadership," *Personnel and Guidance Journal*, 1964, **42**, p. 760–766.

7. Bettelheim, B., and Sylvester, E. "Therapeutic Influence in the Group on the Individual," *American Journal of Orthopsychiatry*, 17, 684–692, 1947.

8. Bradford, L. P., Gibb, J. R., Benne, K. D. (Eds.). T-Group Theory and Laboratory Method, Ch. 8 "From Polarization to Paradox" by Kenneth D. Benne, p. 247, New York: Wiley, 1964.

9. Schwartz, W. "The Social Worker in the Group," *Social Welfare Forum*, New York: Columbia University Press, 1961, pp. 159–172.

10. Klein, A. F. *Social Work Through Group Process*, Albany, New York: School of Social Welfare, 1970, p. 196.

11. Beck, D. F. "The Dynamics of Group Psychotherapy as Seen by a Sociologist," *Sociometry*, **21**, 98–128, June 1958.

12. Gordon, T. "The Functioning of the Group Leader," *Perspectives on The Group Process*, p. 240, Gratton Kemp. Boston: Houghton Mifflin, 1964.

13. Ohlsen, M. M. *Group Counseling*, New York: Holt, Rinehart, Winston, 1970, p. 80.

14. Field, F. *Freedom and Control in Education and Society*, New York: Thomas Crowell, 1970, p. 45.

15. Tropp, E. "The Military Social Worker as a Discussion Leader," *J. Soc. Case Work*, **XXVI**, 377–383, February 1946.

16. Cotton, J. M. "The Psychiatric Treatment Program at Welch Convalescent Hospital," *Research Publications of the Association for Nervous Mental Disease*, 25, 316–321, 1946.

17. Mahler, C. *Group Counseling in the Schools,* New York: Houghton Mifflin, 1969, p. 80.

18. Curry, E. E. "Some Comments on Transference When Group Therapist is Negro," *Int. Journal of Group Psychotherapy,* 1963, **13**, 363–365.

19. Bach, G. R. "Observations on Transference and Object Relations in the Light of Group Dynamics," *International Journal of Group Psychotherapy,* **7**, 64–76, January 1957.

20. Glatzner, H. T. "Transference in Group Therapy," *American Journal of Orthopsychiatry,* **22**, 499, 509, July 1952.

21. Blocksma, D. D. "Leader Flexibility in Group Guidance Situations," *Educational and Psychological Measurement,* **9**, 531–535, 1949.

22. Gorlow, L. *Nondirective Group Psychotherapy: An Analysis of the Behavior of Members as Therapist;* 1950, Columbia University, Microfilm Abstract #2109. Also in *The Nature of Nondirective Group Psychotherapy,* Leon Gorlow, Erasmus L. Hoch, and Earl Telschow. New York: Teachers College Press, 1952.

23. Gordon, T. *Group Centered Leadership,* Boston: Houghton Mifflin, 1955, pp. 197–200.

24. Gibbs, J. R., Platts, G., and Miller, L. *Dynamics of Participation Groups,* St. Louis: J. Swift, 1951.

25. Winder, A., and Stieper, D. "A Prepracticum Seminar in Group Psychotherapy," *International Journal of Group Psychotherapy,* **VI**, 410–417, October 1956.

26. Hadden, S. "Countertransference in the Group Psychotherapist," *International Journal of Group Psychotherapy,* **III**, 417–430, October 1953.

27. Kotkov, B. "Vicissitudes of Student Group Psychotherapists," *International Journal of Group Psychotherapy,* **VI**, 48–52, January 1956.

28. Konopka, G. "Knowledge and Skill of the Group Therapist," *American Journal of Orthopsychiatry,* **19**, 56–60, 1949.

29. Slavson, S. R. "Qualifications and Training of Group Therapists," *Mental Hygiene,* **31**, 386–396, 1947.

30. Korner, I. J. "Ego Involvement and the Process of Disengagement," *Journal of Consulting Psychology,* 1950, **14**, 206–209.

31. Thibaut, J. W., and Coules, J. "The Role of Communication in the Reduction of Interpersonal Hostility," *Journal of Abnormal and Social Psychology,* **47**, 770–777, October 1952.

32. Hansen, J. E., Niland, T. M., and Zani, L. P. "Model Reinforcement in Group Counseling with Elementary School Children," *Personnel and Guidance Journal,* Vol. 47, No. 8, April 1969.

33. Hymes, J. L. *Discipline,* New York: Teachers College Press, 1949.

34. Stendler, C. "Climates for Self-Discipline," *Childhood Education,* **27**, 209–211, January 1951.

35. Sheviakov, G. V., and Redl, F. *Discipline for Today's Children and Youth,* Washington, D. C.: Department of Supervision and Curriculum Development, National Education Association, 1944.

36. Klein, A. F. *Social Work Through Group Process,* Albany, New York: School of Social Welfare, 1970, pp. 138–145.

37. "Promoting Adaptive Behavior" from *Revolution in Counseling,* John Krumboltz (Ed.), p. 19, New York: Houghton Mifflin, 1966.

38. Slavson, S. R. "Criteria for Selection and Rejection of Patients for Various Types of Group Psychotherapy," *International Journal of Group Psychotherapy,* **VI,** 13–30, January 1955.

39. Samuels, A. S. "Use of Group Balance as a Therapeutic Technique," *Archives of General Psychiatry,* 1964, **11,** 411–420.

40. Rieken, H. W. "The Effect of Talkativeness on Ability to Influence Group Solutions of Problems," *Sociometry,* 1958, **21,** 309–321.

41. Stock, D., Whitman, R. M., and Lieberman, M. A. "The Deviant Member in Therapy Groups," *Human Relations,* 1959, **11,** 341–372.

42. Bach, G. *Intensive Group Psychotherapy,* pp. 18–27, New York: Ronald, 1954.

43. Powdermaker, F., Powdermaker, F. J., et al. *Group Psychotherapy—Studies in Methodology of Research and Therapy,* Cambridge: Harvard University Press, 1953.

44. Ash, P. "The Reliability of Psychiatric Diagnoses," *Journal of Abnormal and Social Psychology,* **44,** 272–276, 1949.

45. Cartwright, D. "Achieving Change in People: Some Applications of Group Dynamics Theory," *Human Relations,* 4, 381–392, 1951.

46. Thelen, H. *Dynamics of Groups at Work,* p. 62. Chicago: University of Chicago Press, 1954.

47. Olch, D., and Snow, D. L. "Personality Characteristics of Sensitivity Group Volunteers," *Personnel and Guidance Journal,* Vol. 48, No. 10, June 1970, p. 850.

48. Little, H. M., and Konopka, G. "Group Therapy in a Child Guidance Center," *American Journal of Orthopsychiatry,* **17,** 303–311, 1947.

49. Konopka, G. *Therapeutic Group Work with Children.* Minneapolis: University of Minnesota Press, 1949.

50. Axelrod, P. L., Cameron, M. S., Solomon, J. C. "An Experiment in Group Therapy with Shy Adolescent Girls," *American Journal of Orthopsychiatry,* **14,** 616–627, October 1944.

51. Spotnitz, H. "Observations on Emotional Currents in Interview Group Therapy with Adolescent Girls," *Journal of Nervous Mental Disease,* **106,** 565–582, 1947.

52. Thelen, H. *Dynamics of Groups at Work,* p. 44, Chicago: University of Chicago Press, 1954.

53. Gilmore, J. V. "Parental Counseling and the Productive Personality," in David R. Cook (Ed.), *Guidance for Education in Revolution,* Boston: Allyn and Bacon, 1971, Chapter X.

54. Peck, M. L., and Stewart, R. H. "Current Practices in Selection Criteria for Group Play Therapy," *Journal of Clinical Psychology,* 1964, **20**, 146.

55. Thomas, E. J., and Fink, C. F. "Effects of Group Size," *Psychology Bulletin,* 1963, **60**, 371–384.

56. Middleman, R. R. *The Non-Verbal Method of Working with Groups,* New York: Association Press, 1968.

57. Becker, R. E., Harrow, M., Astrachan, B. M., Detre, T., and Miller, J. C. "Influences of the Leader on the Activity Level of Therapy Groups," *Journal of Soc. Psych.,* 1968, **74**, 99–151.

58. Slavson, S. R. "A Contribution to a Systematic Theory of Group Psychotherapy," *International Journal of Group Psychotherapy,* IV, 3–29, January 1954.

59. Bradford, L. P., Gibb, J. R., Benne, K. D. (Editors). *T-Group Theory and Laboratory Method;* Ch. 7 "Membership and the Learning Process" by Leland P. Bradford, p. 198, New York: Wiley, 1964.

60. Slavson, S. R. "Catharsis in Group Psychotherapy," *Psychoanalytic Review,* **38**, 39–52, January 1951.

61. Klein, A. F. *Social Work Through Group Process,* Albany, New York: School of Social Welfare, 1970, p. 82.

62. Gordon, T. *Group Centered Leadership,* p. 269, Boston: Houghton Mifflin, 1955.

63. Redl, F. "Resistance in Therapy Groups," *Human Relations,* 1, 307–313, 1948.

64. Moreno, J. L., and Kipper, D. A. Chapter II, "Group Psychodrama and Community-Centered Counseling," from *Basic Approaches to Group Psychotherapy and Group Counseling* by George Gazda (Ed.), Springfield, Ill.: Charles C Thomas, 1968.

65. Klein, A. F. *Role Playing in Leadership Training and Group Solving,* New York: Association Press, 1956.

66. Klein, A. F. *Social Work Through Group Process,* Albany, New York: School of Social Welfare, 1970, p. 74.

67. Schwebel, M. "Role Playing in Counselor Training," *Personnel and Guidance Journal,* **XXXII**, No. 4, 196–201, December 1953.

68. Lippitt, R., and Hubbell, A. "Role Playing for Personnel and Guidance Workers: Review of the Literature with Suggestions for Applications," *Group Psychotherapy,* 1956, **9**, 89–114.

6 The Real World— A Changing Society

Those who profess to favor freedom
yet deprecate agitation
are men who want crops
without plowing the ground:
they want rain
without thunder and lightning:
they want the ocean
without the awful roar of its many waters.
FREDERICK DOUGLASS

At least once in every man's life he feels the need to test himself and see if what he believes can stand the ultimate test of working under fire. This chapter contains many personal anecdotes that were selected because they were critical experiences for me. They are not presented in chronological order. Wherever possible each story will terminate with a statement of the principle involved in working with groups whose goal is not therapy, but whose activities contained the seeds for a therapeutic encounter both for the group members themselves and for those whose lives they affected. Most of the illustrations occurred during a six-year period when I served as Coordinator of Pupil Personnel Services for the Rochester City School District of Rochester, New York. Rochester is one of the big six cities in New York State. The school system has approximately 45,000 children in grades kindergarten to 12. It also has contracts to run preschool programs which affect the lives of hundreds of other younger children.

Some readers may question the meaningfulness of these experiences in urban settings for those persons living in more placid suburban or rural areas. It is my belief that we are moving rapidly toward urbanization of our entire country. Megalopolis—a city created by cities that run into one another and form a larger community, is already occurring. It is also possible to demonstrate the ripple effect which seems to originate in urban crisis situations. People in cities who have not studied the works of Gittell (1), Fantini (2) and others cannot recognize how they could learn

213

from the crises at Oceanhill-Brownsville in New York City. It is not always necessary for each group to make the same mistakes. We should be able to profit from experience.

The reader may wonder why, in a book focused on facilitating the growth of the individual through groups, time should be spent in discussing the group workers' responsibility for social action in the real world.

Klein, Meyerson, Rubenstein, and Sirls (3,4,5), facing this issue in the area of social group work, developed what has been called the Pittsburgh position. They believe that there is a unity between social action, individual psychological health, and strength.

> This position rests, in part, upon the assumption that it is debilitating to feel that one has no power to influence one's environment and that the result of such a feeling of being helpless and manipulated leads to apathy and a sense of worthlessness and inadequacy. . . . it can lead also to hostility and anger which could be internalized and directed at one's self or to acting out against others.

I share this view and will try to document its implications in the material which follows.

THERAPEUTIC TECHNIQUE VERSUS THE NEEDS OF CLIENTS

Many inner-city residents were hired to serve as teacher aides in the Rochester school system. In an effort to improve their understanding of the school system, they met on a voluntary basis with various department heads to understand the function of each unit.

Accordingly, one evening I arrived at an inner-city school accompanied by the person responsible for the Mental Health Department, a social worker by training, and his assistant who is a psychologist. We entered a classroom, introduced ourselves, and joined a circle, careful not to sit together.

After an introduction by the chairman of the group I outlined the scope of our responsibilities and asked for questions so we could talk together instead of having a formal presentation. At this point the fireworks started. The aides were angry about the large number of black children in special education classes and wanted to know why we put them there. Attempts to explain the structure of the system, which in Rochester placed Special Education as part of instruction and not under Pupil Personnel, were brushed aside since they held us responsible for the system as a whole. Recognizing the validity of many of their statements, all three of us responded by giving information, accepting feelings, and generally acted as nonjudgmentally as possible. As the evening went on, the abuse grew more violent. Finally, after a long barrage, I became very angry. I told them I did not want to hear any more abuse. That they did not know me as a person. That although they had many reasons to be angry, they had no basis for being angry at me, *until they tried me out to see if I acted as they claimed.* At that point I would be ready to be judged, but until then I would not stand for their behavior. The meeting quieted down, finally ended, and several aides came up to thank me for coming or to talk some more. I went over to the chairlady and offered my apology for "blowing my cool." To my great surprise she said that she liked what I did. When asked for her reasons, she said, "when you answered questions and were being nice [accepting] you were "the man" (the power structure), but when you were mad you were for real!"

This incident forced me to reevaluate how I could be most helpful in acting as a change agent. Although I was trying to do many things to change those activities that tended to be system-oriented instead of people-oriented, as long as I interpreted the system to others, I *was* the system and part of what was putting people down.

It was also relevant to understand the mood changes in the meeting. People in the group were angry. They were catharting their hostility on me as a substitute target for their real target. Because I was not the "real enemy," they were not getting action to meet their needs. The action would not occur unless I could help them examine where and how to direct their fire. To do that I needed credibility as a human being. If readers share the chairlady's estimate of the "success" of the session they may agree that it occurred because:

· I was congruent (together).
· I was strong and respected myself.
· I was rejecting of their behavior, *but not rejecting* of their feelings.

For many of these black women, past experience had taught them that no self-respecting person would tolerate the abuse I was receiving. If I was so weak and so unsure of myself, they could not respect me nor feel I had ability to help them solve their problems. To people whose childhood included "playing the dozens," a game of verbal abuse, dealing with this abuse was necessary to retain group respect. At least at one level, responding to confrontation with equally strong responses is, in a sense, a measure of your confidence in the other individual. It demonstrates your belief that he has the strength to do battle and does not need or want a pyrrhic victory to gain a false sense of strength (6).

What I Learned.   Later on in this chapter, I shall discuss Black Power, student power, and so on, but at this point let me suggest that groups, like individuals, go through stages of development. For the individual seeking his own identity, the process of testing reality to see where he ends and others begin is very important. The child who arm wrestles with his father, and feels his father is "letting him win," gets very angry because he cannot be sure that if the contest was real how much additional strength he really would need to win. Encounter and confrontation taken in this setting are a necessary part of self-definition. The therapeutic stance of being accepting does not always provide the hard crust needed to sharpen your teeth on. In fact, for some people, a permissive stance suggests a "put down," an ill-concealed attempt to cover your belief in their weakness.

I am suggesting that in many situations the height of being therapeutic is to be secure enough to permit yourself to be used in the way the client needs to use you at that moment to work through his problem. Some groups at the adolescent stage of development, where they have ambivalent dependency-independency needs, may at times seek limits to preserve security or to test their strength. At other times they may seek freedom to find their own way. The question is the stance of the helping person to recognize what the work of the group is and how he can facilitate it by his behavior.

The leader or facilitator's ability to perceive the needs of the groups basically depends on his empathic ability. But empathy cannot exist where the leader himself is involved in the problem too. At this point identification or sympathy is the more likely response, but it is not a helpful one.

Liberals rarely understand why their sympathetic claims of being identified with the Black quest for power causes anger. They do not see that in their identification efforts they are repudiating the needs of the blacks to be their "own man" and valued for their difference (7).

For white people working as leaders with minority groups, black, brown, or just plain different, the ability of group members to provoke feelings of guilt puts the white or "different" person in a double bind. If he truly feels personally guilty, he needs to do something to atone. Unless the group has reached the level of maturity where all can accept that each person needs help in some area, the immature group will experience the pleasure of victory over a foe, but in the process they will have reduced the individual in their eyes to the point where they cannot use him as a model of strength or as someone against whom they can test themselves.

The leader who can be aware of his needs can be secure enough to be himself while helping others realize that role models are helpful only as guides for self-determination, not as templates to stamp out mirror images in all group members.

Alan Klein has tried to help group workers recognize that just having a group does not insure positive or therapeutic results (8).

> The group, left on its own, tends to emulate society by establishing a pecking order and a structure which allocates rewards based upon status, position, and power. Sub-groups are formed. . . . Those people who need the most are often the ones who are denied access to them. Again, duplicating the macrocosm, they may sell their souls for a smidgeon of acceptance (p. 196).

It is clear that if the group experience is not to reinforce existing maladaptive postures, it becomes the skillful leader's role to help the group become aware of what is happening so the group can accept responsibility and develop skill in changing conditions. Again quoting Klein (9,10):

> If one wishes members to move toward self determination and to relinquish maladaptive solutions to problems, the worker must facilitate freedom of communication among the members and encourage democratic functioning. This implies that the members are not tools but the prime movers in mutual help. Moreover, the group experience is in the here and now, it is *the* experience, and as such it is in the arena for learning adaptive social functioning (p. 179).

Violent confrontation evokes strong feelings in others just as any expression of anger or hostility does. Yet all of these can produce helpful or positive results.

Turner and Whitten (11) have cited evidence that the confrontation tactics developed by the radical movement can actually increase the moral awareness of the young.

Marlene Pringle (12) differentiates the ways in which aggression can be used. She notes that angry people tend to seek out aggressive scenes. The angry counselor also may tend to seek socially explosive settings to justify his venting of his hostility. Citing the work of Berkowitz (13) and Holt (14), Pringle establishes the idea that the counselor is more helpful when he encourages students to use their anger constructively instead of encouraging them in the direction of sublimation or displacement. Research suggests that when aggression occurs and the results are favorable to the aggressor, this behavior is being reinforced. The counselor therefore must realize that if he accepts aggression as appropriate in some situations, it may well occur in other similar settings. Her summary statement is more than picturesque (12): "The quicker one can become responsive to the rhetoric backed by pillows, the less likely it is that the rhetoric of the pillow fighters will be around to sanction the sticks of those who seek real destruction" (p. 5).

Anxiety, hostility, guilt—these three represent the areas the potential social activist must learn to face and to handle constructively if he is to be effective.

SOURCES OF GROUP STRENGTH FOR SOCIAL ACTION

Black Power.   Shortly after my arrival in Rochester I was drafted for a six-month period, from my job, to serve as the interim director of what later became Action for a Better Community (A.B.C.), the Monroe County poverty program under the Economic Opportunities Act. Along with my codirector, Walter Cooper, a black scientist on loan from East-man Kodak, we tried to formulate a proposal to secure funds to establish a poverty program. In accordance with the requirements of the act we solicited recommendations from people from the poverty community who could work with us in developing plans. The initial group was truly heterogeneous. It included black and white, Puerto Ricans, Italians, refugees from Appalachia, and representatives of all geographic segments of the poverty community. Late at night, after hours of work, they would meet to talk about unmet community needs. They frankly discussed the failures of the existing agencies to recognize their desires, and formulated plans to accomplish their goals. The group was cooperative and often took up the cause of others in the group—"Your area has poor health facilities, let's write it in." They shared a common concern about poverty and were attacking a common goal. One measure of their effectiveness is that although initially we had been told that $700,000 had been earmarked for our area, the proposal developed with their help so clearly refuted the concept of Rochester as an area not needing economic help that first year grants totaled over $3,000,000 and involved many different types of projects.

At about this time an interested group brought in Saul Alinsky (15) to see how he could help the black population organize. As a result of his efforts an organization carrying the acronym, FIGHT was started. Their charter barred membership to anyone who was not black. Using a series of disruptive techniques they tried to capture control of the poverty program. This was certainly in line with Alinsky's philosophy that power can only be taken, not given, since in the latter case it suggests it can be taken away too by the initial giver (16).

Prior to this time the minority group in Rochester had been the Italian population. When they worked together with blacks to formulate plans for the poverty program no problems arose. But when FIGHT took on a chauvinistic stance, each of the other minority groups became threatened and organized, and polarization took place. People facing a common threat now felt the need to seek a different security base (a racial or color base) to meet the new threat. Competition rather than cooperation became the order of the day, and the poverty program had rough sailing as energy was spent adjudicating between groups instead of getting support to implement programs.

Blacks who had not joined FIGHT were put under considerable pressure to conform and to accept this racial umbrella. Presumably the larger the black constituency, the stronger the organization. But as FIGHT began to press demands for the black population on the community, the goals they selected and the tactics they used caused many blacks to be unhappy. So alternate groups arose including the Urban League, NAACP, and Soul Brothers. Each, to attract support, tried to vie with each other in militancy to prove they could get "the bread" for their members. Blacks had to prove their purity by adhering to tighter and tighter definitions of appropriate "soul" behavior. As the leaders of these groups began to confront society, however, they discovered that compromises were necessary. For the membership, fed on unrealistic promises, leaders who talked with, rather than at, the power structure were seen as selling out. They were labeled "Uncle Toms" or "Oreos" (black on the outside, white on the inside). This destructive release of hostility against each other successfully castrated many capable young blacks who were learning leadership skills and were willing to accept responsibility.

What I Learned.   For me this movement (Black Power), which had a very noble goal—providing a group identification which could offer the security needed to take the power associated with achieving manhood in our society, served to be more divisive and more destructive than the initial material gains secured for its members justified. Since the whole methodology was based on power, competition, overtly expressed hostility, and a restrictive definition of membership, the group recapitulated within its structure the very evils of the society they were trying to fight.

Gordon Allport in his study on *The Nature of Prejudice* describes the following traits of those who have been victimized: fantasies of power, desire for protection, indirectness, ingratiation, petty revenge, sabotage, extremes of both self and group hatred and self and group glorification, compassion for the underprivileged, identification with the dominant group's norms, and passivity.

Because in Alinsky's view, Blacks had to make it on their own, he invalidated anything he or others could offer to help. Blacks, therefore, used the only tools they possessed, those which they learned as victims of the society with which they unconsciously identified.

Democracy demands open communication and acceptance of the values and contribution of each *individual*. True personal security is not achieved through the kind of group identification that demands conformity and rejects individual differences which deviate from the defined norm.

Many authors of texts on groups are fond of citing small group research studies that purport to differentiate between task-oriented and personal growth oriented groups. They cite evidence to prove that task-oriented group must be more clearly structured, have a hierarchy of control, and with a line of authority.

Whenever I hear of these studies I am reminded of a book describing Jewish women in a Nazi concentration camp. The guard tells them to pick up a heavy railroad tie. They try but fail. He then brains one of the four women with a shovel. The other three succeed in lifting the beam under fear of death. In other words, *if the threat or reward is great enough we can get people to do almost anything.*

Have we reached the point in our materialistic society where the ultimate effectiveness of the activity is measured only in terms of task completion without regard to the price paid or the lesson learned in the process? Can we truly differentiate task-oriented groups from others, and assume that the self-actualization of individuals needs to be set aside if task effectiveness is to be achieved?

PROFESSIONAL HELPING ROLES AND THE THREAT OF CHANGE

As one of the steps in integrating a Rochester high school, black boys and girls were bussed across the city to a school on the edge of town. The community is composed primarily of upper middle-class skilled craftsmen. It contains a high proportion of people who oppose integration, and the arrival of these students from another area was met with vocal and militant opposition.

One day, a woman looking out of her window saw a black girl take a flower from her lawn. She called the police who responded quickly. Cruising the street they spotted a black girl, placed her in their car and took her to headquarters. As it turned out, the only similarity between the girl they picked up and the real culprit was the color of their skin. The girl they picked up was an honor student, and popular with both students and faculty. The police could not be accused of being color blind!

When her brother learned about her detention he reacted immediately. He and his friends spread the word quickly and black students left their classes and began to roam the school corridors and mass in groups outside the school building. As other students left the building racially insulting words were flung from one group to the other. Fearing their vulnerability if they went home by bus, the black students grouped and began the long hike home, picking up defensive weapons (sticks and rocks) as they went. Shopkeepers seeing the group became very anxious and informed police.

The following day, although black adults succeeded in getting the students to return to school, they had difficulty in calming their fears of being attacked by white toughs who belonged to social clubs from the area. Meanwhile, despite school authorities' requests to the contrary, police massed around the school and began patrolling the corridors. Coming upon a group of black boys and girls they demanded their return to class. A nasty situation was in the making. At this point a black social worker and a white counselor placed themselves physically between the students and the police. Feeling some support and protection from physical harm, the students quieted down and agreed to go as a group to a classroom where the two adults said they would talk with them to see how best to resolve the situation.

Ultimately these two pupil personnel workers were able to meet with the white student leaders and separately with the faculty to deal with their fears and feelings. At a later stage they helped the student groups talk together. One result of this dialogue was that the two groups found they had common grievances about the school and the lack of respect students received from the faculty. They began to explore socially approved ways of changing the school environment.

There were many aspects of this situation that could be explored, but I am going to focus on only one. *The only people able to help in the crisis were the two who by putting their bodies and professional roles on the line retained the respect of all.* Others who had remained in their offices were ignored, since they were seen as impotent. It should be noted that the acceptance by the student body of these two workers caused jealousy in their colleagues. Since by their behavior and their effectiveness they were defining new roles, the threat of change and the insecurity some people felt about their ability to function in new and different ways caused some to direct their frustration and anger toward the perceived cause of the threat.

The same dynamic was seen in a totally different situation. Seeking to use energies in prevention rather than remediation, I approached the more than 50 elementary school principals and asked if any cared to volunteer for an experimental mental health program which was totally new and might, therefore, have some problems. I received 5 offers. Then approaching the pupil personnel staff I made the same offer and 15 people volunteered. Next I asked the 5 principals to interview all 15 candidates and to see which people they would like to work with. In other words, beyond the voluntary nature of the commitment I was seeking compatibility of personalities. The 5 selected came from the fields of psychology (3), social work (1), and guidance (1). I charged these 5 to enter their new schools and to use their skill to improve the mental health of the school. No other job definition was given except to indicate to the principals that these people were not to serve as disciplinarians. Children who had trouble could see them after other authorities had made any decisions in terms of punishment involved.

At the end of the year each of the people who had been called "Elementary Counselors" was asked to describe his job as it had evolved, how he had obtained acceptance by students, faculty, parents, and the local community. To our surprise a comparison of the reports showed that despite differences in professional training, 80 percent of the tasks they worked at in the school were the same. Of greater significance, they were able to perform an equal percentage of these tasks without the help of a different discipline.

When these results became generally known, it was as if a Pandora's box had been opened. Professional staff from all three disciplines attacked the new roles. In their eyes the elementary counselors were generalists and no longer specialists. We were diluting the profession, and so on. It could not be doubted that this experiment was seen as a basic threat to their self-concept and it was therefore attacked with great vigor.

It is worth noting that in subsequent budget hearings when the jobs of these elementary counselors were in jeopardy, the principals and their staff as well as parents came out to fight for the preservation of the new role. The 5 volunteers were faced with the need to decide where their feelings of personal security rested—in a professional role definition and title or in satisfaction of unmet needs felt by the community.

It was the issue of where professional allegiance for helping professions should lie that caused Paul Smith in a speech given before the National Association of Pupil Personnel Administrators to say:

> If our investment in pupil personnel administrators is to continue in view of the changes taking place in our society, there must be some alterations made in their purposes, attitudes and activities, if they are to serve students rather than the educational establishment.

To begin with, the unrest which complicates life in the society is likely to continue. Pupil Personnel workers because of their powerless status can only lend partial assistance to students as they attempt to find solutions to matters they deem important. If the present school organization is to continue, I think the Pupil Personnel administrators and staff should divorce themselves from the chief school officer of institutions and become independent agencies responsible only to students and parents. This could be done on a contractual basis or some form of the "voucher plan." Students and parents would be responsible for selecting the personnel to act in their behalf. They would receive all reports with regard to admission, discipline, placement, human relations, counseling and the entire array of social activities in which students and parents have vested interest.

Those personnel administrators who remain as arms of the chief school officer would serve to coordinate and preserve the position of the administration as they presently do. In matters of dispute and arbitration there would be a balance with one set of workers fighting for the interest of parents and students and the other one for the administration of the system. This arrangement provides personnel workers with the means to be entirely accountable to the population they are intended to serve, and would eliminate conflict of interest with their present boss. In either case, the personnel worker should be representative of the various ethnic groups that comprise the community.

What I Learned.   Although the helping professions profess humanitarian values, their ability to act congruently with their ideals seems to depend on where their security rests. Those in social change roles cannot have divided allegiances. From the incidents reported I've drawn the following conclusions.

1. When security is threatened, even liberal groups act in a reactionary manner.
2. When advisory groups are formed, their purpose and scope of action better be sharply defined or they must test the limits to discover reality. This applies equally well for student groups as it does for community action groups.
3. Society is changing faster than the institutions, and confrontation appears to be the only device that currently produces enough motivation to force institutions to be willing to face the anxiety concomitant with change (17).
4. The closer people are located to those they need to serve, the more effective they can be, not only in providing service but also in effecting changes within the system. The more itinerant the worker, the less he is identified with an institution (18).

STUDENT POWER

The data in this section comes from national survey reports and policy statements rather than from specific incidents. It has long been believed that the mission of the educational establishment was to pass on the culture to those who will follow. Schools, accepting their charge from society, tried to act in "loco parentis" (in place of the parents). Taking their cues from parents, they tried to set up rules that would insure proper behavior. Acceptance of these rules obviously depends on the students' willingness to accept both the mission of the school and inferior or subordinate status.

In January of 1969 the National Association of Secondary School Principals published a report showing that 59 percent of the high school principals surveyed reported some form of student activism. Activism was highest (81 percent) in large suburban schools with urban schools reporting a slightly lower percentage (74 percent).

Adults are distressed and frequently ask "What do these kids want anyway?" The answer found in a book popular with students, *The Student as Nigger* (19), documents the ways in which students are treated in demeaning ways. Because of the increasing number of civil disturbances by students, the Department of Justice surveyed high schools and colleges to isolate causes of grievances. Basically the protests focus on institutional racism, institutional irrelevancy, and the breakdown of communication between administrators and student protestors.

Although the words used differ from setting to setting, students want minority personnel in positions of importance, racism and other forms of discrimination eliminated, internal badgering of minority groups by students and faculty stopped, studies should reflect the contributions of all segments of society (specifically black, brown, and female), and of highest priority: that students share with administration the power needed to run the educational enterprise. Specifically they seek a voice in curriculum planning, the hiring and firing of faculty, and of any codes of behavior designed to regulate student conduct, dress, or rights of assembly.

It is worth noting that violence in schools usually occurred as a last resort when all traditional avenues of democratic redress proved unproductive.

As reported in the *Education Daily* (Friday, October 24, 1969) persons surveyed made the following recommendations:

1. Adopt an open-door policy in colleges and high schools where administrators invite students, teachers, paraprofessionals, and community people to discuss not only statements of demands but also

working terms by which these demands can be met; provisions should be made for a built-in structure to involve students in substantive educational issues.

2. Remove tight laws regarding hair styles and clothing; establish dress codes that respect students' self-image and allow for differences and promote intergroup respect rather than conformity based upon a single value system which by implication is superior. Students with different backgrounds and life styles need to feel accepted in the schools if the school is to be a place of respect instead of rejection.

3. Involve students, faculty, and administration in discussion and institution of black and brown studies, sociology, and other special electives which educate them to understand rather than fear differences in origins, culture, language, etc.

4. Appoint a committee composed of board members, administrators, police, students, teachers, and paraprofessionals to set up guidelines to insure, if possible, the safety and protection of all persons in a school's community and spell out carefully if and how law enforcement agencies will be used during a crisis situation.

5. Review suspension rules and involve members of the student council or a similar organization in participating in the discipline of students. Take steps to stop all corporal punishment and assure that teachers and administrators apply discipline in a fair and equal manner. Get rid of petty regulations such as the suspension of a student for speaking Spanish at school.

6. Set up a mechanism to choose an advisory council of students, parents, teachers, and community to assist in decision making in schools. This process should not be left solely to administrators. Administrators must understand and act in ways to insure minority students that their participation in school affairs will be meaningful to their lives.

7. Coordinate student organizations on campuses to insure student participation in the total school program, implementing the idea that participation and responsibility are prerequisites for self-discipline.

8. Because a considerable polarization between black, brown, and white students exists, a committee of students should be set up to handle human relations problems in the school and work out active programs in this area. This group also should be specifically charged to work to eliminate the need for policemen on campus.

9. Provide massive in-service training for all school personnel, professional, paraprofessional, clerical, and maintenance to sensitize them to respect the dignity of the individual and to value, not reject, diverse cultures. Administrators should be sensitive to minority issues

such as a memorial day for Malcolm X or Martin Luther King, Jr.

10. Examine programs that reinforce a student's sense of unequal treatment by the school such as track systems and groupings that make for segregation within a desegregated institution, compulsory R.O.T.C. training and inferior vocational and technical training.

11. Attack inequities of all kinds in ghetto schools and, where applicable, in the academic community such as discriminative practices; failing to employ or promote blacks and browns at all levels in institutions; letting of building contracts and purchasing of equipment from biased companies; overcrowded classrooms and double shifts; inadequate textbooks; poor libraries; and dirty or nonexistent cafeterias.

12. Assure that extracurricular activities are scheduled during the school day so as not to exclude working students; seek student involvement in improving these activities so that meaningful and relevant activities are available for students whose life styles and backgrounds are not middle-class oriented. Encourage the living of the humanities rather than the mere teaching of them.

13. Consider teaching literate Spanish in elementary schools as a basis for building the English language and reading skills with students with Spanish surnames.

14. Paraprofessionals should be used more constructively to assist administrators, nonteaching professionals, and teachers to establish rapport and better understanding of the black, Chicano, and Puerto Rican student and not merely to patrol halls, check passes, and lock lockers. Paraprofessionals are valuable community resources who could assist and sensitize teachers to the special problems and needs of the students.

15. Encourage decentralization of the educational function and experiment with community control where students, parents, and citizens desire it.

16. "Knock down" the walls of schools, allowing business to come in to train students to insure better careers and economic security for all students.

17. Enlist federal assistance to update schools, to plan programs, and to implement the Supreme Court decision for integrated quality education. Discrimination and inequities of all kinds should be dealt with swiftly and effectively.

18. Ample money and time should be made available for programs that will utilize the innovative, creative, and technological skills to make the necessary changes needed to educate all children.

19. School boards and school advisory councils conducting school affairs should be urged to hold open rather than closed meetings.

The above quotation, if written today, would reflect concern for the American Indian and other minority groups besides the black and brown segments of our society.

In an earlier text (20) I spent considerable time discussing ways in which to make student councils and student groups function. The key concepts were the involvement of students *from the beginning* so that goals, structure, and process reflected student needs and desires to accept responsibility for the setting where they were spending large portions *of their time.*

I concluded that the following points were necessary for a successful student council.

1. The rights, responsibilities, and authority of the group should be clearly defined from the start. Once defined they must be consistently maintained.

2. The purpose of the focus of the student council must reflect the interests and needs of the students rather than serve as extensions of the administration.

3. The student council must serve as a means of feeding responsibility back to the grass roots rather than of relieving them of responsibility by acting for them.

4. Communication about all activities must be designed to reach and involve the entire student body.

5. Faculty and administration can best develop the student council by vesting in the council rights, responsibilities and authority that are indicative of faith in students as mature and interested citizens of the school.

Since those earlier days, students watching the militant minority groups no longer petition for acceptance, but believing that they can only gain respect through power, have adopted the confrontation techniques in popular use today (21,22,23,24,25).

People seeking self-actualization need to emancipate themselves from constraints which at the very least do not permit them the freedom to discover truth in their own way, and to then be free to interpret the action needed to enhance life for all.

Student groups, like minority groups, have grown fearful of cooperating with authorities even when such offers are made in good faith. This seeming irrational response is explained well for another setting where James Statman (26) talks about community mental health as a pacification program. He wonders if regardless of intent, community mental health programs are aimed at pacifying a neighborhood—to mystify and mollify justifiable outrage and thereby prevent action toward meaningful change. He wonders if in using neighborhood leaders as mental health aides, we are succeeding in alienating them from their community, buying them off, and thereby weakening the neighborhood power base. He also questions if "social action" programs are truly free to confront the basic oppressive institutions of our society.

Just substitute student for community aide, and student action for community mental health, and one sees the concern students feel about the dangers of cooperating with the existing power structure.

Associate Commissioner of Education in New York Langworthy, in December of 1969, addressed school administrators and teachers about the Bill of Rights Week to be celebrated in New York. He said, in part:

As the voice of youth has become increasingly audible, relevance becomes as the "cutting edge" that determines what is to be perpetuated or abandoned. In effect, we are challenged to reexamine our democratic system and its documents in terms of relevance to contemporary events and to the world in which today's student lives. Are we merely mouthing empty phrases as we quote the text of the Bill of Rights and other similar guarantees? Do statements concerning the importance of the democratic process fall on unheeding or unhearing ears of youth?

There is a temptation to oversimplify this task of examining what is pertinent for youth by merely reciting the guarantees of personal liberty which, under law, apply to all in this country regardless of age, sex, religion, or racial origin. However, young people are teaching us that communication is more than conversation. Students are disillusioned by those of "the establishment" who talk about fundamental rights, but who want neither to accord them to all, nor to defend the right of everyone to enjoy them. Young people are likely to examine carefully our invitations to them for involvement, disdaining those which are seemingly insincere.

If our goal is to reach the student, to encourage his participation, to make him cognizant of the importance of our guarantees of personal liberty, and ever alert to situations which subvert these guarantees, we must find better ways to communicate with the "now" generation.

Programs of student involvement must include meaningful and responsible opportunities in many phases of decision making. Such experiences should emphasize important aspects of the democratic process. The rule of law should be seen not only as a force to preserve the established order, but also as a framework to provide a means of challenging that order. It is important to remember that the fundamental rights of the individual cannot be voted away, even in a democracy where majority determines the course of action. A real understanding of the guarantees of fundamental rights as expressed in the Bill of Rights should be reflected in indications of greater respect for the individual. Participation in decision making entails responsibility as well as privilege; the mundane and less publicized agenda items of any institution or political agency must be discussed and given thoughtful consideration, as well as those more dramatic subjects which capture the general public interest.

Aspy (27) notes that student activists with their slogans like "peace, brother" and "make love, not war" are urging that we not hurt one another. He notes that to love each other is not enough. The "nice guys" need to also be able to look at their bad feelings. He fears that the frequent avoidance of looking at these feelings is really an evasion technique. Facing these feelings might bring them into violent conflict with other people whom they fear.

He illustrates his point by describing the militant who looks at a nice guy and says "You really hate niggers, don't you!"

The group leader needs skill in helping the nice guys face bad feelings and threatening acts. He needs to confront the militant who claims honesty when he "tells it like it is," but does not recognize that confrontation which does not also communicate a caring for the other person is likely to fail in its implied goal of seeking behavior change.

What I Have Learned.   It would be nice if all that is wrong with education could be changed rapidly. I am convinced that the rate of change can be speeded up. Our major stumbling blocks are not finances, buildings, or materials but people. Change is threatening for no one can guarantee that tomorrow will be better than today. In addition although each person knows how he can function today, he can't be sure he will do as well when asked to function differently. To face the anxiety of change each group needs a source of strength, the kind which can be found in an accepting helping group relationship.

I believe that people prefer more rewarding roles and relationships, if they only dare face change and are willing to consider new possibilities. A group's readiness to face these potentials demands the conditions formerly cited as needed in any counseling group—increased dissatisfaction with what is, a belief that tomorrow can be better, and support to face threat as new skills are developed to meet new situations.

Group leaders, in educational settings, have at least three tasks they need to consider.

1. Helping students learn to accept responsibility along with freedom, while helping them learn how to apply pressure to society to force it to

face problems needing solution—whether it be war, ecology, or the role of education in a changing society (28).

2. Helping school people face the threat of change and helping them change their conception of their helping role from that of "telling" to "open dialogue." Assisting them to consider risk-taking so they can discover that students accept responsibility and grow with it. Help is also needed so that they can learn to test the limits of their own situation. It is necessary to replace the common cop-out of "they won't let you" with "I plan to help the Board see what we need to do and why it will improve our effectiveness."

3. Serving as a mediator so that communication does not break down before we learn how to grow up, while both groups are learning to handle their own agendas (29,30,31,32).

BUILDING UTOPIA

The Model School. Charles Ream (33), in his article on "Youth Culture: Humanity's Last Chance," points out that this is the first generation to live its entire life knowing:

• That total extinction of mankind is but a push-button away.
• That efficient sexual contraception now separates sex from having children.
• That instant global communication via the space satellite makes universal rapid communication possible.
• That America's heritage of being a melting pot may need to change so people will be allowed to live in vastly different ways.
• That past bases for our family structure may be archaic and are severely limiting the number of close human relationships available to children and adults.

Many youth feeling keenly the need for change have adopted a strategy which believes that if people can see a clearly superior alternative they will then feel the need to implement the drastic changes required.

Each of us has a dream, but sometimes when it finally materializes it has changed form and direction. So, too, it has been for me.

One morning in 1965, I arrived at the office early to get some work done before the phones began to ring. I discovered that Superintendent of Schools, Herman Goldberg (now U.S. Associate Commissioner of Education) was already at work. Dropping in to visit, we found ourselves dreaming about a school we wanted to see developed. On impulse, Goldberg turned on the tape recorder and we continued to talk. This discussion ultimately crystallized into plans for a "World of Work" school that would bring the community into the school. We met with staff from the University of Rochester and ultimately formed a joint Center for Cooperative Action in Urban Education. I was charged with developing a formal proposal under Title III of ESEA. We were off and running. Given a planning grant we utilized the funds to hold a workshop at the University of Rochester where many people could work together to evaluate all the facets of what this new school should be like. A name change to the "World of Inquiry School" reflected a change in direction in terms of educational methodology. With the hiring of Elliot Shapiro from New York City as director and the hiring of staff for the school, people were available to draw the blueprint used to activate the school.

Using a school building which had been condemned, they turned to the question of how much structural change was really basic to achieve the type of school they had in mind.

They planned on classes with cross-age groupings, family style, with as much as 6 years age difference possible in one classroom. This last idea really worried me until, much later, I realized that this classroom organization literally made it impossible for a classroom teacher to teach to "the average child in the class." Of necessity individualized instruction took place. Children in the class used age, sex, and skill differences to help each other. Young children had a wide range of role models to use as they tried to clarify their self-concepts. The school incorporated many other new concepts that will not be detailed here. However, the school received national publicity in magazines, press, and television. Theoretically, then, here was one model of the brave new world youth was seeking. The reason for describing this project is that like the "Higher Horizons Project" of New York City, and other experimental models developed for inner-city children in Rochester (Project Beacon), the impact of these programs on the rest of the system was negligible. Efforts to have project participants share their experience with others seemed to cause no behavior change in those who were not part of the projects.

What I Learned. The 1970 White House Conference on Children and Youth, Forum 8 on "Myths in Education" developed a list of ideas which many people believe but which seem to get in the way of change. The major myth seems to be "They won't let you." The ambiguous "they" served as a convenient subterfuge to avoid responsibility for trying anything that deviated from accepted practice.

As I indicated in the preceding section, I found myself repeatedly faced with successful projects which "they," the administration, would not only permit but would also encourage, and yet change was minimal.

It was at this time that a review of Cartwright's concepts about inducing group change proved helpful.

Cartwright (34), in summing up research on techniques of achieving change in people, has developed eight principles that provide a good summary of the goals to be considered in working with groups. The principles are:

1. If the group is to be used effectively as a medium of change, those people who are to be changed and those who are to exert influence for change must have a strong sense of belonging to the same group.
2. The more attractive the group is to its members, the greater is the influence that the group can exert on its members.
3. In attempts to change attitudes, values, or behavior, the more relevant they are to the basis of attraction to the group, the greater will be the influence that the group can exert upon them.
4. The greater the prestige of a group member in the eyes of the other members, the greater the influence he can exert.
5. Efforts to change individuals or subparts of a group which, if successful, would have the result of making them deviate from the norms of the group, will encounter strong resistance.
6. Strong pressure for changes in the group can be established by creating a shared perception by members of the need for change, thus making the source of pressure for change lie within the group.
7. Information relating to the need for change, plans for change, and consequences of change must be shared by all relevant people in the group.
8. Changes in one part of a group produce strain in other related parts which can be reduced only by eliminating the change or by bringing about readjustments in the related parts.

Fullmer (35), in his chapter on research in group counseling, reports a series of studies where the results seem to be a function of the process involved, more than the innovation used. Reviewing studies on the Hawthorne effect which says, in effect, "you are special because you are being studied (or part of a special group)," groups which follow the format developed by a pilot group do not experience the psychic reward of being part of something special.

The implications are clear to me. Each group must live through growth and discovery pains. Group maturation cannot be hastened by handing down experiences. Each group needs to be free to develop in its own way, and possibly deviate enough to feel unique. Reviewing Cartwright's first principle ". . . those who are to exert influence for change must have a strong sense of belonging to the same group," clearly points to the impossibility of someone in administration having a leadership role, as long as the structure is hierarchical in nature, and the threat of change requires a safe way to cop out.

The structure of the classes at the World of Inquiry school brought home the lesson that changes in environmental structure may facilitate people's ability to change. In a sense, if the setting does not set off familiar cues it is easier to try something different.

The shift in title of the school demonstrates that groups are vital and growing. They must be free to shape and revise their goal as their needs and perceptions change.

The vast range of characteristics, problems, and age levels in the classes did *not* seem to bar development of group cohesiveness. It certainly reinforces questions about demands for homogeneity of group members as a criterion for predicting success.

Last of all, the changes that did occur were not really a function of materials or money, but of the ingenuity and involvement of group members.

The Walking Teacher.   Repeatedly, the point has been made that large segments of the population reject institutions in our society. For these institutions to overcome these barriers they need to develop outreach techniques which communicate to potential clients not only that they care but also the ways in which clients could use them.

Staff members in the Rochester City School System realized that we could improve our effectiveness if we could establish contact with children at an earlier age and could secure parental involvement on a cooperative basis. With this goal in mind, Lillian Roemer, working under Dr. Herbert Greenberg, then Director of the Parent Education and Child Development Department, developed the "Walking Teacher" concept.

Mrs. Roemer would drive her car into the inner city and park near a laundromat that was always crowded with mothers and children. Opening the trunk of her car she took out a large piece of plastic which she spread on the ground. On top of this she placed easels and paints, books, and so on. Children who wandered over were encouraged to play with the toys or listen as she read a story. The crowd grew, drawing with it curious mothers.

As she worked with the children, she would tell the adults in a very informal manner why and what she was doing and how it would help the children learn better as they grew older.

As days passed she was able to help the mothers see how they could use empty cereal boxes and other objects to make duplicate toys for their children, at little or no cost. Finally, one mother offered to let the children meet on her porch where there was shade, and where they could get a drink of water or go to the bathroom. Mothers began to take turns helping Mrs. Roemer with the group. Ultimately, it was possible to help

FIGURE 1. The Walking Teacher Program, Rochester City School District, New York.

FIGURE 2. The Walking Teacher Program, Rochester City School District, New York.
234

the mothers see how much more could be done if the group met at the school building.

What I Learned.   A nonthreatening approach that leaves the initiative in the hands of the clients can prove effective in an outreach program. Sharing with people ways in which they can use you to help themselves, when it can be believed, results in warm acceptance and the development of client's willingness to accept responsibility.

DISRUPTIVE GROUP TECHNIQUES

During the period preceding the rise of Hitler, the American public became aware of the potential dangers of propaganda. Recognizing that a democratic society could be very vulnerable to a technique they did not understand, many high schools and colleges introduced units about propaganda into social studies and other related courses.

Today, with confrontations in the streets, in Washington, and involving all age levels, it is timely that we begin to help people recognize disruptive group tactics. One can only cope with techniques one recognizes and understands.

Most readers can vividly recall the many photos showing the shooting of students at Kent State University. Other similar scenes showing people running from tear gas and advancing troops with leveled bayonets, are unfortunately not uncommon. Viewers often wonder about the thoughts of the police or soldiers in these situations. One way to get such an understanding is to read material prepared for their indoctrination. Readers are encouraged to secure Field Manual (FM 19-15) on Civil Disturbances and Disasters (36), March 1968 written by the Department of the Army and published by the Superintendent of Documents, Washington, D. C. Following are a few isolated segments from that document.

1-7.   Techniques of Agitators.   A violent mob can be effectively developed by a trained agitator. By applying his knowledge of group psychology, the skillful agitator can exploit psychological factors to develop the actions desired. By using techniques such as those described in *a* through *e* below, he can trigger sufficient excitement and provide the necessary stimuli to accomplish his purpose. Some of the common techniques used are—

a.   The Use of Extensive Propaganda.   Through the use of extensive propaganda, agitators can get a crowd to form at a particular location, already incensed at real or false inequities. Members of these gatherings are susceptible to the "violence-producing" techniques of agitators. Propaganda can be spread through newspaper and magazine articles,

specially prepared handbills and posters, radio and television broadcasts, or by the spreading of rumors and by aggravating natural
prejudices, grievances, and desires.

   b. A Forceful Harangue by a Fiery Speaker.   The forceful harangue
of a fiery speaker is probably the most effective and best known method
of raising the pitch of the mob to the point where they can be urged or
led to violence. A well-trained speaker, using key words and phrases,
taking advantage of local prejudices, distorting facts, and using em-
phatic movements (e.g., waving of arms, pounding on the rostrum) can
influence individuals to do things they normally would rebel against.
This technique normally follows the following sequence; persons are
first brought to a high emotional peak, then a course of action is
suggested, and finally the course of action is justified.

   c. The Appearance of an Irritating Individual or Object.   The timely
appearance of an individual or object irritating to the crowd can be just
the spark to explode them into violence. The crowd may, for example,
be brought to a fever pitch by a speaker, then by either planned or
coincidental appearance of the individual or object the crowd will
explode into violence. An irritating object frequently used is a newspaper photograph depicting alleged police brutality.

   d. The Successful Accomplishment of an Act of Violence.   The successful accomplishment of an act of violence can set off a chain reaction
of violence within a previously peaceful crowd. Agitators can plan this
initial act or take advantage of an unplanned act. The success of the
act is all-important for further violence to be attempted, since failure
dulls the interest of most individuals. For instance, if a few individuals
succeed in their efforts to burn down a building, others may follow by
looting the building and destroying other property.

   e. The Use of an Emotion-Provoking Rumor.   Nothing can increase
the tempo of disorder or incite an orderly demonstration to violence
more than the circulation of an emotion-provoking rumor. Forces
committed to civil disturbance control duty will discover the need for
an extensive network aimed at picking up and promptly reporting
rumors—no matter how inaccurate those rumors may seem.

1–10. Mental Preparation of Troops.   Troops engaged in civil disturbance operations will be subjected to the noise and confusion created
by large numbers of people facing them. Individual soldiers may be
shouted at, insulted or called abusive names. They must learn to ignore these taunts and not allow personal feelings to interfere with
the execution of their mission. In addition, troops can expect objects
to be thrown at them, but must learn to avoid thrown objects by
evasive movements; they must never throw the objects back. Troops

must subdue their emotions and carry out their orders determinedly and aggressively whether in formation, patrolling, or posted as guards. They must be emotionally prepared for unusual actions, such as members of the crowd screaming and rushing toward them, tearing off their own clothes, or deliberately injuring or maiming themselves. Troops should understand that the well-disciplined execution of orders is the most effective force applied against rioters. They must be indoctrinated in all aspects of self-control so they may be mentally prepared for participation in civil disturbance operations (page 1–7).

. . . .

. . . .

Section III.   Agitators and Mob Action

1–8. General.   Agitation of a mob to accomplish a socio-political objective can be part and parcel of an entire disturbance from the initial apparently casual gathering of people to the outbreak of violence, or it can be the insertion at any point in this development of highly trained agitators to stimulate and exploit an otherwise spontaneous gathering. Both approaches involve no more than the insertion of a "shadow chain of command" to give direction and purpose to otherwise "herdlike" behavior. It is hazardous, in terms of controlling group behavior, to deny or disregard the presence of such internal control. Always present in the agitation technique is a "shadow" effect of blending with the other participants to give the "appearance" of spontaneity, lack of direction, etc. If a group, however, demonstrates resilience and flexibility in reacting to traditional control techniques— wedge formations and fixed bayonets, etc.—it is quite probable that an internal control apparatus is present. The paragraphs below describe the organization and tactics/techniques of such an apparatus, and the most effective counter-organization for prevention or reaction.

1–9. Preconditioning.   After militant group cadre have infiltrated (by joining or recruiting from existing membership) such organizations as labor unions, youth groups, farm and agrarian organizations, they are in a position to manipulate such groups' drives. Legitimate grievances are couched in the language of "the movement." The first objective is to create the image of the common enemy, be it the "capitalist exploiters," the police, "whitey," the "papist cleric," or "the Jew." In addition to the "anti-cause" cry, the propaganda apparatus seeks to "Precondition" a mental attitude that, in the crucial moment, can be whipped into a fury of righteous, self-justifying violence. The militants literally try to create temporary compulsive obsessions, or "hot places" of consciousness. They may aim these preconditioning campaigns at the general public, or at specific target groups such as political parties, professional organizations, students, workers, unemployed, national or ethnic minorities—in short, at any segment of a pluralistic society deemed vulnerable or recruitable as mob participants, sympathizers, or militant group converts. Constant hammering on the chosen themes— in meetings, informal conversations, bus stop harangues, pamphlets and leaflets, newspaper or radio and TV bits—is intended to insure that, at the crucial time, the "hot place" will inhibit normal social restraints and obsessive compulsions against the *personalized enemy* will take over behavior. So thorough has this preconditioning been in many areas that any time a local issue stirs controversy, agitators can direct the generalized excitement against legal-traditional bases of government *within a few hours.*

1–10. Selection of Proper Slogans. The militant group catalogs its slogans in accordance with circumstances, with a view to mobilizing the group on the broadest possible scale of activity and on the highest level of emotional intensity. When a riotous situation is still developing, the agitators advance "transitional" slogans and partial demands corresponding to a concrete situation; but these demands and slogans are "stepping stones" toward the aim of the "movement." If the legal authority appears disorganized and the people are in a state of emotional ferment, the agitators' slogans become increasingly radical. If there is no emotional upsurge, the agitators continue *partial slogans* and demands based on the *everyday* needs of the target groups, linking them up with the goals of the movement. An example of the needed *simplicity in slogans* is that few people think in terms of a billion dollars, but almost anyone can understand a *pair of shoes.* The movement's goals are ideological, but its militant agitators know that "bread and butter" issues *move* people and that is *their mission.*

1–11. Creating the Nucleus. This involves little more than mobilizing a specified number of agitators of the local militant group organization. This group inevitably attracts an equal number of the curious, the excitement seekers, and the chronic malcontents. And, of course, the militant group always mobilizes as many sympathizers as well as sincere citizens harboring legitimate grievances as possible. Each militant subunit is assigned quotas to fill and missions to accomplish. Militant group agitators go into areas where the criminal element lives and hire available hoodlums, arming them with wooden clubs, iron bars, and placards whose wooden poles can be used as battering rams or clubs. During "partial" demonstrations in days before the climax, it is standard practice for agitators to visit employment offices and hire all applicants present for an unspecified "job." These "paid recruits" are

necessary even with the presence of many, perhaps legitimate, grievances, because they provide a nucleus *responsive to orders* which
sincere citizen protestors might *not* be.

1–12. Execution—Mob Agitation. Through a tiny minority the militant group—by carefully disguising the direction of demonstrations,
rallies, and riots—is able to give an impression of great size and support. Using the tactics described in subparagraphs *a* through *g* below,
a deployed force of 2–300 agitators can create a riot in which 10–20,000
actually take part. The agitators' tactics are *concentration* of efforts in
"preconditioning" march/rally demonstrations, then *dispersal* to continue agitation of rioting, burning, and looting throughout a large
area. But in both the concentrated and dispersed phases, one will
find these tactics being employed.

a. External Command. This is composed of commanders well removed from the activity, stationed so that the entire "battlefield" can
be observed. In a moving march/demonstration, it will stay apart from
the crowd. An actual "observation post" is required—tall building,
overpass, top row in an auditorium or stadium—and a war room with
operations map and communications net is acceptable only when
absolutely necessary. The spontaneous nature of the ebb and flow in
mob behavior places a premium on constant visual reconnaissance *by
the commander.* In a dispersed phase—widespread rioting, burning,
looting—the *number* of command/observation posts increases, but *the
tactic remains the same.*

b. Internal Command. These are the militant group agitator element within the crowd. They are responsible for directing the demon-
stration/rally or rioting, under the external command's orders. *Great importance is attached to protecting the leaders of these units.* In any
demonstration, key agitators can be found keeping close to certain
conspicuous banners or placards, and in the dispersed rioting phase
near inscriptions on walls or large poster/billboard slogans. They will
avoid locations of incidents or fights, *after* initiation.

c. "Bull Fighters." This group acts as a "loose," (covert), bodyguard
surrounding the internal command, protecting the leader from police
and screening his escape if necessary. A loose, ill-defined line of these
guards will flank processions and protect banner carriers as well. They
are neither militant group fanatics or naturally pugilistic, but they
are also highly-disciplined and will normally react with violence *only
on verbal order.*

d. Couriers. They stay close to leaders, carrying orders *between
internal and external commands.* Generally, they will use radio, tele-
phone, foot mobility, or bicycles and motorcycles/scooters which they

can wheel along sidewalks, into small doorways and basement stair-wells or over back-yard fences, keeping abreast of but removed from the mob. Young adolescents and females predominate in this element.

e. Shock Force. These men are armed with concealed clubs, switch-blades, etc., and accompany the militant group faction, but march or linger along the sidewalk and in alleys where they are screened by spectators. They will move into the mainstream of mob action only as "reinforcements" if the agitators are attacked by police. Their sudden and violent descent on the battle scene is designed to provide sufficient diversion to enable an orderly *retreat of the internal command element* who, upon signal from the external command, will *melt quickly into the ranks of spectators,* leaving the milling bystanders, unwitting excitement seekers, and other "fellow travelers" to the police.

f. Banner/Placard Bearers. The slogans used by this group and the "cheerleaders" are adapted to suit the prevailing mood. At first they display slogans expressing "partial" or "transitional" grievances, but as the demonstration/riot gains momentum, and frenzy drives out reason so that real issues lose meaning, the slogans are exchanged for direct riot propaganda. The bearer may be a sincere non-militant group protestor, entirely innocent of his true role as an important part of the internal command's communication network. By assigning key agitators to stay near specified banners/placards, the command knows their location at all times and can dispatch couriers to them with orders for stepping up the tempo, shifting slogans, or inciting violence. The same is true for key locations in the dispersed, rioting phase.

g. Cheerleaders. Specifically briefed agitators are carefully rehearsed on the slogans they are to chant and the order in which the cries are to be raised. Thus, "bread, bread, bread" phases into "his head, his head, get the cop" or "freedom, freedom, freedom" into "burn, baby, burn." Their job, and their technique of agitating mass behavior, is very much like that of high school football game cheerleaders. It differs only in that, in a mob situation, *the fans will join the game and riot* when all of the above "plays" have been properly executed.

. . . .

. . . .

b. Mores of the Members. Crowd behavior is limited by the con-viction of the members as to what is "right." The concept of what is "right" is based on the customs or folkways, the conventional be-haviors, of the times and places in which people live. A crowd rarely does anything which does not claim a measure of moral approval. Lynchings used to occur where a large proportion of the people felt that a lynching was morally justified, even necessary, under certain circumstances. The members of the lynching party normally considered themselves public benefactors, not guilty law breakers. The crowd functions not so much to paralyze the moral judgments of its members, as to isolate and neutralize some of a person's judgments, so that certain others can find unrestrained expression.

c. Crowd Leadership. Leadership profoundly affects the intensity and direction of crowd behavior. Given a collection of frustrated, resentful people, a skillful agitator can convert them into a vengeful group and direct their aggression at any "enemy" who is included among their antagonisms. Likewise, an individual can sometimes calm or divert a crowd by a strategic suggestion or command. Since most crowd behavior is unstructured, with no designated leaders, leadership is evidently "up for grabs." In many crowd situations, the members, frustrated by confusion and uncertainty, *want* to be directed, and the first person who starts giving clear orders in an authoritative manner is likely to be followed. The leader's role includes the following elements:

(1) The leader must establish rapport. By rapport is meant a responsive trusting attentiveness. It is most easily established by a leader who has the same background as the members. He senses their wants, recognizes their antagonisms, speaks their language, and can predict their reactions; he can establish with them a relationship of harmony, conformity, and accord.

(2) The leader builds emotional tensions. For some types of crowds, the leader builds up emotional tensions by an impassioned reminder of problems and grievances. In other kinds of crowds. the leader need not arouse emotional tension, for it already exists, and he passes directly to the next function.

(3) The leader suggests "justifiable" action to release the tension. The leader provides an outlet to the tension and emotional pitch of the crowd which is now ready and eager to "do something" about the perceived grievances, for example, when the lynch leader calls, "Let's get him!" Seldom does a crowd respond instantly to suggestion; the repetition of suggestion and its justifications is necessary; this repetition permits emotional contagion to mount and the need for release of tension continues to grow.

d. External Controls. Most group behavior occurs in the summertime when people are normally standing around and gathering in large outdoor assemblies. Cold weather and rain discourage group actions. Riotous behavior is rare on military posts, where discipline can be invoked to maintain order. The principal external controls on crowd behavior, however, are those exerted by the police. With few exceptions, serious riots are evidence of police failure. School integration disorders are an example. Where local police and public officials have let it be known that no disorders would be tolerated, practically no disorders occurred. Where officials have not shown determination, or have invited violence by predicting it, violence has developed.

It should be obvious that the above manual presents one concept of the way to cope with confrontation, threat of violence, and the motivations that govern the actions of the protestors.

For readers who have not experienced the tactics used to disrupt meetings, or who wonder why people would be motivated to circumvent typical institutional procedures, following is a list of recommended readings.

Suggested Readings

1. Counseling and the Social Revolution, the May 1971 issue (Vol. 49, No. 9) of the *Personnel Guidance Journal.*
2. Brown, G. W. "Teacher Power Techniques," *American School Board Journal,* Vol. **CLII**, No. 2, February 1966, pp. 11–13.
3. Freidland, W. H. "Confrontation at Cornell," *Trans-action,* Vol. **VI**, No. 7, June 1969, pp. 29–36.
4. Howe, H. "Community Interest." *Vital Speeches,* Vol. **XXXV**, No. 6, January 1, 1969, pp. 178–180.
5. Hunter, C. A. "On the Case in Resurrection City," *Trans-action,* Vol. **V**, No. 10, October 1968, pp. 47–55.
6. McEvoy, J. "On Strike—Shut It Down," *Trans-action,* Vol. **VI**, No. 5, March 1969, pp. 18–23.
7. Trimberger, E. K. "Why a Rebellion at Columbia Was Inevitable," *Trans-action,* Vol. **V**, No. 9, September 1968, pp. 28–38.
8. U.S. National Commission on the Causes and Prevention of Violence. *The Politics of Protest.* Government Printing Office, Washington, D. C., 1969.
9. Von Eschen, D. "The Conditions of Direct Action in a Democratic Society," *Western Political Quarterly,* Vol. **XXII**, No. 2, June 1969, pp. 309–325.
10. Wildman, W. A. "Representing the Teacher's Interests," *U.S. Monthly Labor Review,* Vol. **LXXXIX**, No. 6, June 1966, pp. 617–623.
11. Cloward, R. A. *Delinquency & Opportunity: A Theory of Delinquent Gangs.* Glencoe Press, 1961.
12. Cunningham, J. V. *The Resurgent Neighborhood.* Fides Publishers, 1965.

13. Short, J. F., and Strodtbeck, F. L. *Group Process and Gang Delinquency*, Chicago: University of Chicago Press, 1965, pp. 102–115.
14. Landsberger, H. A. *Power, Participation and Ideology*, New York: David McKay, 1971.
15. Miller, S. M., and Riessman, F. *Social Class and Social Policy*. New York: Basic Books, 1968.
16. Schelling, T. C., and Halperin, M. H. *Strategy of Conflict* (Chapter on Bargaining). New York: 20th Century Fund, 1961.
17. Kramer, R., and Specht, H. *Readings in Community Organization Practice*. New Jersey: Prentice Hall, 1969.
18. Lakey, G. *Non-Violent Action: How it Works* (orig.) 1969, Pendle Hill.
19. Lakey, G., and Oppenheimer, M. *Manual for Direct Action*. Quadrangle, 1965.
20. The Center Magazine, 1970, 3, 3, Second Edition, Civil Disobedience.
21. The Radical Therapist, 23 Hancock Street, Somerville, Mass. 02144.
22. Social Policy, P.O. Box 534, Cooper Station, New York City 10003.
23. Journal of Conflict Resolution, Center for Research on Conflict Resolution, University of Michigan, Ann Arbor, Michigan 48104.
24. The New Left, Memorandum prepared for the Subcommittee to Investigate the Administration of the Internal Security Act and Other Internal Security Laws, Committee on the Judiciary, Oct. 9, 1968, U.S. Gov't Printing Office.
25. Peace Research Abstracts Journal, 25 Dundana Ave., Dundas, Ontario, Canada. (See especially Education IX–74, Social Change IX–66, Small Groups III–68, Pressure Groups IX–33.)

SUMMARY

Our society is crying out in pain. Those of us who claim to be in the helping professions will find ourselves being called on to assist in many new and alien situations. Sometimes techniques and approaches that are helpful in carefully controlled therapeutic settings do not work in the emotion ridden group confrontations that are part of our current daily life.

Many social agencies, much to their chagrin, are discovering that their perception of their clients' needs and the perceptions of the clients themselves are worlds apart, and that there exists a gap in communication. Clients express their resentment at the dependency status implied when they are not given a share in planning. Being independent implies freedom of choice.

One of the female members of a group guidance class phrased it very well when she said: "I enjoy having a boy take my arm to cross the street, but if I felt he did this because he thought I couldn't make it across myself, I'd resent his action."

We need to evaluate how we feel about our personal involvement in the social issues of the day. There may be times when we shall need to question whether our role is to assist people to adjust to their environment or to change it (37). It may be helpful to remember that aggression seems to be inversely proportioned to the amount of participation.

If we feel social concern we need to ask what steps can we take to prevent explosive situations instead of trying to heal deep wounds after a battle has occurred (38).

It would pay to read a report of a study by Kenneth Tye, which appeared in the SRIS Quarterly, where he reviewed research about dissemination of innovative or new ideas (39).

This chapter pointed out that groups do not exist in a vacuum and we therefore need to understand the effect of society on agendas developed by a group.

The ability of the group leader to function in a wide variety of groups depends on the breadth of his social awareness, his willingness to take risks, and his ability to cope with hostility and anger. He will need to become familiar with the techniques of social activists. He then will be able to understand what is going on instead of reacting to the threats involved. To cope with social action, the leader will need to recognize his own ties to the power structure and the ways in which these ties limit his ability to help groups to explore goals which may change the status quo.

The following chapter covers the group worker's role as the dispenser of mass information.

Bibliography

1. Berube, M. R., and Gittell, M. (Eds.). *Confrontation at Ocean Hill–Brownsville*, New York: Frederick A. Praeger, 1969.

2. Fantini, M., Gittell, M., and Magat, R. *Community Control and the Urban School*, New York: Praeger Publishing Co., 1970.

3. Klein, A. F. *Social Work Through Group Process*, New York: School of Social Welfare, SUNY at Albany, 1970, p. 40.

4. Weiner, H., Sr. "Social Change and Social Group Work Practice," *Journal of Social Work*, Vol. IX, No. 3, July 1964, 106–112.

5. Klein, A. F. et al. "Social Group Work Practice Elaborated: A Statement of Position," Pittsburgh: University of Pittsburgh, Graduate School of Social Work, 1964.

6. Gochros, J. S. "Recognition and Use of Anger in Negro Clients," *Social Work*, Vol. 11, No. 1, January 1966.

7. Vanden Haag, E. *The Jewish Mystique*, New York: Stein and Day, 1969, p. 110.

8. Klein, A. F. *Social Work Through Group Process*, New York: School of Social Welfare, SUNY at Albany, 1970, p. 196.

9. Klein, A. F. *Social Work Through Group Process*, New York: School of Social Welfare, SUNY at Albany, 1970, p. 179.

10. Papanek, H. "Psychotherapy Without Insight: Group Therapy as Milieu Therapy," *Journal of Individual Psychology*, Vol. XVII, No. 2, November 1961, p. 187.

11. Hampden-Turner, C., and Whitten, P. "Morals Left and Right," *Psychology Today*, April 1971, p. 39.

12. Pringle, M. B. "Responding to Aggression," *Eric Capsule*, Winter 1971, Vol. 4, No. 2, published by the Counseling and Personnel Services Information Center, School of Education, University of Michigan, Ann Arbor.

13. Berkowitz, L. "Experimental Investigations of Hostility Catharsis," *Journal of Consulting and Clinical Psychology*, 1970, 35 (1) 1–7.

14. Holt, R. R. "On the Interpersonal and Intrapersonal Consequences of Expressing or Not Expressing Anger," *Journal of Consulting and Clinical Psychology*, 1970, 35 (1) 8–12.

15. Alinsky, S. "The Professional Radical, 1970," *Harpers*, Vol. CCXL, No. 1436, January 1970, pp. 35–42.

16. Dodson, D. W. "Sociological Perspectives on Educational Materials," Chapter II in *Educating for Tomorrow,* Walter M. Lifton (Ed.), New York: John Wiley, 1970.

17. Rainwater, L. "Crucible of Identity: The Negro Lower-Class Family," *Daedalus,* Summer, 1966, p. 211.

18. Rosenbaum, M., Snadowski, A., and Hartley, E. "Group Psychotherapy and the Integration of the Negro," *International Journal of Group Psychotherapy,* 1966, **16**, 86–90.

19. Farber, J. *The Student as Nigger,* New England: Free Press (no date).

20. Lifton, W. *Working With Groups: Group Process and Individual Growth,* New York: John Wiley, 1960.

21. Dodson, D. W., *High School Racial Confrontation* (White Plains, New York: White Plains Board of Education, 1969).

22. Arentdt, H. *On Violence,* New York: Harcourt, Brace and World, 1969.

23. Flacks, R. "The Liberated Generation: An Exploration of the Roots of Student Protest," *Journal of Social Issues,* **23**, 52–75, 1967.

24. Johnston, J. R. "Student Revolt and Social Revolution" *Ed. Rec.* **51**: 22, 27, Winter 1970.

25. Cook, D. R. "Guidance and Student Unrest," in *Guidance for Education in Revolution,* Cook, D. (Ed.), Boston: Allyn and Bacon, 1971, pp. 492–516, Chapter 19.

26. Statman, J. "Community Mental Health as a Pacification Program: A Radical Critique," digest of paper presented at Convention of American Orthopsychiatric Association, (p. 274), 1969, *Journal of Orthopsychiatry.*

27. Aspy, D. "Empathy—Congruence—Caring are Not Enough," *Personnel and Guidance Journal,* Vol. 48, No. 8, April 1970, p. 638.

28. Grambs, J. D. "The Self-Concept Basis for Reeducation of Negro Youth," in *Negro Self-Concept,* Kvaraceus; W. C. et al., New York: McGraw-Hill 1965.

29. Walton, M., Reeves, G. D., and Shannon, R. F. "Crisis team intervention in School–Community Unrest," *Social Casework,* January 1971, pp. 11–17.

30. Hoffnung, R. J., and Mills, R. B. "Situational Group Counseling with Disadvantaged Youth," *Personnel and Guidance Journal,* Vol. 18, No. 6, February 1970.

31. Gazda, G. (Ed.). *Proceedings of a Symposium on Group Procedures for the Disadvantaged,* Georgia: Center for Continuing Education, University of Georgia, Athens, Georgia, February 1969.

32. Wyers, N. L. "Adaptations of the Social Group Work Method," *Social Casework,* November 1969, p. 513, Vol. 50, No. 9.

33. Ream, C. "Youth Culture: Humanity's Last Chance," *Personnel and Guidance Journal,* Vol. 49, No. 9, May 1971.

34. Cartwright, D. "Achieving Change in People: Some Applications of Group Dynamics Theory," *Human Relations,* **IV**, 381–392, 1951.

35. Fullmer, D. *Counseling: Group Theory and System,* Pennsylvania: Intern Textbook Co., 1971.

36. Department of the Army, Field Manual (FM 19–15), *Civil Disturbances and Disasters,* March 1968, Washington, D.C.: Superintendent of Documents.

37. Halleck, S. "Therapy is the Handmaiden of the Status Quo," *Psychology Today,* April 1971, p. 98.

38. Stubbins, J. "The Politics of Counseling," *Personnel and Guidance Journal,* Vol. 48, No. 8, April 1970.

39. Hearn, N. E. "Dissemination: Bangkok, What?" *SRIS Quarterly,* Summer 1968, p. 10.

7 Group Guidance, Orientation Programs and Other Vehicles for Mass Dissemination of Information

Knowledge is of two kinds. We know a subject ourselves or we know where we can find information upon it.
SAMUEL JOHNSON (Boswell's Life of Johnson)

BLOCKS TO LEARNING

Counselors find themselves basically concerned with "Blocks to Learning." This phrase is really a play on words because it encompasses two meanings. One meaning involves the building blocks necessary to be ready for future experiences. The second meaning involves the removal of the blocks or inhibitors to be able to learn. Preceding sections have devoted considerable time to the group techniques useful in helping people develop the security needed to be willing to face and deal with aspects of self which are blocking the realization of the type of self-actualization sought. After facing these factors, individuals and groups recognize the need for data to implement their desire to accept responsibility toward moving themselves toward the defined goal.

Traditionally, when textbooks have described programs designed to provide this needed information, whether it be in group guidance classes or orientation programs, they have geared their approach to the concept that these groups are most effective when the client faces crises or decision points. These include transition from one setting to another, facing the need for maturational skills, or values requiring clarification.

The approach implies that the major job to be done at these crises points is to help clients gather data and assess their meaning. Theoretically, the job is one of synthesis instead of development of new concepts. Unfortunately, the approach frequently fails because it does not recognize that the significant factors affecting a person's decision were experienced many years before, and they now operate as unconscious determiners of choice.

It should be obvious that the school must have a role in helping youngsters secure and understand experiences that form the building blocks for later decisions. Basically, the experiences in school must facilitate helping a student answer two questions: "Who am I?" and "What could I be?" It must also recognize that children start getting their answers to these questions from infancy on. Deutsch (1) and Goodman (2) have documented the early effects of race awareness on four-year-olds' feelings about themselves and others. Studying a different dimension, Cowen et al. (3) have found it possible to "red tag" children in primary grades. The holders of the "red tag" are prime candidates for future mental difficulty, which probably will reflect itself through poor school adjustment. In their studies they found that almost one-third of the children needed preventive help to avoid future difficulties.

Orientation, to be effective, ought to occur *before* the student is moved into the new setting. In some cases students may need help to develop new skills. Nowhere is this seen more sharply than in the adjustment problems of the youngster from cultures that lack an emphasis on academic experience. It is partially because of the size of the adjustment required that we now find a major emphasis on preschool education designed to overcome the cultural deficiency.

Concern over early childhood experiences is reawakening interest in some of the concepts developed by Maria Montessori (4). Although her techniques, which are still slavishly copied today, are inappropriate for modern society and may be overly compulsive in their format, the concepts she espoused merit our attention.

Dr. Montessori was convinced that there are definite sensitivity periods during which certain types of learning need to occur. She was convinced of the irreversibility of learning and pessimistic about what could be achieved if the sensitivity periods were missed.

Her focus was on the differences in a child's tempo from those of an adult's, and the way school, being adult-oriented, misses its goal. In the area of work, adults want division of labor if it makes the job easier; they want maximum results with minimum effort; and they tend to be product-oriented. By contrast, children enjoy repetition, want to do the job themselves, and are process-oriented, enjoying doing the job over and over again, with the payoff coming from self-perfection. Montessori also focused on the needed "working conditions" suited to the child's pace and taste. Just as we must recognize the possible value of different rewards for different segments of our society, so too must we pay attention to the differences that reflect levels of maturity.

Although a major role of orientation is to provide information, it falls on deaf ears if the hearers have not been helped first to perceive

the need for the information and then to face the anxieties the new situation may provoke.

THE USE OF INFORMATION

It is fairly well accepted that clients will incorporate information when:

1. The information is presented in a way which enables them to use the facts with a minimum of transfer.
2. They are secure enough to allow themselves to perceive the situation broadly, rather than using tunnel vision to protect themselves from seeing potentially threatening situations.
3. They have perceived that this information is necessary to achieve a goal important to themselves.

In group settings people seek two kinds of information: (1) about themselves and their relationships with others (group counseling) and (2) information about the external world (traditionally group guidance or orientation).

I look forward to the day when terms like group guidance are obsolete. In very large measure they reflect a concept of efficiency for an institution where by providing the same data to many people at once, time is saved. Programs are planned on a statistical basis to that they may be relevant to most people in a specific group. But if we recognize that information is incorporated best at the point where the need is perceived, individuals will differ markedly not only in the timing of their desire for the data but also in their need for it to be presented in a different form.

INFORMATION (ABOUT THE EXTERNAL WORLD)

Stiller (5), writing on the role of the guidance counselor in the emerging school, has this to say.

It is in the field of information-dispensing that educational media will likely offer the greatest immediate impact. Currently, information is maintained primarily in written form; books, college catalogues, reference sources, and occupational briefs. These written materials are static and require literacy. . . . Some information is available in sight/sound filmstrips, motion pictures, audio tapes, and disc recordings. The filmstrips and motion pictures likely provide greater impact upon the student than do the written materials, but they are more expensive to purchase and revise, and cover only a small segment of the needed information. The audio tapes and disc recordings typically utilize some expert talking about his field of work and do not require student involvement at all.

It is usually assumed that youngsters will seek information which is stored. What is ignored is the fact that youngsters will seek information when *they think they need it*. . . . Schools do little to increase student readiness or desire for information. When youngsters do seek information they want it in a form that can be used immediately. If it is not in that form, youngsters are unlikely to put much effort into translating the existing material into the desired form. They are also unlikely to know how to search for the desired information if it does not appear where they expect it to be, or to conduct the search if it appears to be a laborious process. Frequently, youngsters do not know what questions to ask themselves in order to elicit desired information.

Despite these problems of use of educational media, assuming that the same data given by a human being will necessarily solve these problems is fallacious.

Failure of handbooks and other inanimate devices to complete the orientation process represents a lack of awareness that receptivity and acceptance of any information given through impersonal devices is based upon several prior assumptions:

1. That all people want to know the facts available through the booklet, film, etc.

2. That the words used in these devices are understood by the recipient in the same fashion as the author intended.

3. That the recipient is able to transfer the meaning of an answer from one situation to another.

4. That the material not only reflects the needs of the agency but also meets needs of the recipients.

THE COUNSELOR'S FACILITATING ROLE IN INDIVIDUALIZING INFORMATION

The answer to problems of dissemination of information in groups obviously is to attempt to individualize the process. The selection of time, media, and associated counseling help redefine the counselor's role from the current one where he is the source of information to one where he will help individuals learn how to use facilities that will represent primary sources of information retrieval. Youst (6) in an attempt to demonstrate this interrelationship in the Rochester Career Guidance Project developed the representation pictured in Figure 1.

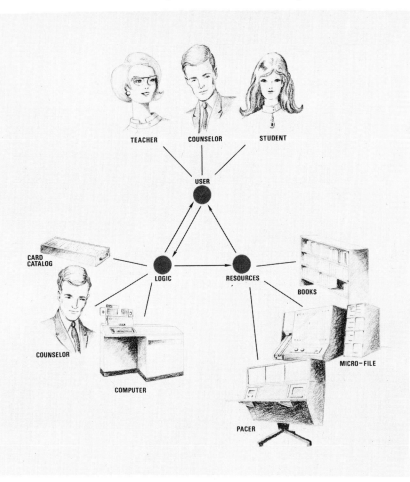

FIGURE 1. Representation of the Rochester Career Guidance Information System.

The Rochester Career Guidance Project was based on the following concepts:

· The information system should be developed in close proximity to the user, and where possible, should actively involve the user.
· Better ways should be found to interest and involve students in career exploration and planning.
· Greater priority should be given to nonprinted communication.

· Components in any machine configuration should be available for independent use and should not be computer-dependent.
· Guidance, wherever possible, should be integrated into the students' on-going school activities.

In an attempt to mesh the process of client definition of needs for data with instant availability of accurate data (7) they mated the use of the computer with a battery of display devices (see Figure 2).

FIGURE 2.   PACER display console and computer terminal.

Stiller (5) recognizes how the introduction of nonhuman devices cause anxiety in some people.

Arguments for greater use of inanimate objects in counseling often raise the spectre of a dehumanized, impersonal, manipulating relationship. The introduction of media will neither personalize nor depersonalize counseling; it will be the understanding and intent of the counselor that will determine the nature of the relationship. A common complaint of students today is that counselors do not understand them and/or do not devote sufficient time to them. The cruel realities of excessive workload and the need to satisfy a variety of pressure groups have already depersonalized what passes for counseling in many schools, suburban as well as urban, large as well as small. This chapter argues that proper utilization of media will free counselors to do that which they can do best: engage in interpersonal relations with students to help them achieve fullest possible development for themselves.

PLANNING FOR AND PREPARING THE INFORMATION NEEDED

Information does not exist in a vacuum. Information that is offered before the need is perceived functions as advice, since it implies that this is what people ought to pay attention to or be thinking about.

When youngsters claim that the older generation does not recognize their needs or desires they partially reflect accurately the differences in their experiences from those of their parents. Consider the following changes in society.

1. We are in the midst of four basic changes in our society, reflected by the use of systems analysis in long-range planning, a cybernetic revolution involving the use of computers and automation, an increase in direct social engineering with active participation by people at the grass-roots level in determining policy and organization, and a biological revolution which has dramatic implications for population control and longevity (8).

2. Partially as a result of these forces for change, work and leisure are both undergoing dramatic shifts in meaning, as is the traditional Protestant ethic which, historically, had an influence on educational and career planning in the United States (9,10,11).

3. New strategies for teaching, along with the vast explosion of new technological advances in the area of educational media, are combining to create a tremendous lag between the school as it exists today and resources currently available but not yet incorporated into the fabric of the school. The school as an institution has been greatly resistant to change. Impatience by society over the widening cultural gap is being reflected by increased use of industry as either the educators or as the change agents to influence the school environment (12,13,14,15,16,17).

4. The pendulum has returned to an earlier position where recognition of the critical importance of early childhood experience is again emphasized. Research is documenting the major influence of environmental factors on the developing intelligence of children. Guidance and counseling theorists are now concerning themselves with the relationship of the way early school and family experiences shape children's attitudes toward themselves and affect their feelings about the role school can play in helping them achieve meaningful goals.

The helping person serving as the mediating agent needs to be sensitive to the different forces operating on clients, other than just physiological maturation, and to try to select media or experiences that may best reflect the needs of his client at that stage of development.

Thompson (18) facing this issue in the area of vocational maturation, has conceptualized the following hierarchy in the use of media.

10. On-the-job tryout: part-time; summer jobs; work-study programs.
9. Directed exploratory experiences: work samples; work evaluation tasks.
8. Direct observation: visits to work settings.

Provides direct —contact with actual work situations

7. Synthetically created work environments: combination of stimuli and environmental manipulation.
6. Simulated situations: career games; role playing.

Simulation of work —settings and occupational roles

5. Interviews with experts: questioning representatives of occupations; career days.
4. Computer-based systems: computer systems which store, retrieve and process occupational data in response to individual requests.
3. Programmed instructional materials: books and workbooks.

Information is processed by —and adapted to the needs of the individual

2. Audiovisual aids: films, tapes, slides, etc.
1. Publications: books, monographs, charts, etc.

Information is pre- —structured, fixed, and designed for general use

Spectrum of occupational information media

He has explained the sequence as follows:

1. *Publications.* Here the materials are printed, are prestructured, fixed, and usually expected to have general application. Books, pamphlets, occupational monographs, charts, etc., are examples. They, of necessity, must be written for a group of readers and must be rather general. As words on paper, they are several steps removed from a specific work situation and require interpretation by the reader.

2. *Audio-Visual Aids.* Here are slides, motion pictures, tape recordings, video tapes, etc. They can present *pictures* or *representations*

of the world of work which require less interpretation by the reader. The materials, like printed materials, are fixed, prestructured, and are difficult to be adapted to individual needs (such as Types 3 or 4, or 5).

3. *Programmed Instruction Materials.*   In their simplest form, much of the programmed instructional materials are a form of printed materials—books or workbooks. But they differ in that they permit the individual to work his way through the material in an individualized fashion, taking into account his particular learning needs. The "interaction" between the individual and materials is thus a variable one and the materials are not prestructured or fixed, but under the control of the reader. It is thus possible to develop a World of Work text and guidance workbook through which the individual works his way at his own pace and in the particular sequence appropriate to his needs.

4. *Computer Based Systems.*   These may be regarded either as a fancier "programmed instruction" device or as an "information source" with which the individual interacts. To the extent that they provide data in response to the individual's questions, they are a source of expert information available to the individual. To the extent that the individual engages in a "dialogue" with the computer, it is like an interview, individualized to meet the individual's needs and "guiding" him in data gathering and decision making. The systems being developed at IBM, Harvard, and Penn. State, are examples. The use of computers is also applicable in the "simulation" methods described later.

5. *Interviews.*   This is the traditional method. Young people talk formally or informally with others (usually their elders) who provide information, advice, persuasion, etc., in response to career questions raised by the younger person. The elders may be parents, counselors, representatives of the occupation, etc. Career Days represent an organized form of this approach, in which persons knowledgeable about an occupation *come to* the student and give information either in prepared presentations or in answer to specific questions.

All of the methods so far discussed (Nos. 1 to 5) provide *information* about rather than *direct contact* with the world of work. Between the individual and the *real* occupational world is some mediating agent—a book, a picture, a computer, a person. The remaining media (Nos. 6 to 10) are designed to provide *direct experience* in the work situation.

6. *Simulated Situations.*   These are exemplified by the *Career Games*

developed by James Coleman and Sarane Boocock, which enable an individual to engage in a simulated career decision exercise. To the extent that they provide opportunities to role-play or act out a situation analogous to the real one, they provide an experience which hopefully transfers to the real situation. As presently constituted, they simulate career decision-making or the planning process more than occupational behavior.

7. *Synthetically Created Work Environments.* I know of no examples of another type of simulation which seems to be theoretically possible, i.e., a combination of visual, auditory, and other sensory stimuli designed to reproduce as closely as possible an actual work situation. The technical means for such a procedure are certainly available; we now have "3-D movies" which make the viewer feel as if he were in the middle of the scene and which create an illusion of reality. The sights, sounds, odors, vibrations, etc., of being a subway motorman could be synthetically duplicated. It is not too much out of this world to visualize a youngster checking out an electronic tape from the Occupational Library, going to a Job Experiencing Room, and threading the tape into a device which would create a reasonably accurate and complete simulation of the environment and activities of a real job. The youngsters could "live" rather than just "view" the occupation for an hour or so.

8. *Direct Observation.* This is the traditional technique of visiting an actual job setting and observing a real worker engaged in real tasks. A son's visit to see his father at work or a group tour are common events, although to make them really significant requires considerable planning, preparation, orientation, and interpretation by a counselor or teacher.

9. *Direct Exploratory Experiences.* Here an attempt is made to provide a series of work samples through which the individual can explore the world of work and learn about his likes, dislikes, aptitudes, sources of satisfaction, etc. Let us assume that the 20,000-plus separate occupations in our occupational structure are really just various combinations of a relatively few basic work tasks. The DOT with its Things-Data-People profiling of twenty-three worker functions is one such attempt to identify the basic tasks. The TOWER system of work evaluation developed at the Institute for Crippled and Disabled, and the Job Exploration Project of the Jewish Employment and Vocational Service at Philadelphia are also directed toward providing work experiences which sample the occupational world. Let us visualize 30 work

stations where an individual could actually try out, under supervision and expert assessment, a preselected sample of these 30 basic work tasks and obtain from this experience some clarification as to the kinds of work for which he has potential. To the extent to which the tasks sample the real tasks of real occupations, the exploratory experience would provide "occupational information" based on direct experience and immediate contact with real activities.

10. *On-the-Job Tryout.*   In a real sense, the *only* way to learn what an occupation entails and what life is really like in a given field is to *be in* the occupation. Research has shown that most young people go through a trial or floundering period during which a sequence of jobs is held before settling down to one field of work; and recent studies show there may be several such trial or exploratory sequences in one's work history. Research also shows that a large proportion of young people hold part-time or summer-time jobs. If properly planned and if choices are available, these jobs can have considerable exploratory value and can be a means of testing one's self in real work situations instead of merely providing some income.

Since some readers are not yet ready or able to individualize these developmental experiences, they may find the following concept of developmental tasks of some help in selecting appropriate experiences for their clients (see Figure 3). They should realize, however, that prepackaged curriculums for groups is doomed to be ineffective for some in the groups.

SOURCES OF OTHER REFERENCE MATERIALS

In the American culture, with the Calvinist heritage of "work for the night cometh," work is a basic part of our society. It determines for many people how they feel about themselves, who their friends will be, where they live, and reflects the types of rewards they feel are most meaningful (for example, economic, political, social service). Thus discussions of careers entail most facets of life which determine a person's self-concept. Super and Bachrach (19) have charted two tables that set forth the developmental tasks typical in our society (see Tables 1 and 2).

A very comprehensive survey of concepts, learning experiences, and materials has been published for grades kindergarten to fourteen, for teaching mental health concepts in the classroom, by the American School Health Association Committee on Mental Health in the Classroom (20).

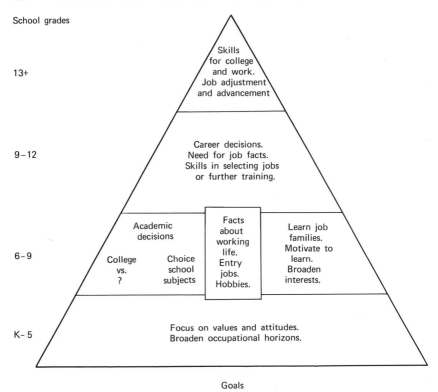

School grades

13+

9–12

6–9

K–5

Goals

FIGURE 3. Planning the content for group guidance. Vocational maturity: a pyramid of decisions and experiences. (Parts of this section appeared in a paper, "Where Is the Guidance Movement Heading? The Publisher's Role in Determining Direction" written by W. Lifton in *The SRA Newsletter*, February 1961.

All of these charts can be useful if they are used to assist one in determining the possible needs of a specific individual or the media or material available to meet that need. They can be harmful if they are accepted as a lockstep curriculum all must pass through at specific grade levels without regard to readiness or individual preference.

SOCIETY'S ANSWER TO PROBLEMS—"START A GROUP IN THE AREA!"

It seems as if whenever society gets upset about a common problem they solve it by mandating a course in the area. This seems to hold true for driver education, sex education, and more recently for drug education

TABLE 1. Developmental Stages, with Illustrative Sociocultural Factors and Vocational Developmental Tasks and Opportunities[a]

Developmental Stages	Cultural Emphases	Vocational Developmental Tasks	Vocational Developmental Opportunities
Preschool	Father's job; father's earnings Parental attitudes Parental values Parental expectancies Place of residence Family status	Learn dependency Learn self-help Learn self-direction Maturational tasks	Opportunity to: React to parental handling, attitudes Explore environment Begin to develop peer relations Begin to develop authority and important-figure relationships
Elementary school	Urban-rural environment Family class identification Religion School	Conform to school Deal with family attitudes Begin to develop own attitudes and values Choose JHS curriculum Pass school subjects	Opportunity to: Learn about world of work Explore world of work Develop attitudes to school and school subjects Have after-school work experiences
High school	Family associates Family attitudes and behavior Values of teacher Class values	Choose HS curriculum Develop study habits Make tentative vocational choices Implement self-concept	Opportunity for: Academic exploration Work experience (summer) Tentative occupational choice
Young adult	Courtship and marriage Family finances Availability of college Military service	Postpone gratification of immediate needs Defer marriage Gain college admission Find job Move toward career decision	Opportunity for: Choice of educational major; choice of educational minor Continued academic exploration; change of educational major; job changes In-service training Returning to school
Mature adult	Status in family Economic responsibilities Realities of the marketplace: war, depression, prosperity, technological change	Vocational establishment and advancement Acquire new skills	Opportunity for: Changes of jobs or fields of work Job promotion Further schooling

[a] Super, D. B., and Bachrach, P. *Scientific Careers and Vocational Development Theory.* New York: Teachers College Press, 957, pp. 106–107.

(21,22). The fallacy seems to be that lectures by adults on the dangers of particular activities appears to have no effect in reducing the problem. There is even some evidence that material produced to inform students, as a way of preventing anti-social behavior, actually may work in reverse. If the facts presented run counter to the audience's experiences or values, they tend to reject all the material, not just part. The material may also

TABLE 2. An Integrated Approach to the Process of Vocational Development[a]

Developmental Stages	Cultural Variables	Intra- and Inter-Personal Variables		Vocational Developmental Tasks	Vocational Developmental Opportunities
		Traits and Factors	Personality Development		
Preschool	Father's job income Parental attitudes, values, expectations, residence, social status	Sex Constitutional factors Intelligence Early interests Early aptitudes Physical appearance	Constitutional factors Early psychosexual development Position in family Parental handling and need satisfaction Identifications	To learn: Dependency Independence Social interaction Industriousness Goal setting Persistence	Opportunity to: React to parental handling and attitudes Explore environment Develop peer relations Develop authority relationships
Elementary school	Urban-rural Religion Class affiliations School	Scholastic aptitude Emerging personality patterns Developing interests and attitudes Physical capacities	Parental relations Peer relations Authority relations Emerging identity or self-concept Success-failure reactions	Socialization Coping with school Dealing with family attitudes and values Developing own attitudes and values Passing school subjects	Opportunity to: Learn about world of work Develop attitudes toward school and school subjects Have after-school work experiences
High school	Family associates Family behavior Class values Peer values Teacher values	Special aptitudes and abilities Crystallization of interests Emergence of values	Heterosexual relationships Psychosexual development Adult role playing Clarification of self-concept Changes in role Crystallization of self-concept	Choosing curriculum Developing study habits Making tentative educational-vocational choices Implementing self-concept	Opportunity for: Academic exploration Occupational exploration Social role exploration

TABLE 2. (*Continued*)

Developmental Stages	Cultural Variables	Intra- and Inter-Personal Variables		Vocational Developmental Tasks	Vocational Developmental Opportunities
		Traits and Factors	Personality Development		
Young adult	Courtship patterns Marriage patterns Family finances Educational patterns Military service Labor market Occupational requirements	Crystallization of values, attitudes, and personality Motivation and drive at peak Intellectual and physical capacities at peak	Success-failure reactions Changes in identity or self-concept Crystallization of self-concept	Evaluation of need gratifications: marriage college job Specification of goals Launching of career	Opportunity for: Choice of educational major, minor Further exploration in study and work Change of curriculum or occupation Return to student or beginner status in new field
Mature adult	Family status Economic responsibilities Realities of the market place: war, depression, prosperity, technological change	Aptitudes on developmental plateau Gradual narrowing of interests	Role acceptance or rejection	Vocational establishment and advancement Resolution of conflicts	Opportunity for: Change of job or occupation Promotion In-service training

a Super, D. B., and Bachrach, P. *Scientific Careers and Vocational Development Theory.* New York: Teachers College Press, 1957, pp. 114–117.

open up new arenas, formerly unknown, which seem exciting and challenging to try. It also provides avenues to rebel against adult authority and to test one's own power, even if the activity itself initially did not have appeal.

SUMMARY

The movement in society, especially in education, is to attempt to individualize methods of instruction, content, and pace. Where a group develops out of the needs of group members who require a group setting to clarify their own perceptions and skills as well as the reactions of others to their ideas, such settings are congruent with all the concepts of group counseling discussed so far. However, when groups are used as settings for mass dissemination of facts, they will function like a shotgun. Some pellets will hit the target but many will be wasted. Exploration of the use of appropriate educational media that can be used by an individual as and when he needs it, seems to be clearly part of society's future efforts to solve this problem (23).

In the next chapter, I shall explore ways in which the leader and the group can assess if the experience is proving effective.

Bibliography

1. Deutsch, M. "Minority Group and Class Status as Related to Social and Personality Factors in Scholastic Achievement," *Monograph 2, Society for Applied Anthropology,* pp. 10, 11, 19, 1960.

2. Goodman, M. E. *Race Awareness in Young Children,* New York: Crowell-Collier, 1964.

3. Cowen, E. L., Izzo, L. D., Miles, H., Telschow, E. F., Trost, M. A., and Zax, M. "A Mental Health Program in the School Setting: Description and Evaluation," *Journal of Psychology,* **56** (Part 2), 307–356, 1963.

4. Standing, E. G. *Maria Montessori: Her Life and Work.* Fresno, Calif.: Academy Library Guild, 1957.

5. Stiller, A. Chapter V in *Educating For Tomorrow: The Role of Media, Career Development, and Society.* W. Lifton (Ed.), New York: John Wiley, 1970.

6. Youst, D. Chapter IX, in *Educating For Tomorrow: The Role of Media, Career Development, and Society.* W. Lifton (Ed.), New York: John Wiley, 1970.

7. Vriend, J. Chapter 17, "Computer Power for Guidance and Counseling," in *Guidance for Education in Revolution.* David Cook, Ed., Boston: Allyn & Bacon, 1971.

8. Michael, D. *The Next Generation: Prospects Ahead for the Youth of Today and Tomorrow,* New York: Random House, 1965.

9. Wilensky, H. L. "Work and Leisure: Implications for Career Development and the Curriculum," *Conference on Implementing Career Development Theory and Research Through the Curriculum*; Washington, D. C.: NVGA, 1966, 194 pp., Project No. ERD-556, Grant No. OEG-2-6-000556-0582, pp. 93–112.

10. Levenstein, A. "Work and Its Meaning in an Age of Affluence," *Conference on Implementing Career Development Theory and Research Through the Curriculum*; Washington, D. C.: NVGA, 1966, 194 pp. Project No. ERD-556, Grant No. OEG-2-6-000556-0582, pp. 55–66.

11. Murphy, G. "Work on the Productive Personality," *Conference on Implementing Career Development Theory and Research Through the Curriculum*; Washington, D. C.: NVGA, 1966, 194 pp. Project No. ERD-556, Grant No. OEG-2-000556-0582, pp. 67–92.

12. Miles, M. (Ed.). *Innovation in Education,* New York: Bureau of Publications, Teachers College, Columbia University, 1964.

13. DeGrazia, A., and Sohn, D. A. (Eds.). *Revolution in Teaching: New Theory, Technology, and Curricula,* New York: Bantam Books, 1964.

14. Ontario Curriculum Institute Committee on Instructional Aids and Techniques, *Technology in Learning,* Toronto, Canada, May 1965.

15. Hillson, M. (Ed.). *Change and Innovation in Elementary School Organization,* New York: Holt, Rinehart, and Winston, 1965.

16. Boocock, S. S., and Coleman, J. S. "Games and Simulated Environments for Social Studies," paper presented at the University of Pittsburgh Conference on Improving the Content, Structure, and Methods of Communication in Vocational Guidance, March 1966.

17. Michael, W. B. et al. (Eds.). "Instructional Materials: Educational Media and Technology," *Review of Educational Research,* April 1962, Vol. **XXXII**, No. 2.

18. *The Spectrum of Occupational Information Media,* Albert S. Thompson, Teachers College, Columbia University. Paper delivered to Panel on Counseling and Selection, National Manpower Advisory Committee, May 22, 1967 in Stiller, Alfred, Chapter V, in *Educating for Tomorrow: The Role of Media, Career Development, and Society.* Walter Lifton (Ed.), New York: John Wiley, 1970.

19. Super, D. Chapter VI, in *Educating for Tomorrow: The Role of Media, Career Development and Society.* Walter Lifton (Ed.), New York: John Wiley, 1970.

20. American School Health Association Committee on Mental Health in the Classroom, "Some suggested areas for guidance in teaching Mental Health in the classroom," Appendix A, *Educating for Tomorrow: The Role of Media, Career Development, and Society.* Walter Lifton (Ed.), New York: John Wiley, 1970.

21. Lewis, B. "How One High School Licked Its Drug Problem," *Family Circle,* Vol. **78**, No. 6, June 1971, p. 46.

22. Jalkanen, A. W. Chapter 16, "Drug Use and the Guidance Counselor," in *Guidance for Education in Revolution,* David R. Cook (Ed.), Boston: Allyn and Bacon, 1971, pp. 356–373.

23. Kirby, J. H. "Group Guidance," *Personnel and Guidance Journal,* Vol. 49, No. 8, April 1971, pp. 593–599.

8 Professional Problems of the Group Counselor

Truth is within ourselves; it takes no rise
From outward things, whate'er you may believe
There is an inmost centre in us all
Where truth abides in fullness
ROBERT BROWNING (Paracelsus)

MEASURING GROUP AND LEADER EFFECTIVENESS

In the preceding chapters it has been pointed out that an effective group climate produces an atmosphere where group members are continually trying to clarify their ideas and behavior. The protocols in the preceding chapters demonstrated how as a group matures, it becomes increasingly concerned about the yardstick to use in measuring its growth and present status. As the question is explored by the group it becomes apparent that there are at least three aspects of the problem of evaluation worth looking at.

1. The growth of the group as a group.
2. The growth of an individual from the beginning session to the present.
3. A comparison of an individual's present functioning with "norms" described from society's expectations.

The problems involved in measurement came basically from several areas—the selection of an appropriate yardstick (criterion), the selection of tools and designs that enable one to measure the variable being assessed, an assessment of how the evaluation process itself affects the group being studied and, ultimately, the need to recognize the way in which the philosophy and assumptions accepted by the evaluator determine the meaning given to the results obtained.

RESEARCH AND EVALUATION

Chapter 8 differentiates between research and evaluation. The difference comes from the emphasis on collecting data under controlled conditions to provide answers to predetermined questions versus data used for descriptive purposes and with a more heuristic purpose.

WHAT ARE THE ISSUES?

The topic of research and evaluation is loaded with threat for most people. On a personal level it implies that we are willing to be accountable for our behavior and can face the threat of potential feedback, which might imply our relative ineffectiveness as compared to others. On a professional level, the issue is even more complex because the procedures used in evaluation frequently involve esoteric mathematical formulas and complex designs.

One way to deal with threat is to define it and to cope initially with those aspects with which you feel most secure. Using that logic, this chapter could not hope to discuss in any meaningful way all the variables or designs open to consideration. The beginning researcher would be better off going directly to texts designed to teach research methodology.

This chapter does raise specific questions about research problems and indicates that most current research on groups, in the opinion of the author, tends to be meaningless because they do not control the critical variables and they tend to ignore those aspects they do not know how to measure (1). The person planning research on group process is faced with a choice of possibilities for establishing a control group against which to measure the effects of the experimental variable. One method involves one group only, with data gathered during a period where the variable is not operating, then an equal period involving the experimental variable, and then another equal period where the experimental variable is again absent. This approach avoids the major problem of matching groups on the basis of the atmosphere that characterizes each group as unique. It has the weakness of not being able to assess the effects of uncontrolled variables, maturation, or the effect of the second phase on the third. Although maturation would appear to be controlled, the assumption is being made that the growth resulting from maturation during all three phases is constant.

An alternative and traditional method of control is to try to establish a control group that matches the experimental group on the significant variables in the research. Many studies have dodged the issue involved here by assuming that if characteristics such as age, diagnosis, personality type, and I.Q. were comparable, the groups could be considered matched. Although this is a convenient escape hatch, it ignores the fact that the major variable in most studies of groups is the group climate itself. Admittedly this is a difficult variable to quantify, but I believe that it is this problem which most needs our present attention.

A scholarly summary of problems of research by Strupp and Bergin (2) documents the first of many assumptions currently being made, which are very open to question. Strupp and Bergin believe that since the purpose of group counseling is to change individual behavior, research on principles of individual change may provide the foundation on which group research techniques can be built. For them, groups actually represent a setting where each client is seen as being treated individually, and the interrelationship between group members is seen as less meaningful. Moreover, they applaud the tendency to plan research that avoids theoretical bases.

It has been the thesis of this book that no interaction between people can be considered as divorced from values or should be considered apart from the social setting where the actual encounter occurs. Golembiewski (3) documents his concern over the transferability of results achieved in a laboratory setting to real-life situations.

The most basic issue about research seems to be the tendency on the part of scientists to assume that using scientific methods insure objectivity. Does not the selection of the topic itself reflect a value judgment on the part of the researcher? Does not the selection of certain measurement devices imply an acceptance of the assumptions on which they were developed? The most difficult issue of all to face is the requirement, in the use of most statistical procedures, of the assumption of a normal distribution. This assumption by its very nature directs attention away from the specific case and toward grouped data where ability to predict improves—but at the expense of the understanding needed to work with a unit of one, whether that unit be one client or one group.

I am not impressed by most research on groups because few made any serious attempt to deal with the following questions.

1. Can any two groups be found that are actually comparable enough to assume the similarity needed to use one for control purposes? Matching group members on any number of characteristics tells us nothing about the climate produced when people interrelate with each other. It is this group atmosphere that must be matched.

2. Can any group leader, regardless of training, ignore his own personality, values, and needs sufficiently to be equally competent and effective when employing two different leadership styles? I do not believe technique is divorced from values and so I believe any research that attempts to control for the leader by using the same

person differently for research purposes is making an assumption that cannot be defended.

3. Can we assume that groups contrived under laboratory conditions would perform similarly in real life where many additional variables affect their behavior? Field research or action research may be less controllable, but it may provide leads that are more helpful when working with other groups exposed to similar societal stresses.

4. Does use of statistical procedures insure objectivity? It is distressing to discover the number of studies that ignore the conditions necessary to defend the use of a specific statistical procedure. For example Hays (4) states that it is necessary in the use of analysis of variance to assume independent errors in order for justification of the F test to be made. He states that great care must be taken to see that data treated by the fixed effects analysis of variance are based on independent observations, both *within and across groups* (italics, mine), that is, each observation in no way is related to any other observation. The desired intragroup relationship that is necessary in group counseling can contaminate the assumption that each person, and each measure of that person, is independent.

5. On a personal level I am most offended by procedures that force me to overlook the uniqueness of a person or group, since statistically we are usually concerned with grouped data and cannot defend our predictions for the single case. As a clinician I *am* concerned with the client or group I am trying to help. Although I know my ability to predict for any given client is improved if I predict for the mean of many clients, he (the client), cherishing his uniqueness, will not find me therapeutically helpful if I focus on his commonness.

WHAT IS THE ALTERNATIVE?

Moustakas (5), in his chapter on heuristic research, quotes Rogers on emphases needed in future research. The Rogers' quote cites the need to do away with the fear of creative subjective speculation. He focuses on the need for a disciplined commitment—personal commitment, not methodology. Rogers also stresses the need to provide free rein for phenomenological thinking in behavioral science, efforts to understand man from the inside. He points out that no type of hypothesis has any special virtue in science except in its ability to relate to a meaningful pattern in the universe. Last, he emphasizes the need for the scientist to remain a human being. Certainly in a period when science has been used to dehumanize man, no more important point could be made.

Much that now passes for research is form without substance. I am concerned about our society's tendency to value the crowd over the individual. I want science to be the servant of mankind not its master. Since I believe process determines ends, the impact of research procedures on subjects concerns me equally as much as the research findings. All that is old is not necessarily bad. A review of nomothetic versus idiographic studies as first presented by Allport (6) still offers help for researchers seeking objective ways of studying individual subjective behavior. Techniques do exist that focus on group climate and group characteristics. Many recent texts recognize the points I am making. All too many, however, seeking to retain the aura of scientific methodology, have conveniently overlooked the problems raised in this section, and the alternative solutions available are not currently equally acceptable (7,8,9,10,11).

EVALUATION

One concept presented repeatedly in this text is that the group provides a vehicle through which society can help individuals solve problems. Groups have a life of their own. As members accept responsibility for making the group work, they tend to constantly redefine the goal of the group, based on their increasing maturity and corresponding changes in desired goals. It is partially for this last reason that I find objectionable the suggestions by some authors that groups ought to be evaluated in terms of their initially defined purpose, or by the contract agreed to by group members initially. It denies the group the chance to change and grow since, by definition, to succeed they must meet criteria that initially made sense, but do not necessarily make sense later on.

In the last stages of maturation a group begins to examine the bases by which they can determine if they have reached their goal. As the criteria involved are put into words, the associated discussion provides a synthesis of all that has gone before. Criteria labels become associated with specific group experiences and are remembered long after the group dissolves. This association also causes the criteria and the subsequent label to have personal meaning for each group member.

Because the group has learned that it is easier to face threat when others help, and that the perceptions of others are meaningful, it is not surprising that final evaluations typically take the form of sociometric ratings. Sociometric ratings are tools that have been developed to measure the relative standing or distance between people on a given dimension. The data are gathered in the following way. Members of a group are asked to indicate the names of other people in the group with whom they would prefer to be closely associated in a defined activity. By tallying the number of times each person is chosen, and by examining the way a person both chooses and is chosen by others, one get a clear picture of the intended relationships between group members. Group sociometric ratings differ from the typical classroom use of sociometric ratings in several important ways. Typically sociometrics are used as a basis for objectifying group structure so that the teacher or leader can locate individuals who need help and people who are in positions of leadership (12). They often provide the basis for a diagnosis which is then followed by a manipulation of the environment to promote change in the direction the manipulator thinks is best. One rather forceful reaction to this type of activity is the concern now being expressed in our gregarious society whether the individual diagnosed by this device as an "isolate" needs to be socialized. Increasingly we are concerned over the need for "isolates" in our society who represent the well-adjusted person who feels better able to create by himself rather than with others. To put it differently, we are becoming concerned over the meaning of the behavior to the person himself, and we are recognizing that society requires many different kinds of people. Of equal concern with this diagnostic use of sociometric data is the effect on the people completing the instrument. Since people typically are asked to rank others in terms of a specified characteristic, the effect of this action is to focus the perception of people on each other in terms of the status derived from their acceptance (or rejection) by their peers. Since studies tend to focus on one dimension rather than on the differing strengths of different people, they tend to create a status hierarchy in the group. Smucker (13) raises an interesting and provocative question when he points out that negative sociometric data is equally diagnostically useful in revealing the tension and disruptive potentials in a group.

In contrast to the foregoing description, groups have frequently used sociometric ratings to give the person being rated an objective picture of how others see him. It not only provides a basis for helping a person compare one of his characteristics with other traits he possesses, but also, if the group shares the total group data it allows each person to see how he compares with all others on each characteristic. Since the pooled data can be kept anonymous, no person need feel threatened by others knowing how the total group perceived him. The major threat comes, instead, from facing the differences between his own self-concept and the opinions of others. To provide this help, groups typically insist that sessions be held after ratings are made available, so that anyone who desires can ask the group for help. At that time, not only is support given, but also, where confusion exists in the mind of a group member about the reasons for the disparity between his own perception and those of the group, the group tries to help by providing examples of behavior which caused their perception to develop.

Probably the most threatening aspect of this approach is the unexpectedly high (in the group's eyes) agreement between group members in the way they perceive specific characteristics in the person being rated. The ratings also demonstrate to the group that even when all attributes are considered, some people are more effective than others. At this point, if the group can examine the pattern of total ratings for the entire group, it is relatively easy to assign labels or grades, if that has importance to the sponsoring institution. Since this is done without awareness of the scores of specific individuals it carries no implication of group rejection of an individual.

Presented here are two instruments developed by different groups. In both cases the groups were concerned with developing skills in group process. Although derived independently, it is interesting to see the characteristics that both deemed important.

Obviously not all of these qualities were rated in the same way. The group had to make value judgments, for example, as to their attitude toward the person who always conformed as compared to the one who never conformed. The result of the rating process in Group B was a

Group A

	(Less) 1 2 3 4 5 6 7 (More)
How much did Joe	
(a) solve his problems through identification with others' problems	1 2 3 4 5 6 7
(b) solve problems by accepting responsibility for his actions	1 2 3 4 5 6 7
(c) understand (empathy) others' feelings	1 2 3 4 5 6 7
(d) understand (diagnosis) others' actions	1 2 3 4 5 6 7
(e) help others feel accepted	1 2 3 4 5 6 7
(f) show concern with others' problems	1 2 3 4 5 6 7
(g) show preoccupation with own problems	1 2 3 4 5 6 7
(h) use others to gain information	1 2 3 4 5 6 7
(i) offer help to others on request	1 2 3 4 5 6 7
(j) show consistency between what he says and does (judge from classroom situation)	1 2 3 4 5 6 7
(k) effectively make himself understood	1 2 3 4 5 6 7
(l) efficiently make himself understood	1 2 3 4 5 6 7
(m) change within this group	1 2 3 4 5 6 7
(n) How competent would this person be as a group leader?	1 2 3 4 5 6 7

Group B

(Rating scales available with each factor)

1. Awareness of group process   Helps structure limits, helps group solve problems)

 (*a*) Observer (doing nothing)   (*b*) Participant (cohesiveness)

2. Does he use others to get answers for himself (parasite)?
3. Does he let others know when he feels the same way?
4. Does he express feelings?

         (*a*) Positive   (*b*) Negative

5. When he serves as a therapist can he understand another's feelings without getting emotionally involved himself the same way? (Does he cry when you do?)
6. Does he try out new ideas (new behavior, new ways)?
7. Listening—does he respond:

         (*a*) Verbally   (*b*) Physically

8. Is he a conformist?
9. Is he getting through audibly and clearly
10. Does he dig you? (Do you feel understood?)
11. Does he focus on others' needs?
12. Does he focus on my needs?
13. Does he contribute when he has something to contribute?
14. Does he assume a client role?
15. Does he assume a therapist role?

---

sharper perception of the specific areas needing attention by the group members who wanted to improve their over-all effectiveness.

GROUP GROWTH

Although authors differ in the areas they emphasize, almost all authors would agree that the following characteristics are typical of mature groups.

   1. An increasing ability to be self-directed (not dependent on leader).
   2. An increased tolerance in accepting that progress takes time.
   3. An increasing sensitivity to their own feelings and the feelings of others.
   4. Marked improvement in the ability to withstand tension, frustration and disagreement.
   5. A perception of the common denominators which bind the group as well as areas of individual difference.
   6. A better ability to anticipate realistic results of behavior and to

channel emotions into more socially acceptable ways of expressing these emotions.

7. An increased ability to change plans and methods as new situations develop.

8. A decrease in time needed to recover from threatening group situations. Peaks and valleys of emotional group crises become less pronounced.

9. Increased efficiency in locating problems, engaging in problem solving, and providing help to individuals as needed.

10. A willingness to face one's own responsibilities and to assist others when help is needed.

11. An acceptance of the right of the other person to be different.

12. An acceptance of the idea that people are different.

It seems odd that there are still people who insist that there can be no such thing as group counseling or therapy and who claim that what is being observed is actually counseling of individuals in a group. This point of view conveniently overlooks some of the characteristics of the group setting which cannot be equated with a one-to-one relationship. The growth that comes about by identifying with another person who is working out a similar problem, the attempt to define reality by testing how many peers need to see something the same way for it to be real, and the learning involved in assuming a leadership role are all samples of phenomena that are based on group life. No equivalent experience can be presented in the individual therapy session.

Despite the many problems in research design discussed in this chapter, the frequency with which studies demonstrate significant findings must make the objective individual wonder if all this smoke cannot help but suggest a fire underneath.

EVALUATING THE LEADER

A recent issue of the *Journal of Counseling Psychology* (Vol. 2, No. 2, 1970) was devoted to the issue of encounter groups. The contributing authors differed markedly on many things, but their differences were most sharply perceivable in their discussion of the characteristics and skills needed for a group leader. Coulson (p. 29) states there is a slight negative correlation between training and ability in group work. He emphasizes the need for a leader to be well rounded, adventuresome, with a deep feeling for people along with a capacity to drive them forward. Although I can accept Coulson's selection of desirable characteristics, I do not accept that training has to result in developing a leader who has lost the enthusiasm and sensitivity Coulson prizes.

The sensitive untrained person certainly can communicate a sense of caring, can provide a climate where people can feel free to explore and may, because of his background, be especially able to communicate or understand the jargon of a special group (14). All of these skills are desirable and provide the rationale for use of paraprofessionals as group leaders for those groups where the composition of its membership is essentially normal and where supervision is available to help the paraprofessional recognize and deal with situations holding dangers for individuals or for the group.

One illustration may help to document the different levels of response possible as a result of training. Sensitive individuals seeing a person under pressure try to alleviate their anxiety by reducing the pressure. Helping a person cathart without helping them see the underlying emotions they are ignoring will provide temporary relief but no ultimate resolution of the problem. Beginning group leaders are always amazed as they analyze protocols of their groups to discover that emotions that are expressed but are not recognized or dealt with continue to come up until they are faced.

The skills discussed in this text need to be practiced to be effective. Leaders who are unaware of the way in which their needs (see section on countertransference) limit their ability to help others, cannot hope to become more effective until they themselves are helped to see and face their own needs. This is a basic part of training a group leader and results in more open, sensitive, and effective behavior. It provides the basis for empathic instead of sympathetic relationships.

Many readers will welcome the chance to secure formal training, but reality factors make the possibility remote. Although pulling oneself up by one's bootstraps is difficult, there are specific criteria one can apply as a means of gauging whether growth is taking place. After each group session it would help to ask oneself the following questions:

1. How much of the time was I concerned with the content of the group's discussion rather than on the interaction taking place or needs being covertly expressed?

2. How active was I in this session? Were my contributions a reaction to group needs, or was I meeting personal needs?

3. Did I have any trouble in communicating with the group?

4. How accepting was I of the right of each person to see things in his own way? Do I in fact accept the idea that no two people are really alike?

5. Could I really accept the fact that a group moves slowly and that it takes time to mature?

6. Was I able to experience tension in the group without getting upset?

7. How effective was I in helping the group develop leadership skills so they wouldn't need me?

LEADERSHIP TRAINING STANDARDS

Because of the popularity of many group approaches and their seeming simplicity, many untrained and unethical people are leading groups with disastrous results. Many professional groups including the American Personnel and Guidance Association, The American Psychological Association, and The National Training Laboratories have set down criteria which their organization uses to recognize competent and professional behavior.

Hopefully, this book will have demonstrated that effective group leadership is a skill that requires training and preparation. As one reviews the many techniques employed by group leaders it is easy to conceive of the role as involving only the mastery of a series of tricks of the trade. Of greater importance is an awareness that each technique's effectiveness is dependent not only on how it was employed but also on why it was used. Each technique becomes but an extension of the needs, values, and biases of the group leader. Although all of us will find ourselves involved in groups and with leadership functions, our ultimate success as a person and as a nation depends upon an increased awareness of our need to develop group process skills.

One of the most serious weaknesses of a book of this type is that it must advocate the value of an experience that many have not shared. As we have seen, an intellectual acceptance of the rights of the individual is not enough. To live out one's beliefs, each person needs to have had the chance to experience the rewards that come from a supportive group where individual difference is truly valued.

New behaviors need to be rewarded and need to be equally effective as older modes of behavior. If, then, the approach described in this text makes sense to a reader, further implementation of the approach will require more than additional reading.

For the highly motivated person there are specific kinds of preparation that will be helpful. Included are:

1. Courses covering personality theory and the dynamics of human behavior.

2. Courses covering semantics and effective verbal communication.

3. Courses providing background of an anthropological or sociological nature which will assist the reader in recognizing the meaning or symbolic significance of various roles or acts in our culture.

4. Courses training a person in specific counseling skills.

5. Courses providing supervised practicum experiences where the student is helped to discover the way in which his needs are effecting his behavior.

6. Experiences as a group leader or member to sensitize the person to typical experiences in the life of a group.

The NTL Institute trainers and consultants (15) are expected to have mastered the following skills and to have completed the following group participation experiences.

Skills

- Ability to conduct a small group and to provide individual consultation using the theory and techniques of laboratory method.
- Ability to articulate theory and to direct a variety of learning experiences for small and large groups and for organizations.
- Ability to recognize their own behavior styles and personal needs and to deal with them productively in the performance of their professional roles.
- Ability to recognize symptoms of serious psychological stress and to make responsible decisions when such problems arise (p. 10).

Participation Experiences

- Participation in at least one NTL Institute Basic Human Relations laboratory.
- Supervised cotraining with senior staff members.
- Participation on laboratory staff with experienced trainers in programs for a variety of client groups.
- Participation in an NTL Institute or university program specifically designed to train trainers (p. 11).

Readers seeking more information on standards are encouraged to write to the various professional organizations, since at the time this book is being written many final position statements are still in process.

GROUP SKILLS AND THE GENERAL PUBLIC

There is concrete evidence (19,20,21) that laymen working with their peers to explore feelings and attitudes can, with minimal training, learn how to help members of a group use each other as a source of support.

Just as professional group leaders need to be selected, so too screening is necessary in choosing lay leaders. In addition to providing support and consultation to lay leaders, trained group counselors need to recognize that self-help groups have some unique characteristics that can differ from formally organized groups (22). Self-help groups share the properties of small groups in that they are an instrument for the satisfaction of the needs of the individual members. They tend to be problem centered and group-action oriented toward group selected goals. Members of the group tend to be peers and accept helping others as the norm of the group. The role of the "professional" is not clear, if it exists at all. The leadership is an accepted instead of a status or inherited role. Since group goals arise from the group, they tend not to feel an allegiance to any outside group or institution.

Since much learning occurs through identification with role models, the involvement of potential group leaders in a group experience where they can experience concepts that at a later date they may recognize and incorporate can be helpful. There is increasing recognition that the supervisory process lends itself well to use in a group setting (23).

ETHICS

Group leaders should also be evaluated in terms of the way they behave as professionals. Although existing codes of ethics cover many aspects of a group counselor's functioning there are several that deserve special comment.

Because our society values productive behavior, many organizations are applying coercive tactics to insure participation by their members in group settings. Students are being required to participate in sensitivity sessions as part of a class, without prior warning, and with no freedom of choice.

The group leader has a clear responsibility to insist that any group for which he is responsible require the orientation of potential members to the purpose and potential activities of the group. All members should be volunteers. In addition, there must be established safeguards that protect participants from violations of confidentiality and freedom from physical assault, sexual advance, or severe emotional attacks (16,17).

Zimpfer (18) has examined the many unique problems of ethics faced in groups and has developed the following minimum guidelines for the group leader.

1. He should have articulated a philosophical base and rationale regarding interpersonal relationships that permit peer and group activity to be an important part of the growth/change process.
2. He should have the mandate or at least the approval of the authorities in his institution or agency.
3. He should restrict his goals for groups to those that are appropriate for his institution or agency and that he is competent to achieve.
4. He should have the ability to perceive the advantages, dynamics,

and limitations of group procedures, and to either activate or control the process as needed.

5. He should provide adequate screening of and orientation for potential participants.

6. He should ascertain the integrity of the members to be of a helpful disposition and willing to work with each other.

7. He should use only those strategies and tools in which he is a skilled practitioner.

8. He should build in adequate safeguards and backup supports such as referral resources, consultation on special problems, and supervision of his work.

SUMMARY

This chapter has focused on the concept of accountability as reflected by ways in which individuals or groups can assess the degree to which they have accomplished defined goals. It has reraised the questions of "accountable for whom, for what, and why."

Research design and research techniques can best be learned through reading texts specifically designed for the purpose. This chapter limited itself to problems associated with group assessment.

Specific problems associated with research on groups were explored and a recommendation was made that focus return to an evaluation of the single case, and in a reality setting.

The chapter also explored the relationship of training to levels of group leadership. The ethical responsibilities of the group leader was defined.

Bibliography

1. Maloney, W. P. *A Review and Analysis of the Reported Experimental Research on Group Counseling in Higher Education Between 1955 and 1967.* Ed. D. University of Virginia, 1970.

2. Strupp, H. W., and Bergin, A. E. "Some Empirical and Conceptual Bases for Coordinated Research in Psychotherapy: A Critical Review of Issues, Trends, and Evidence," *International Journal of Psychiatry,* Vol. 7, 18–90, Feb. 1969.

3. Golembiewski, R. T. *The Small Group: An Analysis of Research Concepts and Operations,* Chicago: University of Chicago Press, 1962, p. 46.

4. Hays, W. L. *Statistics for Psychologists,* Holt, Rinehart, and Winston, 1963, p. 379.

5. Moustalas, C. *Individuality and Encounter,* Mass.: Doyle Publishing Co., 1968, pp. 115–116.

6. Allport, G. W. *The Use of Personal Documents in Psychological Science,* New York: Social Science Research Council Bulletin, 49, 1942.

7. Dinkmeyer, D., and Muro, J. *Group Counseling: Theory and Practice,* Illinois, Peacock, 1971, p. 320.

8. Fullmer, D. W. *Counseling—Group Theory and System,* Pennsylvania: Intext Ed. Publ., 1971, pp. 136–153.

9. Gazda, G. M., and Larsen, M. J. "A Comprehensive Appraisal of Group and Multiple Counseling Research," *Journal of Research and Development in Education,* pp. 57–132.

10. Ohlsen, M. M. *Group Counseling,* New York: Holt, Rinehart and Winston, 1970.

11. Anderson, A. R. "Group Counseling." In *Review of Educational Research,* Vol. 39, No. 2, pp. 209–226, April 1969.

12. Jennings, H. H. "Sociometric Grouping in Relation to Child Development." In Caroline Tryon (Ed.), *Fostering Mental Health in Our Schools,* Washington, D.C.: ASCD, National Education Association, 1950.

13. Smucker, O. "Measurement of Group Tension through the Use of Negative Sociometric Data," *Sociometry,* 10, 376–383, November 1947.

14. Keith-Spiegel, P., and Spiegel, D. "Perceived Helpfulness of Others as a Function of Compatible Intelligence Levels," *Journal of Counseling Psychology,* 14: 61–62, 1967.

281

15. *Standards for the Use of Laboratory Method,* Washington, D.C.: National Training Laboratories, 1969.

16. Lakin, M. "Some Ethical Issues in Sensitivity Training," *American Psychologist,* 24 (10), 923–928, Oct. 1969.

17. Hill, W. F. *Bulletin on Group Counseling, Supervision, and Group Psychotherapy.* Issues One and Two, U. of So. Cal. Youth Studies Center (no dates).

18. Zimpfer, D. "Needed: Professional Ethics for Working with Groups," *P & G Journal,* December 1971.

19. Hereford, C. F. *Changing Parental Attitudes Through Group Discussion,* Austin, University of Texas Press, 1963.

20. Auerbach, A. B. *Parents Learn Through Discussion,* New York: Wiley, 1968.

21. Lifton, W. *Leading Groups: A Leader's Guide for They Ask Why,* Chicago: National Dairy Council, 1963.

22. Katz, A. H., "Self-Help Organizations and Volunteer Participation in Social Welfare," *Social Work,* Vol. 15, No. 1, Jan. 1970, pp. 51–60.

23. Klein, A. F. *Supervision: The Why and the Wherefore,* A Social Welfare Paper No. 5, State University of New York at Albany: School of Social Welfare, 1970.

9 Conclusion

*Independence? That's middle class blasphemy. We are all de-
pendent on one another, every soul of us on earth.*
GEORGE BERNARD SHAW, Pygmalion

TERMINATING GROUPS

Groups, like all things, reach a point where they end. For continuous groups, the ending is not clearly perceived, for it may represent merely the moving out of one group of people who are immediately replaced by others. For finite groups, however, closure represents a distinctive part of the group's life. As the terminal date approaches, the discussions become more superficial as the anxiety increases.

Think of the last day before graduation and the feelings discussed in this chapter may come back to you. Remember the sense of loss of close friendships, the sudden acceptance of characteristics which symbolized a group that was formerly rejected (labels, etc.), the frantic copying of addresses to insure that the bond really wasn't being broken, and the apprehension over your capacity to face the next step alone. In a very real sense, groups go through a weaning process. Almost like an ill child, they may revert to infantile behavior as one way of saying they really are not ready to go off on their own.

The leader who anticipates the sudden upsurge of anxiety and dependency will not become anxious himself. He will be able, instead, to accept these feelings as natural. Discovering that the leader remains calm helps the group achieve perspective and enables them to go on to their next level of responsibility. If, in the end, members of a group can perceive what the group as a group achieved and if they can see what they personally have gained, the value of the group as a social force will remain in their memory for future reference.

Groups can be used in at least three ways. They can serve as a way of helping a person discover how others might help him in an individual counseling situation. For the person receiving individual counseling, it might often be helpful to relate concurrently to a group; the group might serve as a testing ground for ideas developed in the individual sessions. Lastly, the person who terminates individual counseling may wish to use a group as a weaning process. Having been secure in a two person setting, he now moves to a comfortable group situation before tackling the world at large.

TO BE OR NOT TO BE?

For me the real problem presented by this text was to discover a way to communicate that our current stress on the existential moment with its frequent hedonistic emphasis on satisfying current needs as perceived by each individual is understandable in a world faced with possible immediate termination. It is only when the individual or the group clarifies what they are that they can begin to consider what they would like to become in the future. The current alienation in our society reflects feelings of impotence in having any real impact on the forces that seem to decide our fate.

The security needed to face tomorrow is both a moral and an emotional one. As man seeks the strength to do battle he will increasingly turn either to his fellow man or to a concept of a Supreme Being. History teaches us that people who reject the risks of doing something about their fate are very prone to seeking easy solutions by trusting a charismatic leader. Totalitarianism suggests rapid solutions to problems, but asks that man pay the price of loss of any personal identity.

Groups, properly developed, in all areas of our life can help people discover that democracy can work. It can also provide the security base needed to face the outer darkness. The steps are clear. Each person needs to find himself with the help of others. Groups then need to define their group identity and goals. And then, finally, groups need help to secure the information, skills, and techniques needed to reach their defined objectives.

SUMMARY

The chapter discussed issues involved in terminating groups. Problems also exist in ending a book. Tradition decrees that we attempt to secure closure, a sense of finality, a final amen. For the person who espouses an existential philosophy with an emphasis on "becoming" it is more appropriate to use today as a starting place for tomorrow. Accordingly, with the special help of David Zimpfer, a special appendix has been prepared for this book. It represents a source for finding answers to as yet unseen or unanswered questions. The final evaluation of this text rests on how many readers seek more training, feel the need for more knowledge, or who question themselves more closely. Although I have placed great confidence in the constructive role of groups in our society, in the last analysis the success of any group rests on the willingness of each person to be responsible for his own behavior although aware of his interdependence on others.

A Bibliography of Recent Publications on Group Procedures in Guidance

DAVID G. ZIMPFER

Associate Professor of Education
University of Rochester

College of Education
University of Rochester
Rochester, New York

Contents

Introduction

This bibliography is intended to have both resource and heuristic value to its user. It classifies into 12 major categories and an additional 71 subcategories the discursive literature and research on group procedures both with respect to basic knowledge and as applied in the helping professions. Because of space limitations and the greatly increased recent output of materials on the subject of group procedures, it was necessary to decide whether to represent the field in breadth over a short span of time, or in depth longitudinally on a few subtopics. Since the Lifton style swings freely through counseling and guidance, then to the whole of education, on through the related helping professions of psychotherapy and social work, and finally into the area of organizational and social change, it quickly became clear that a broad-based approach would be most suited. The bibliography therefore represents only the most recent publications, being limited to the years 1969 to 1971 (through the end of May). This decision in no way reflects pejoratively on the quality of older materials, nor is it intended to suggest to the reader that newer materials are adequately representative of the tradition and scope of group procedures. In fact, there are areas of interest and research in group work that have been highlighted in former literature, but that happen not to be represented in the years included here. Such areas are labeled but show simply the word "None" beneath them.

As a companion volume to the present listing a full bibliography on group procedures in guidance has been published also. Using the same topical headings, it covers such area in depth, including classical studies and going back to the earliest systematic presentations and researches. (David G. Zimpfer, *Group Procedures in Guidance: a Bibliography*. New York: Wiley, 1972.)

This present listing reports comprehensively, for the years named, the literature and research on group procedures in guidance and counseling in educational settings. Books, dissertations, journal articles, and unpublished documents as they became available, are included. None were eliminated because they were judged to be inadequate, biased, or otherwise inappropriate. The literature and research in psychotherapy are represented whenever they appear to have direct application in group guidance and counseling with normal populations. The literatures of other than educational settings were sampled, and an indicative listing is presented.

Many periodicals were searched systematically. These are named at the end of the topical listing. Other periodicals appear as I happened to discover useful materials within them. Author listings for the bibliography are included in the general author index for the text. Specific publications are listed under as many topical headings as seem appropriate. The "general" categories that occasionally appear (such as Section III—General) comprise those items that span a whole major topical area. Such listings could readily be included under each of the subcategories for that general topic.

July, 1971

David G. Zimpfer

I. GROUPS: FOUNDATIONS, PHILOSOPHY, PURPOSES, DEFINITIONS

Books

Kemp, C. Gratton, *Foundations of Group Counseling*. New York: McGraw Hill, 1970. Chapter 3, "The Concept of the Group."

Kemp, C. Gratton (Ed.), *Perspectives on the Group Process* (2nd ed.). Boston: Houghton Mifflin, 1970. "Issues in Group Process," 3–17.

Rogers, Carl, *Carl Rogers on Encounter Groups*. New York: Harper and Row, 1970. Chapter 1, "The Origin and Scope of the Trend Toward 'Groups.'"

Periodicals

Burks, Herbert, and Pate, Robert, "Group Procedures Terminology: Babel Revisited," *School Counselor*, 1970, **18**, 53–60.

II. THEORETICAL FORMULATIONS IN INTERPERSONAL RELATIONSHIPS

Books

Bales, Robert, *Personality and Interpersonal Behavior*. New York: Holt, Rinehart and Winston, 1970.

Carson, Robert, *Interaction Concepts of Personality*. Chicago: Aldine, 1969.

Heine, Patrick, *Personality in Social Theory*. Chicago: Aldine, 1971.

Luft, Joseph, *Group Processes: An Introduction to Group Dynamics* (2nd ed.). Palo Alto: National Press, 1970. Chapter 5, "Interaction Patterns and Metacommunication."

Luft, Joseph, *Of Human Interaction*. Palo Alto: National Press, 1969.

III. THE DYNAMICS AND RELATIONSHIPS OF GROUP PROCESS

GENERAL

Books

Davis, James, *Group Performance*. Reading, Massachusetts: Addison-Wesley, 1969.

Dimock, Hedley, *Factors in Working with Groups*. Montreal, Quebec: Sir George Williams University, 1970.

Lindzey, Gardner, and Aronson, Elliot (Eds.), *The Handbook of Social Psychology* (2nd ed.). Reading, Massachusetts: Addison-Wesley, 1969. Vol. 4, "Group Psychology and Phenomena of Interaction."

Mills, Theodore, and Rosenberg, Stan (Eds.), *Readings on the Sociology of Small Groups*. Engelwood Cliffs, New Jersey: Prentice Hall, 1970.

Schmuck, Richard, and Schmuck, Patricia, *Group Processes in the Classroom*. Dubuque, Iowa: Brown, 1971.

Periodicals

Watson, Eugene, "Group Communications and Developmental Process," *High School Journal*, 1969, **52**, 431–440.

III. A. SOCIAL STRUCTURE, CLIMATE, NORMS, GOALS, FORCES

Periodicals

Sapier, Herman, "Group Learning: Note on Undivided vs. Equally Divided Task Information," *Psychological Reports,* 1969, 24, 847–848.

III. B. LEADERSHIP, POWER, STATUS

Books

Kemp, C. Gratton, *Perspectives on the Group Process* (2nd ed.). Boston: Houghton Mifflin, 1970. Part IV, "Leadership," 153–240.

III. C. MEMBERSHIP

Books

Kemp, C. Gratton, *Perspectives on the Group Process* (2nd ed.). Boston: Houghton Mifflin, 1970. Part V, "The Group Member," 241–333.

III. D. PHASES OF GROUP EVOLUTION; TYPICAL PROBLEMS OF GROUPS

Books

Mills, Theodore, "Toward a Conception of the Life Cycle of Groups," in Theodore Mills and Stan Rosenberg (Eds.), *Readings on the Sociology of Small Groups.* Englewood Cliffs, New Jersey: Prentice Hall, 1970, 238–247.

III. E. ROLE BEHAVIOR; INTERACTION PROCESS ANALYSIS

Books

Amidon, Peggy, *Nonverbal Interaction Analysis.* Minneapolis: Paul Amidon and Associates, 5408 Chicago Avenue South, 1971.

Bales, Robert, *Personality and Interpersonal Behavior.* New York: Holt, Rinehart and Winston, 1970.

Gallagher, James, Nuthall, Graham, and Rosenshine, Barak, *Classroom Observation.* Chicago: Rand McNally. American Educational Research Association Monograph Series on Curriculum Evaluation, No. 6, 1970.

McCarthy, Terry, *Identity: A Handbook on Group Interaction.* Salt Lake City: Institute for the Study of Interaction Systems, 1969.

Simon, Anita, and Boyer, E. Gil (Eds.), *Mirrors for Behavior II: An Anthology of Observation Instruments.* Volume B. Philadelphia: Research for Better Schools, Inc., 1700 Market Street, 1970.

Strickland, Ben, and Wood, Nolan, *Interpersonal Proximity, An Avenue for Contact.* Fort Worth: Guidance Vistas. 1969.

Periodicals

Hill, William, "The Hill Interaction Matrix," *Personnel and Guidance Journal,* 1971, 49, 619–622. Comment by Richard Rank, 623.

Sata, Lindbergh, and Derbyshire, Robert, "Breaking the Role Barrier—A Psychotherapeutic Necessity," *Mental Hygiene,* 1969, **53**, 110–117.

III. F. INDIVIDUAL AND INTERPERSONAL PERCEPTION AND BEHAVIOR

Books

Luft, Joseph, *Group Processes* (2nd ed.), Palo Alto: National Press, 1970. Chapter 3, "The Johari Window—A Graphic Model of Awareness in Interpersonal Relations."

Periodicals

Holt, Robert, "On the Interpersonal and Intrapersonal Consequences of Expressing or Not Expressing Anger," *Journal of Consulting and Clinical Psychology,* 1970, **35**, 8–12.

III. G. SOCIOMETRIC CONSIDERATIONS

Books

Myers, Eddie, *Classroom Sociometric Analysis.* Cleveland, Ohio: Educational Research Council of America, Child-Educational Psychology Program, 1970.

Periodicals

Moreno, J. L., "The Triadic System, Psychodrama-Sociometry-Group Psychotherapy," *Group Psychotherapy and Psychodrama,* 1970, **23**, 16.

III. H. DECISION MAKING IN GROUPS

Books

Kemp, C. Gratton, *Perspectives on the Group Process* (2nd ed.). Boston: Houghton Mifflin, 1970. "Making Better Decisions," 211–214.

III. I. SILENCE IN GROUPS

None

III. J. PROCESS RESEARCH; PROPOSITIONS ABOUT GROUP PROCESS

Books

Ahearn, T. R., *An Interaction Process Analysis of Extended Group Counseling With Prospective Counselors.* Unpublished doctoral dissertation. University of Georgia, 1969. Abstract in *Dissertation Abstracts,* 1969, **29**, 4271–A.

Brown, Jerome, *Some Factors in Response to Criticism in Group Therapy.* Unpublished doctoral dissertation. University of Houston, 1969. Abstract in *Dissertation Abstracts International,* 1969, **30**, 376–B.

Fox, W. T., *The Relationship Between Group Counselor Functioning and the Counseling Group's Perception of the Campus Environment.* Unpublished master's thesis. Chico State College, 1970.

Kemp, C. Gratton, *Foundations of Group Counseling.* New York: McGraw-Hill, 1970. Part Three, "Contrasts in Theory and Process," 81–135.

Luft, Joseph, *Group Processes* (2nd ed.). Palo Alto: National Press, 1970. Chapter 4. "Basic Issues in Group Processes."

Ohlsen, Merle, *Group Counseling.* New York: Holt, Rinehart and Winston, 1970. Chapter 6, "Resistance"; Chapter 7, "Transference."

Periodicals

Berger, Irving, "Resistances to the Learning Process in Group Dynamics Programs," *American Journal of Psychiatry,* 1969, **126**, 850–857.

Bouchard, Thomas, and Hare, Melana, "Size, Performance, and Potential in Brainstorming Groups," *Journal of Applied Psychology,* 1970, 54, 51–55.

Danish, Steven, "Factors Influencing Changes in Empathy Following a Group Experience," *Journal of Counseling Psychology,* 1971, **18**, 262–267.

Grand, Stanley, Freedman, Norbert, and Jortner, Sidney, "Variations in REM Dreaming and the Effectiveness of Behavior in Group Therapy," *American Journal of Psychotherapy,* 1969, **23**, 667–680.

Hall, Douglas, "The Impact of Peer Interaction During an Academic Role Transition," *Sociology of Education,* 1969, **42**, 118–140.

Heckel, Robert, Holmes, George, and Rosecrans, Clarence, "A Factor Analytic Study of Process Variables in Group Therapy," *Journal of Clinical Psychology,* 1971, **27**, 146–150.

Lucas, Richard, and Jaffee, Cabot, "Effects of High-Rate Talkers on Group Voting Behavior in the Leaderless-Group Problem-Solving Situation," *Psychological Reports,* 1969, **25**, 471–477.

Minton, Henry and Miller, Arthur, "Group Risk Taking and Internal-External Control of Group Members," *Psychological Reports,* 1970, **26**, 431–436.

III. K. EXTERNAL INFLUENCES ON GROUP BEHAVIOR

None

III. L. OBSERVATION OF GROUPS

Books

Dimock, Hedley, *How to Observe Your Group.* Montreal, Quebec: Sir George Williams University, 1970.

Periodicals

Jenkins, David, "Feedback and Group Self-Evaluation," *Journal of Social Issues,* 1948, 4, 50–60. (Also in Kemp, *Perspectives on the Group Process,* 2nd ed., 1970, 130–138.)

III. M. NONVERBAL BEHAVIOR IN GROUPS

Books

Amidon, Peggy, *Nonverbal Interaction Analysis.* Minneapolis: Paul Amidon and Associates, 5408 Chicago Avenue South, 1971.

Birdwhistell, Ray, *Kinesics and Context*. Philadelphia: University of Pennsylvania Press, 1970.

Fast, Julius, *Body Language*. New York: Evans, 1970.

Pesso, Albert, *Movement in Psychotherapy: Psychomotor Techniques and Training*. New York: New York University Press, 1969.

Periodicals

Wilson, Stephen, "The Effect of the Laboratory Situation on Experimental Discussion Group," *Sociometry*, 1969, **32**, 220–236.

IV. DEVELOPMENT OF GROUPS

GENERAL

Books

Dimock, Hedley, *Planning Group Development*. Montreal, Quebec: Sir George Williams University, 1970.

Mahler, Clarence, *Group Counseling in the Schools*. Boston: Houghton Mifflin, 1969. Chapter 3, "Formation of the Group."

Periodicals

Yunker, John, "Essential Organizational Components of Group Counseling in the Primary Grades," *Elementary School Guidance and Counseling*, 1970, **4**, 172–179.

IV. A. COMPOSITION AND SELECTION

Books

Kauffman, John, *The Effects of Group Composition on an Experimental Group Counseling Program*. Unpublished doctoral dissertation. University of Iowa, 1970. Abstract in *Dissertation Abstracts International*, 1970, **31**, 2685–A.

Ohlsen, Merle, *Group Counseling*. New York: Holt, Rinehart and Winston, 1970. Chapter 5, "Establishing a Group."

Periodicals

DeLara, Lane, "Listening Is a Challenge: Group Counseling in the School," *Mental Hygiene*, 1969, **53**, 600–605.

IV. B. SIZE

Periodicals

Zimet, Carl, and Schneider, Carol, "Effects of Group Size on Interaction in a Small Group," *Journal of Social Psychology*, 1969, **77**, 177–187.

IV. C. PROCEDURES

Books

Dimock, Hedley, *Planning Group Development*. Montreal, Quebec: Sir George Williams University, 1970.

Glass, Sheldon, *The Practical Handbook of Group Counseling.* Baltimore: BCS Publishing, 1969. Chapter 2, "How to Organize a Group"; Chapter 3, "The Role of the Group Leader"; Chapter 4, "The Mechanics of Group Counseling"; Chapter 5, "Techniques to Stimulate Group Interaction"; Chapter 6, "The Important Group Sessions."

New York State Education Department, *Planning Models for Group Counseling.* Albany, New York: The Department, Bureau of Continuing Education Curriculum Development, 1969.

Pesso, Albert, *Movement in Psychotherapy: Psychomotor Techniques and Training.* New York: New York University, 1969.

Periodicals

Clack, Ronald, "Encouraging Participation in Group Counseling," *School Counselor,* 1971, **18**, 286–289.

Vordenberg, Wesley, "A Technique for Goal-Setting in Group Work," *Personnel and Guidance Journal,* 1970, **48**, 479–480.

IV. D. AUDIOVISUAL TECHNIQUES AND DEVICES

Books

Dinkmeyer, Don, and Muro, James, *Group Counseling: Theory and Practice.* Itasca, Illinois: Peacock, 1971. Appendix I, "Visual Aids."

Edwards, William, *The Use of Focused Audio Feedback in Group Counseling with Adolescent Boys.* Unpublished doctoral dissertation. University of Georgia, 1969. Abstract in *Dissertation Abstracts International,* 1970, **30**, 5232–A.

Hum, Sterling, *An Investigation of the Use of Focused Video Tape Feedback in High School Group Counseling.* Unpublished doctoral dissertation. University of Southern California, 1969. Abstract in *Dissertation Abstracts,* 1969, **29**, 4284–A.

Krumboltz, John, and Thoresen, Carl (Eds.), *Behavioral Counseling.* New York: Holt, Rinehart and Winston, 1969. Chapters 24–28.

Pennsylvania Department of Education, *Elementary School Guidance: Resource Materials.* Harrisburg: The Department, Bureau of Pupil Personnel Services, Division of Guidance Services, 1970.

Stoller, Frederick, "Videotape Feedback in the Marathon and Encounter Group," in M. Berger (Ed.), *Videotape Techniques in Psychiatric Training and Treatment.* New York: Brunner-Mazel, 1970, 170–178.

Periodicals

Stevens, Helen, Doerr, J. Joseph, and Chatten, Roger, "Audiovisual Materials for Group Workers," *Personnel and Guidance Journal,* 1971, **49**, 657–658.

Stoller, Frederick, "Videotape Feedback in the Group Setting," *Journal of Nervous and Mental Disease,* 1969, **148**, 457–466.

IV. E. USE OF ART OR MUSIC AS PART OF GROUP WORK

None

V. TYPES OF GROUP EXPERIENCE

V. A. COUNSELING (OTHER THAN IN EDUCATION)

Books

Klein, Alan, *Social Work Through Group Process*. Albany, New York: State University of New York; School of Social Welfare, 1970.

Rose, Sheldon, *A Behavioral Approach to Group Treatment with Children: The Social-Behavioral Approach to Social Work*. New York: Council on Social Work Education, 1969.

Periodicals

Johnson, Robert, and Chatowsky, Anthony, "Game Theory and Short-Term Group Counseling," *Personnel and Guidance Journal*, 1969, **47**, 758–761.

Sullivan, Dorothy, "Group Guidance in an Employment Setting," *Journal of Employment Counseling*, 1970, **7**, 75–80.

V. B. PSYCHOTHERAPY

Books

Kaplan, H. I., and Sadock, B. J. *Comprehensive Group Psychotherapy*. Baltimore: Williams and Wilkins, 1971.

Luft, Joseph, *Group Processes* (2nd ed.). Palo Alto: National Press, 1970. Chapter 6, "Group Processes and Clinical Psychology."

Pesso, Albert, *Movement in Psychotherapy: Psychomotor Techniques and Training*. New York: New York University, 1969.

Ruitenbeek, Hendrik (Ed.), *Group Therapy Today: Styles, Methods, and Techniques*. New York: Atherton, 1969.

Sahakian, William, *Psychotherapy and Counseling*. Chicago: Rand McNally, 1969.

Yalom, I. D., *The Theory and Practice of Group Psychotherapy*. New York: Basic Books, 1970.

Periodicals

Bernstein, Stephen, Wacks, Jerry, and Christ, Jacob, "The Effect of Group Psychotherapy on the Psychotherapist," *American Journal of Psychotherapy*, 1969, **23**, 271–282.

Brandes, Norman, "Group Psychotherapy in the Treatment of Emotional Disturbance," *Mental Hygiene*, 1969, **53**, 105–109.

Cohn, R. C. "The Theme-centered Interactional Method: Group Therapists as Group Educators," *Journal of Group Psychoanalysis and Process*, 1970, **2**, 19–36.

Gordon, Myron, and Norman Liberman, "Group Psychotherapy: Being and Becoming," *Personnel and Guidance Journal*, 1971, **49**, 611–617. Comment by Milton Schwebel, 617–618.

Grand, Stanley, Freedman, Norbert, and Jortner, Sidney, "Variations in REM Dreaming and the Effectiveness of Behavior in Group Therapy," *American Journal of Psychotherapy*, 1969, **23**, 667–680.

Hanson, Philip, Rothaus, Paul, O'Connell, Walter, and Wiggins, George, "Training Patients for Effective Participation in Back-Home Groups," *American Journal of Psychiatry,* 1969, **126**, 857–862.

Heckel, Robert, Holmes, George, and Rosecrans, Clarence, "A Factor Analytic Study of Process Variables in Group Therapy, " *Journal of Clinical Psychology,* 1971, **27**, 146–150.

Lomont, James, Gilner, Frank, Spector, Norman, and Skinner, Kathryn, "Group Assertion Training and Group Insight Therapies," *Psychological Reports,* 1969, **25**, 463–470.

Moreno, J. L., "The Triadic System, Psychodrama-Sociometry-Group Psychotherapy," *Group Psychotherapy and Psychodrama,* 1970, **23**, 16.

Papanek, Helene, "Therapeutic and Antitherapeutic Factors in Group Relations," *American Journal of Psychotherapy,* 1969, **23**, 396–404.

Pierce, Richard, and Drasgow, James, "Teaching Facilitative Interpersonal Functioning to Psychiatric Inpatients," *Journal of Counseling Psychology,* 1969, **16**, 295–298.

Sata, Lindbergh, and Derbyshire, Robert, "Breaking the Role Barrier—A Psychotherapeutic Necessity," *Mental Hygiene,* 1969, **53**, 110–117.

Slavson, Samuel, "Eclecticism versus Sectarianism in Group Psychotherapy," *International Journal of Group Psychotherapy,* 1970, **30**, 3–14.

Smith, R. J., "A Closer Look at Encounter Therapies," *International Journal of Group Psychotherapy,* 1970, **20**, 192–209.

Stoller, Frederick, "Videotape Feedback in the Group Setting," *Journal of Nervous and Mental Disease,* 1969, **148**, 457–466.

Tenenbaum, Samuel, "A Discussion of the Therapy That Resides in a Group," *Psychotherapy: Theory, Research and Practice,* 1970, **7**, 253–255.

V. C. SMALL GROUP DISCUSSION; PROBLEM SOLVING GROUPS
Books

Magoon, Thomas, "Developing Skills for Solving Educational and Vocational Problems," in John Krumboltz and Carl Thoresen (Eds.), *Behavioral Counseling.* New York: Holt, Rinehart and Winston, 1969, 343–396.

Prazak, Janice, "Learning Job-Seeking Interview Skills," in John Krumboltz and Carl Thoresen (Eds.), *Behavioral Counseling.* New York: Holt, Rinehart and Winston, 1969, 414–428.

Periodicals

Bouchard, Thomas, "Personality, Problem-solving Procedure, and Performance in Small Groups," *Journal of Applied Psychology Monograph,* 1969, **53** (No. 1, Part 2), 1–29.

Rotter, George, and Portugal, Stephen, "Group and Individual Effects in Problem Solving," *Journal of Applied Psychology,* 1969, **53**, 338–341.

V. D. ROLE PLAYING, PSYCHODRAMA, SOCIODRAMA
Books

Ohlsen, Merle, *Group Counseling.* New York: Holt, Rinehart and Winton, 1970. Chapter 8, "Role Playing: A Group-Counseling Technique."

Periodicals

Amaro, Jorge Ferreira, and Soeira, Alfredo, "Psychodrama at a Psychiatric Clinic," *Group Psychotherapy,* 1969, **22**, 157–163.

Bonilla, Eduardo, "Spiritualism or Psychodrama," *Group Psychotherapy,* 1969, **22**, 65–71.

Friedman, Sam, "Role-Playing in a Youth Employment Office," *Group Psychotherapy and Psychodrama,* 1970, **23**, 21–26.

Moreno, J. L., "The Triadic System, Psychodrama-Sociometry-Group Psychotherapy," *Group Psychotherapy and Psychodrama,* 1970, **23**, 16.

Moreno, Zerka, "Practical Aspects of Psychodrama," *Group Psychotherapy,* 1969, **22**, 213–219.

O'Connell, Walter, and Hanson, Philip, "The Protagonist in Human Relations Training," *Group Psychotherapy and Psychodrama,* 1970, **23**, 45–55.

Sturm, Israel, "Note on Psychodrama in a 'Helping Relationship,'" *Group Psychotherapy,* 1969, **22**, 191–193.

V. E. GROUP PLAY THERAPY

None

V. F. LABORATORY TRAINING; T-GROUPS

Books

Gazda, George, and Porter, Thomas (Eds.), *Proceedings of a Symposium on Training Groups.* Athens, Georgia: University of Georgia, College of Education, 1970.

Golembiewski, Robert, and Blumberg, Arthur (Eds.), *Sensitivity Training and the Laboratory Approach: Readings About Concepts and Application.* Itasca, Illinois: Peacock, 1970.

National Training Laboratories, *Standards for the Use of Laboratory Method.* Washington, D. C.: The Laboratories, 1969.

Thompson, George, *Intellectualizing: Philosophic Inquiry in the Group Process.* Unpublished doctoral dissertation. University of Cincinnati, 1968. Abstract in *Dissertation Abstracts,* 1969, **29**, 3642–3643–A.

Periodicals

Cooper, Cary, "The Influence of the Trainer on Participant Change in T-Groups," *Human Relations,* 1969, **22**, 515–530.

Eddy, William, and Lubin, Bernard, "Laboratory Training and Encounter Groups," *Personnel and Guidance Journal,* 1971, **49**, 625–635. Comment by James Beck, 635.

Gottschalk, Louis, and Pattison, E. Mansell, "Psychiatric Perspectives on T-Groups and the Laboratory Movement: An Overview," *American Journal of Psychiatry,* 1969, **126**, 823–839.

Peck, H. (Ed.), "Encounter and T-groups: The Current Use of the Group for Personal Growth and Development," *International Journal of Group Psychotherapy,* July, 1970. Whole issue.

V. G. HUMAN POTENTIAL GROUPS; BASIC ENCOUNTER, SENSITIVITY AND CONFRONTATION GROUPS

Books

Berzon, Betty, "Encounters for Black/White Groups: A New Approach to Race Relations," in George Gazda (Ed.), *Group Procedures for the Disadvantaged.* Athens, Georgia: University of Georgia, Center for Continuing Education, 1969, 113–140.

Blank, L., Gottsegen, G. G., and Gottsegen, M. (Eds.), *Encounter Confrontations in Self and Interpersonal Awareness.* New York: Macmillan, 1970.

Burton, Arthur (Ed.), *Encounter: Theory and Practice in Encounter Groups.* San Francisco: Jossey Bass, 1969.

Cobbs, Price, "Racial Confrontation Groups," in George Gazda (Ed.), *Group Procedures for the Disadvantaged.* Athens, Georgia: University of Georgia, Center for Continuing Education, 1969, 74–112.

Egan, G., Encounter: *Group Processes for Interpersonal Growth.* Belmont, California: Brooks-Cole, 1970.

Gazda, George, and Porter, Thomas (Eds.), *Proceedings of a Symposium on Training Groups.* Athens, Georgia: University of Georgia, College of Education, 1970.

Howard, June, *Please Touch: A Guided Tour of the Human Potential Movement.* New York: McGraw-Hill, 1970.

O'Banion, Terry, and O'Connell, April, *The Shared Journey—An Introduction to Encounter.* Englewood Cliffs, New Jersey: Prentice Hall, 1970.

Otto, Herbert, *Group Methods Designed to Actualize Human Potential: A Handbook.* Beverly Hills, California: Holistic Press, 1970.

Pfeiffer, J., and Jones, J., *Handbook of Structured Experiences for Human Relations Training.* (Two volumes.) Iowa City: University Associates Press, 1969.

Rogers, Carl, *Carl Rogers on Encounter Groups.* New York: Harper and Row, 1970.

Stoller, Frederick, "Videotape Feedback in the Marathon and Encounter Group," in M. Berger (Ed.), *Videotape Techniques in Psychiatric Training and Treatment.* New York: Brunner-Mazel, 1970, 170–178.

Thompson, George, *Intellectualizing: Philosophic Inquiry in the Group Process.* Unpublished doctoral dissertation. University of Cincinnati, 1968. Abstract in *Dissertation Abstracts,* 1969, **29**, 3642–3643–A.

Watson, Goodwin, *48 Exercises and Games.* Union, New Jersey: Newark State College, Laboratory of Applied Behavioral Sciences.

Periodicals

Birnbaum, Max, "Sense About Sensitivity Training," *Saturday Review,* November 15, 1969, 82–83 and 96–98.

Blanchard, William, "Ecstasy Without Agony Is Baloney," *Psychology Today,* 1970, **3** (8), 8–10 and 64.

Coulson, William, "Inside a Basic Encounter Group," *Counseling Psychologist,* 1970, **2** (2), 1–27. Responses, 28–60.

Eddy, William, and Lubin, Bernard, "Laboratory Training and Encounter Groups," *Personnel and Guidance Journal,* 1971, **49,** 625–635. Comment by James Beck, 635.

Gottschalk, Louis, and Pattison, E. Mansell, "Psychiatric Perspectives on T-Groups and the Laboratory Movement: An Overview," *American Journal of Psychiatry,* 1969, **126,** 823–839.

Halleck, Seymour, "You Can Go to Hell with Style," *Psychology Today,* 1969, **3** (6), 16 and 70–73.

Hurewitz, Paul, "Ethical Considerations in Leading Therapeutic and Quasi-therapeutic Groups: Encounter and Sensitivity Groups," *Group Psychotherapy and Psychodrama,* 1970, **23,** 17–20.

Maliver, Bruce, "Encounter Groups Up Against the Wall," *New York Times Magazine,* January 3, 1971. Pp. 4–5, 37–40, and 43.

Morris, Sumner, Pflugrath, Jack, and Emery, John, "Personal Encounter in Higher Education," *Personnel and Guidance Journal,* 1969, **47,** 1001–1007.

O'Connell, Walter, and Hanson, Philip, "The Protagonist in Human Relations Training," *Group Psychotherapy and Psychodrama,* 1970, **23,** 45–55.

Olch, Doris, and Snow, David, "Personality Characteristics of Sensitivity Group Volunteers," *Personnel and Guidance Journal,* 1970, **48,** 848–850.

Peck H. (Ed.), "Encounter and T-groups: The Current Use of the Group for Personal Growth and Development," *International Journal of Group Psychotherapy,* July 1970. Whole issue.

Rogers, Carl, "The Group Comes of Age," *Psychology Today,* 1969, **3** (7), 27–31 and 58–61.

Smith, R. J., "A Closer Look at Encounter Therapies," *International Journal of Group Psychotherapy,* 1970, **20,** 192–209.

V. H. ACTIVITY APPROACHES TO GROUP WORK

Periodicals

Burnside, Irene, "Sensory Stimulation: An Adjunct to Group Work with the Disabled Aged," *Mental Hygiene,* 1969, **53,** 381–388.

Steiner, Jerome and Kaplan, Seymour, "Outpatient Group 'Work-For-Pay' Activity for Chronic Schizophrenic Patients," *American Journal of Psychotherapy,* 1969, **23,** 452–462.

VI. APPLICATIONS IN EDUCATION
GENERAL

Books

Bernard, Harold, and Fullmer, Daniel, *Principles of Guidance.* Scranton, Pennsylvania: International Textbook, 1969. Chapter 14, "Group Procedures in Guidance and Counseling," 285–306.

Gutsch, Kenneth, and Alcorn, John, *Guidance in Action: Ideas and Innovations for School Counselors.* West Nyack, New York: Parker Publishing, 1970. Chapter 4, "Using a Group Approach Effectively."

Hill, George, and Luckey, Eleanore, *Guidance for Children in Elementary Schools.* New York: Appleton, 1969. Chapter 6, "Group Guidance."

Kemp, C. Gratton (Ed.), *Perspectives on the Group Process* (2nd ed.). Boston: Houghton Mifflin, 1970.

Periodicals

Foulds, Melvin, and Guinan, James, "On Becoming a Growth Center," *Journal of College Student Personnel,* 1970, 11, 177–181.

Myrick, Robert, "Growth Groups: Implications for Teachers and Counselors," *Elementary School Guidance and Counseling,* 1969, 4, 35–42.

VI. A. COUNSELING

Books

Bentley, Joseph, "Sensitivity Training, Encounter Groups, Laboratory Learning —Implications for Counselors," in Carlton Beck, *Philosophical Guidelines for Counseling* (2nd ed.). Dubuque, Iowa: Brown, 1971, 74–88.

Berg, Robert, and Johnson, James (Eds.), *Group Counseling: A Source Book of Theory and Practice.* Fort Worth: American Continental Publishing, 1971.

Cahill, Robert, *Group Counseling—a Syllabus.* Unpublished doctoral dissertation. United States International University, 1969. Abstract in *Dissertation Abstracts International,* 1969, 30, 2324–A.

Dinkmeyer, Don, and Caldwell, Edson, *Developmental Counseling and Guidance.* New York: McGraw-Hill, 1970. Chapter 7, "Group Counseling."

Dinkmeyer, Don, and Muro, James, *Group Counseling: Theory and Practice.* Itasca, Illinois: Peacock, 1971.

Fullmer, Daniel, *Counseling: Group Theory and System.* Scranton, Pennsylvania: International Textbook, 1971.

Gazda, George, *Group Counseling: A Developmental Approach.* Boston: Allyn and Bacon, 1971.

Gazda, George (Ed.), *Proceedings of a Symposium on Group Procedures for the Disadvantaged.* Athens, Georgia: University of Georgia, Center for Continuing Education, 1969.

Gazda, George (Ed.), *Theories and Methods of Group Counseling in the Schools.* Springfield, Illinois: Thomas, 1969.

Glass, Sheldon, *The Practical Handbook of Group Counseling.* Baltimore: BCS Publishing, 1969.

Golembiewski, Robert, and Blumberg, Arthur (Eds.), *Sensitivity Training and the Laboratory Approach.* Itasca, Illinois: Peacock, 1970. Part V, "Where Can T-Group Dynamics Be Used?: Applications in the Home, School, Office, and Community."

Grenfell, John, "Group Counseling for Adult College Students," in Clarence Thompson (Ed.), *Counseling Adults: Contemporary Dimensions.* Washington, D.C.: American College Personnel Association, 1969, 76–78.

Hayes, Robert, "Group Counseling," in David Cook (Ed.), *Guidance for Education in Revolution.* Boston: Allyn and Bacon, 1971. Chapter 9.

Kemp, C. Gratton, *Foundations of Group Counseling.* New York: McGraw-Hill, 1970.

Mahler, Clarence, *Group Counseling in the Schools.* Boston: Houghton Mifflin, 1969.

New York State Education Department, *Group Counseling in the Schools: A Panel Discussion.* Albany, New York: The Department, Bureau of Guidance, 1970.

New York State Education Department, *Planning Models for Group Counseling.* Albany, New York: The Department, Bureau of Continuing Education Curriculum Development, 1969.

Ohlsen, Merle, *Group Counseling.* New York: Holt, Rinehart and Winston, 1970.

Peterson, James, *Counseling and Values.* Scranton, Pennsylvania: International Textbook, 1970. "The Counselor and the Group," 212–220.

Sahakian, William, *Psychotherapy and Counseling.* Chicago: Rand McNally, 1969.

Wrenn, C. Gilbert, "Group Counseling and Problems of Communication in the Large Universities," *Conseiller Canadien,* 1970, 4, 117–127. (Also in Koziey, *Selections for an Introduction to Guidance,* 202–213.)

Zimpfer, David, "Multi-leader Approaches to Groups in Counseling and Therapy," in Stanley Cramer and James Hansen, *Group Guidance and Counseling in the Schools.* New York: Appleton, 1971, 305–320.

Periodicals

Clack, Ronald, "Encouraging Participation in Group Counseling," *School Counselor,* 1971, **18**, 286–289.

Cohn, R. C., "The Theme-centered Interactional Method: Group Therapists as Group Educators," *Journal of Group Psychoanalysis and Process,* 1970, **2**, 19–36.

DeLara, Lane, "Listening Is a Challenge: Group Counseling in the School," *Mental Hygiene,* 1969, **53**, 600–605.

Dinkmeyer, Don, "Developmental Group Counseling," *Elementary School Guidance and Counseling,* 1970, 4, 267–272.

Dinkmeyer, Don, "Group Counseling Theory and Techniques," *School Counselor,* 1969, **17**, 148–152.

Mahler, Clarence, "Group Counseling," *Personnel and Guidance Journal,* 1971, **49**, 601–608. Comment by Carl Thoresen, 608–610.

Meadows, Mark, and Taplin, Jaci, "Premarital Counseling with College Students: A Promising Triad," *Journal of Counseling Psychology,* 1970, **17**, 516–518.

Moore, John, and Haley, Margaret, "Reflections: An Approach to Group Counseling in the Junior High School," *Elementary School Guidance and Counseling,* 1970, 4, 215–217.

Tenenbaum, Samuel, "School Grades and Group Therapy," *Mental Hygiene,* 1970, 54, 525–529.

Yunker, John, "Essential Organizational Components of Group Counseling in the Primary Grades," *Elementary School Guidance and Counseling,* 1970, **4**, 172–179.

VI. B. ORIENTATION

Books

Fitzgerald, Laurine, Johnson, Walter, and Norris, Willa (Eds.), *College Student Personnel: Readings and Bibliographies.* Boston: Houghton Mifflin, 1970. Part Two, Section A, "Orientation."

Franks, Mamie, *An Evaluation of Student Reaction to Orientation Programs in Selected Institutions of Higher Learning.* Unpublished doctoral dissertation. University of Mississippi, 1969. Abstract in *Dissertation Abstracts International,* 1969, **30**, 2330–A.

Periodicals

Harrold, Roger, "College Orientation and the Black Student," *Journal of College Student Personnel,* 1970, **11**, 251–255.

Nelson, Richard, "A Prekindergarten Orientation Program," *Elementary School Guidance and Counseling,* 1970, **5**, 135–139.

VI. C. GROUP GUIDANCE; SMALL GROUP DISCUSSION; TESTING INFORMATION

Books

Bloom, A. Martin, *Successful Programs and Practices for Counseling the College-Bound Student.* Englewood Cliffs, New Jersey: Prentice Hall, 1969. Chapter 11, "Ten Actual Programs for Group Guidance."

Isaacson, Lee, *Career Information in Counseling and Teaching* (2nd ed.). Boston: Allyn and Bacon, 1971. Chapter 15, "Using Career Information With Classes and Groups."

Marshall, Marvin, *The Tenth Grade Guidance Course in the Los Angeles City High Schools.* Unpublished doctoral dissertation. University of Southern California, 1969. Abstract in *Dissertation Abstracts,* 1969, **29**, 4288–A.

Periodicals

Bullock, Lyndal, "Group Guidance Seminars Designed for Junior High School Pupils," *School Counselor,* 1970, **17**, 174–177.

Kelly, Gary, "Group Guidance on Sex Education," *Personnel and Guidance Journal,* 1971, **49**, 809–814.

Kirby, Jonell, "Group Guidance," *Personnel and Guidance Journal,* 1971, **49**, 593–599.

Milling, Margaret, "An Elementary School Teacher and Group Guidance? You Bet!" *School Counselor,* 1969, **17**, 26–28.

Sisco, John, "Interpersonal Small-Group Communication," *National Association of Secondary School Principals Bulletin,* 1970, **54**, 77–85.

VI. D. CAREER DAYS AND CAREER CONFERENCES

Books

Bloom, A. Martin, *Successful Programs and Practices for Counseling the College-Bound Student.* Englewood Cliffs, New Jersey: Prentice Hall, 1969. Chapter 11, "Ten Actual Programs for Group Guidance."

Periodicals

Hoppock, Robert, "How to Conduct an Occupational Group Conference with an Alumnus," *Vocational Guidance Quarterly,* 1970, **18**, 311–314.

VI. E. STUDENT ACTIVITIES AND ACTIVITY GROUP APPROACHES

Books

Blakeman, John, and Day, Sherman, "Activity Group Counseling," in George Gazda (Ed.), *Theories and Methods of Group Counseling in the Schools.* Springfield, Illinois: Thomas, 1969. Chapter 3.

Moates, Hugh, *The Effects of Activity Group Counseling on the Self-Concept, Peer-Acceptance and Grade Point Average of Disadvantaged Seventh Grade Negro Boys and Girls.* Unpublished doctoral dissertation. Auburn University, 1969. Abstract in *Dissertation Abstracts International,* 1970, **30**, 3795–A.

Periodicals

Vriend, Thelma, "High Performing Inner-City Adolescents Assist Low-Performing Peers in Counseling Groups," *Personnel and Guidance Journal,* 1969, **47**, 897–904.

VI. F. CASE CONFERENCES

Books

Roeber, Edward, Walz, Garry, and Smith, Glenn, *A Strategy for Guidance.* New York: Macmillan, 1969. Chapter 7, "Helping Relationships: Pupil-Study Conferences."

Periodicals

Torrance, E. Paul, "Small Group Behavior of 5-Year-Old Children Under Three Kinds of Educational Stimulation," *Journal of Experimental Education,* 1970, **38**, 79–82.

VI. G. GUIDANCE IN CLASSROOM GROUPS; GUIDANCE COURSES

Books

American School Health Association Committee on Mental Health in the Class-room, "Some Suggested Areas for Guidance in Teaching Mental Health in the Classroom," in Walter Lifton (Ed.), *Educating for Tomorrow: The Role of Media, Career Development, and Society.* New York: Wiley, 1970. Appendix A.

Bradford, Leland, "Developing Potentialities Through Class Groups," in C. Gratton Kemp, *Perspectives on the Group Process* (2nd ed.). Boston: Houghton Mifflin, 1970, 74–82.

Dinkmeyer, Don, and Caldwell, Edson, *Developmental Counseling and Guidance.* New York: McGraw-Hill, 1970. Chapter 14, "Sociometric Techniques"; Chapter 16, "Group Guidance"; Chapter 17, "Role-Playing."

Dinkmeyer, Don, and Muro, James, *Group Counseling: Theory and Practice.* Itasca, Illinois: Peacock, 1971. Chapter 10, "Group Dynamics in the Classroom: The Teacher as Group Leader."

Isaacson, Lee, *Career Information in Counseling and Teaching* (2nd ed.). Boston: Allyn and Bacon, 1971. Chapter 15, "Using Career Information With Classes and Groups."

Koplitz, Eugene, "The Sensitivity Training Movement—Professional Implications for Elementary and Secondary School Counseling and Teaching," in Carlton Beck, *Philosophical Guidelines for Counseling* (2nd ed.). Dubuque, Iowa: Brown, 1971, 42–50.

Ligon, Mary, and McDaniel, Sarah, *The Teacher's Role in Counseling.* Englewood Cliffs, New Jersey: Prentice-Hall, 1970. Chapter 10, "Group Situations."

Luft, Joseph, *Group Processes: An Introduction to Group Dynamics* (2nd ed.). Palo Alto: National Press, 1970. Chapter 8, "The Teacher and Group Processes."

Schmuck, Richard, and Schmuck, Patricia, *Group Processes in the Classroom.* Dubuque, Iowa: Brown, 1971.

Yabroff, William, "Learning Decision Making," in John Krumboltz and Carl Thoresen (Eds.), *Behavioral Counseling.* New York: Holt, Rinehart and Winston, 1969, 329–343.

Periodicals

Adkins, Winthrop, "Life Skills: Structured Counseling for the Disadvantaged," *Personnel and Guidance Journal,* 1970, **49**, 108–116.

Dahms, Alan, "A Teacher-Counselor Program in Higher Education," *Journal of College Student Personnel,* 1971, **12**, 116–119.

Morris, Sumner, Pflugrath, Jack, and Emery, John, "Personal Encounter in Higher Education," *Personnel and Guidance Journal,* 1969, **47**, 1001–1007.

VI. H. HANDBOOKS FOR PUPIL AND LEADER USE IN GROUP GUIDANCE

Books

Bloom, A. Martin, *Successful Programs and Practices for Counseling the College-Bound Student.* Englewood Cliffs, New Jersey: Prentice-Hall, 1969. Chapter 11, "Ten Actual Programs for Group Guidance."

Dimensions of Personality Series: Grade Four: *Here I Am.* Grade Five: *I'm Not Alone.* Grade Six, *Becoming Myself.* Dayton, Ohio: Pflaum. (Also *Teacher's Edition.*)

Hill, William, *Learning Thru Discussion* (Rev. ed.). Beverly Hills, California: Sage, 1969.

Lewis, Howard, and Streitfeld, Harold, *Growth Games.* New York: Harcourt, Brace and Jovanovitch, 1971.

Munson, Harold, *My Educational Plans.* Chicago Science Research Associates, Group Guidance for Junior High School Students series, 1970.

New York State Education Department, *Planning Models for Group Counseling*. Albany, New York: The Department, Bureau of Continuing Education Curriculum Development, 1969.

Otto, Herbert, *Group Methods Designed to Actualize Human Potential: A Handbook*. Beverly Hills, California: Holistic Press, 1970.

Pfeiffer, J., and Jones, J., *Handbook of Structured Experiences for Human Relations Training*. (Two volumes.) Iowa City: University Associates Press, 1969.

Watson, Goodwin, *48 Exercises and Games*. Union, New Jersey: Newark State College, Laboratory of Applied Behavioral Sciences.

Wrenn, C. Gilbert, Hein, Reinhard, and Schwarzrock, Shirley, *Planned Group Guidance: A Group Discussion Manual*. Circle Pines, Minnesota: American Guidance Service, 1970.

VI. I. ORGANIZATIONAL DEVELOPMENT (ESPECIALLY EDUCATIONAL INSTITUTIONS) THROUGH GROUP PROCEDURES

Books

Cook, David, *Guidance for Education in Revolution*. Boston: Allyn and Bacon, 1971. Chapter 18, "Guidance and Institutional Change"; Chapter 19, "Guidance and Student Unrest."

Davis, Joe, *The Effect of Group Counseling on Teacher Affectiveness*. Unpublished doctoral dissertation. University of South Dakota, 1969. Abstract in *Dissertation Abstracts International*, 1969, 30, 2328–2329A.

Dinkmeyer, Don, and Muro, James, *Group Counseling: Theory and Practice*. Itasca, Illinois: Peacock, 1971. Chapter 11, "Group Counseling and Consulting with Teachers."

Glass, Sheldon, *The Practical Handbook of Group Counseling*. Baltimore: BCS Publishing, 1969. Chapter 8, "Group Counseling as an Adjunct to the Teacher"; Chapter 9, "Group Counseling as an Adjunct to the Administrator."

Havighurst, Robert, "The Sociology of Guidance," in David Cook (Ed.), *Guidance for Education in Revolution*. Boston: Allyn and Bacon, 1971. Chapter 3.

Henderson, Ann, *Small Group Treatment Effects on Behaviors and Perceptions of Secondary School Counselors*. Unpublished doctoral dissertation. Arizona State University, 1969. Abstract in *Dissertation Abstracts International*, 1969, 30, 2333–A.

Kavanaugh, Michelle, *An Investigation Into the Relative Effectiveness of the Teacher-Counselor Team Method versus Counseling in Facilitating Classroom Behavior Change*. Unpublished doctoral dissertation. University of Miami, 1969. Abstract in *Dissertation Abstracts International*, 1969, 30, 1868–1869A.

Levine, Daniel, "Guidance and the School as a Social System," in David Cook (ed.), *Guidance for Education in Revolution*. Boston: Allyn and Bacon, 1971. Chapter 4.

Owens, Robert, *Organizational Behavior in Schools*. Englewood Cliffs, New Jersey: Prentice-Hall, 1970.

Zimpfer, David, "Multi-leader Approaches to Groups in Counseling and Therapy," in Stanley Cramer and James Hansen, *Group Guidance and Counseling in the Schools*. New York: Appleton, 1971, 305–320.

Periodicals

Hansen, Lorraine, and Wirgan, Otto, "Human Relations Training: A Response to Crisis," *School Counselor*, 1970, **17**, 253–259.

Jones, B. A., and Karraker, R., "The Elementary Counselor and Behavior Modification," *Elementary School Guidance and Counseling*, 1969, 4, 28–34.

Lake, Dale, Ritvo, M. R., and O'Brien, G. M., "Applying Behavioral Science: Current Projects," *Journal of Applied Behavioral Science*, 1969, **3**, 67–90.

Myrick, Robert, "Growth Groups: Implications for Teachers and Counselors," *Elementary School Guidance and Counseling*, 1969, 4, 35–42.

Stubbins, Joseph, "The Politics of Counseling," *Personnel and Guidance Journal*, 1970, **48**, 611–618.

Walton, Maxine, Reeves, Gloria, and Shannon, Robert, "Crisis Team Intervention in School-Community Unrest," *Social Casework*, 1971, **52**, 11–17.

Walz, Garry, and Miller, Juliet, "School Climates and Student Behavior: Implications for Counselor Role," *Personnel and Guidance Journal*, 1969, **47**, 859–867.

Watson, Drage, "Group Work with Principals: Implications for Elementary Counselors," *Elementary School Guidance and Counseling*, 1969, **3**, 234–241.

VI. J. GROUP PROCEDURES FOR PARENTS

Books

Dinkmeyer, Don, and Muro, James, *Group Counseling: Theory and Practice*. Itasca, Illinois: Peacock, 1971. Chapter 12, "Parent and Family Group Counseling-Consultation."

Gilmore, John, "Parental Counseling and the Productive Personality," in David Cook (Ed.), *Guidance for Education in Revolution*. Boston: Allyn and Bacon, 1971.

Glass, Sheldon, *The Practical Handbook of Group Counseling*. Baltimore: BCS Publishing, 1969. Chapter 11, "Group Counseling with Parents."

Periodicals

Danforth, Joyce, Miller, Diane, Day, Anne, and Steiner, George, "Group Services for Unmarried Mothers: An Interdisciplinary Approach," *Children*, 1971, **18**, 59–64.

VI. K. GROUP PROCEDURES DIRECTED TOWARD UNDERACHIEVEMENT

Periodicals

Brown, Robert, "Effects of Structured and Unstructured Group Counseling with High- and Low-Anxious College Underachievers," *Journal of Counseling Psychology,* 1969, **16**, 209–214.

Finney, Ben, and Van Dalsem, Elizabeth, "Group Counseling for Gifted Underachieving High School Students," *Journal of Counseling Psychology,* 1969, **16**, 87–94.

Moulin, E. K., "The Effects of Client-Centered Group Counseling Using Play Media on the Intelligence, Achievement, and Psycholinguistic Abilities of Underachieving Primary School Children," *Elementary School Guidance and Counseling,* 1970, **5**, 85–98.

VI. L. GROUP PROCEDURES FOR CHILDREN

Books

Dinkmeyer, Don, and Muro, James, *Group Counseling: Theory and Practice.* Itasca, Illinois: Peacock, 1971. Chapter 9, "Group Counseling with Children."

Gazda, George, and Folds, Jonell, "Group Procedures in the Elementary School," in George Gazda (Ed.), *Theories and Methods of Group Counseling in the Schools.* Springfield, Illinois: Thomas, 1969. Chapter 2.

Ohlsen, Merle, *Group Counseling.* New York: Holt, Rinehart and Winston, 1970. Chapter 11, "Counseling Children in Groups."

Periodicals

Hoppock, Robert and Brown, S. H. "Occupational Group Conferences in Grade Two," *Elementary School Guidance and Counseling,* 1969, 4, 150–151.

Meyer, Roy, Rohen, Terrence, and Whiteley, A. Dan, "Group Counseling with Children: A Cognitive-Behavioral Approach," *Journal of Counseling Psychology,* 1969, **16**, 142–149.

Milling, Margaret, "An Elementary School Teacher and Group Guidance? You Bet!" *School Counselor,* 1969, **17**, 26–28.

Nelson, Richard, "A Prekindergarten Orientation Program," *Elementary School Guidance and Counseling,* 1970, **5**, 135–139.

Stormer, G. E., and Kirby, J. H., "Adlerian Group Counseling in the Elementary School: Report of a Program," *Journal of Individual Psychology,* 1969, **25**, 155–163.

Yunker, John, "Essential Organizational Components of Group Counseling in the Primary Grades," *Elementary School Guidance and Counseling,* 1970, **4**, 172–179.

VI. M. GROUP PROCEDURES FOR THE EMPLOYMENT-BOUND

Books

Walker, Robert, " 'Pounce': Learning to Take Responsibility for One's Own Employment Problems," in John Krumboltz and Carl Thoresen (Eds.), *Behavioral Counseling*. New York: Holt, Rinehart and Winston, 1969, 399–414.

Winger, Leland, *A Study of the Otto Self-Concept Improvement Counseling Technique (OSCICT) Applied to Dropouts*. Unpublished doctoral dissertation. University of Utah, 1969. Abstract in *Dissertation Abstracts International*, 1969, **30**, 1883–1884A.

Periodicals

Friedman, Sam, "Role-Playing in a Youth Employment Office," *Group Psychotherapy and Psychodrama*, 1970, **23**, 21–26.

Jones, Mark, "Roleplaying as an Educational and Training Device in a Poverty-Oriented, Multiracial Group," *Group Psychotherapy*, 1969, **22**, 195–201.

Neel, Elsie, "Preparing Students for Employment," *School Counselor*, 1971, **18**, 294–296.

Sullivan, Dorothy, "Group Guidance in an Employment Setting," *Journal of Employment Counseling*, 1970, **7**, 75–80.

Waterland, Jean, "Group Counseling with Disadvantaged Youth in an Employment Setting," *Journal of Employment Counseling*, 1970, **7**, 3–8.

Winder, Alvin, and Nicholai, Savenko, "Group Counseling with Neighborhood Youth Corps Trainees," *Personnel and Guidance Journal*, 1970, **48**, 561–567.

VI. N. GROUP PROCEDURES DIRECTED AT BEHAVIOR PROBLEMS

Periodicals

Hinds, William, and Roehlke, Helen, "A Learning Theory Approach to Group Counseling With Elementary School Children," *Journal of Counseling Psychology*, 1970, **17**, 49–55.

Kelly, Eugene, and Matthews, Doris, "Group Counseling with Discipline-Problem Children at the Elementary School Level," *School Counselor*, 1971, **18**, 273–278.

Mann, Philip, "Modifying the Behavior of Negro Educable Mentally Retarded Boys Through Group Counseling Procedures," *Journal of Negro Education*, 1969, **38**, 135–142.

Shaffer, Marcia, "Group Counseling in a Senior High School," *School Counselor*, 1969, **17**, 22–25.

VI. O. GROUP PROCEDURES WITH MINORITY GROUPS AND CULTURALLY DISADVANTAGED POPULATIONS

Books

Gazda, George (Ed.), *Proceedings of a Symposium on Group Procedures for the Disadvantaged*. Athens, Georgia: University of Georgia, Center for Continuing Education, 1969.

Moates, Hugh, *The Effects of Activity Group Counseling on the Self-Concept, Peer Acceptance and Grade Point Average of Disadvantaged Seventh Grade Negro Boys and Girls.* Unpublished doctoral dissertation. Auburn University, 1969. Abstract in *Dissertation Abstracts International,* 1970, **30**, 3795–A.

Potts, John, *Selected Effects of Required Group Counseling in the Regular Curriculum for Disadvantaged Ninth Grade Students.* Unpublished doctoral dissertation. Arizona State University, 1969. Abstract in *Dissertation Abstracts International,* 1970, **30**, 3736–A.

Richardson, Duane, *Use of Small Group Confrontation for Changing Attitudes Between Ethnic Groups in a Senior High School.* Unpublished doctoral dissertation. Washington State University, 1969. Abstract in *Dissertation Abstracts International,* 1970, **30**, 4233–A.

Periodicals

Adkins, Winthrop, "Life Skills: Structured Counseling for the Disadvantaged," *Personnel and Guidance Journal,* 1970, **49**, 108–116.

Amaro, Jorge Ferreira, and Soeira, Alfredo, "Psychodrama at a Psychiatric Clinic," *Group Psychotherapy,* 1969, **22**, 157–163.

Friedman, Sam, "Role-Playing in a Youth Employment Office," *Group Psychotherapy and Psychodrama,* 1970, **23**, 21–26.

Harrold, Roger, "College Orientation and the Black Student," *Journal of College Student Personnel,* 1970, **11**, 251–255.

Jones, Mark, "Roleplaying as an Educational and Training Device in a Poverty-Oriented, Multiracial Group," *Group Psychotherapy,* 1969, **22**, 195–201.

Klitgaard, Guy, "A Gap is Bridged: Successful Group Counseling of College Potential Mexican-Americans," *Journal of Secondary Education,* 1969, **44**, 55–57.

Mann, Philip, "Modifying the Behavior of Negro Educable Mentally Retarded Boys Through Group Counseling Procedures," *Journal of Negro Education,* 1969, **38**, 135–142.

Milling, Margaret, "An Elementary School Teacher and Group Guidance? You Bet!" *School Counselor,* 1969, **17**, 26–28.

Moulin, E. K., "The Effects of Client-Centered Group Counseling Using Play Media on the Intelligence, Achievement, and Psycholinguistic Abilities of Underachieving Primary School Children," *Elementary School Guidance and Counseling,* 1970, **5**, 85–98.

Nelson, Richard, Smith, Helen, and Nivens, Maryruth, "The Group and Racial Understanding," *Elementary School Guidance and Counseling,* 1970, **4**, 211–214.

Vriend, Thelma, "High Performing Inner-City Adolescents Assist Low-Performing Peers in Counseling Groups," *Personnel and Guidance Journal,* 1969, **47**, 897–904.

Waterland, Jean, "Group Counseling with Disadvantaged Youth in an Employment Setting," *Journal of Employment Counseling,* 1970, **7**, 3–8.

VI. P. GROUP PROCEDURES FOR ADOLESCENTS

Books

Ohlsen, Merle, *Group Counseling*. New York: Holt, Rinehart and Winston, 1970. Chapter 10, "Counseling Adolescents in Groups."

Periodicals

Bullock, Lyndal, "Group Guidance Seminars Designed for Junior High School Pupils," *School Counselor*, 1970, 17, 174–177.

DeLara, Lane, "Listening Is a Challenge: Group Counseling in the School," *Mental Hygiene*, 1969, 53, 600–605.

Moore, John, and Haley, Margaret, "Reflections: An Approach to Group Counseling in the Junior High School," *Elementary School Guidance and Counseling*, 1970, 4, 215–217.

VI. Q. GROUP PROCEDURES WITH EXCEPTIONAL STUDENTS (PHYSICALLY HANDICAPPED, MENTALLY RETARDED, EMOTIONALLY DISTURBED)

Periodicals

Cormany, Robert, "Returning Special Education Students to Regular Classes," *Personnel and Guidance Journal*, 1970, 48, 641–646.

Mann, Philip, "Modifying the Behavior of Negro Educable Mentally Retarded Boys Through Group Counseling Procedures," *Journal of Negro Education*, 1969, 38, 135–142.

Maynard, Peter, Warner, Richard, Jr., and Lazzaro, Joseph, "Group Counseling with Emotionally Disturbed Students in a School Setting," *Journal of Secondary Education*, 1969, 44, 358–365.

VI. R. HUMAN POTENTIAL, ENCOUNTER, SENSITIVITY AND CONFRONTATION GROUPS IN EDUCATION

Books

Koplitz, Eugene, "The Sensitivity Training Movement—Professional Implications for Elementary and Secondary School Counseling and Teaching," in Carlton Beck, *Philosophical Guidelines for Counseling* (2nd ed.). Dubuque, Iowa: Brown, 1971, 42–50.

Periodicals

Hansen, Lorraine, and Wirgan, Otto, "Human Relations Training: A Response to Crisis," *School Counselor*, 1970, 17, 253–259.

Myrick, Robert, "Growth Groups: Implications for Teachers and Counselors," *Elementary School Guidance and Counseling*, 1969, 4, 35–42.

Rueveni, Uri, "Using Sensitivity Training With Junior High School Students," *Children*, 1971, 18, 69–72.

VII. GROUP OUTCOMES, PRODUCTIVITY, EVALUATION

VII. A. CRITERIA AND PROCEDURES

Books

Dimock, Hedley, *How to Analyze and Evaluate Group Growth.* Montreal, Quebec: Sir George Williams University, 1970.

Fullmer, Daniel, *Counseling: Group Theory and System.* Scranton, Pennsylvania: International Textbook, 1971. Chapter 8, "Research in Group Counseling."

Goldstein, Arnold, and Simonson, Norman, "Social Psychological Approaches to Psychotherapy Research," in Allen Bergin and Sol Garfield (Eds.), *Handbook of Psychotherapy and Behavior Change: An Empirical Analysis.* New York: Wiley, 1971, 154–195.

Golembiewski, Robert, and Blumberg, Arthur (Eds.), *Sensitivity Training and the Laboratory Approach.* Itasca, Illinois: Peacock, 1970. Part VI, "How Can T-Group Dynamics Be Studied? Conceiving and Executing Research."

Kemp, C. Gratton, *Foundations of Group Counseling.* New York: McGraw-Hill, 1970. Chapter 16, "Research and Evaluation."

Mahler, Clarence, *Group Counseling in the Schools.* Boston: Houghton Mifflin, 1969. Chapter 9, "The Current Status of Group Counseling Research."

Ohlsen, Merle, *Group Counseling.* New York: Holt, Rinehart and Winston, 1970. Chapter 12, "Appraisal of Group Counseling."

Robinson, John, and Shaver, Phillip, *Measures of Social Psychological Attitudes.* Appendix B to *Measures of Political Attitudes.* Ann Arbor: University of Michigan, Institute for Social Research, 1969.

Periodicals

Papanek, Helene, "Therapeutic and Antitherapeutic Factors in Group Relations," *American Journal of Psychotherapy,* 1969, **23**, 396–404.

VII. B. RESEARCH SUMMARIES AND BIBLIOGRAPHIES

Books

Bednar, Richard, and Lawlis, G. Frank, "Empirical Research in Group Psychotherapy," in Allen Bergin and Sol Garfield (Eds.), *Handbook of Psychotherapy and Behavior Change: An Empirical Analysis.* New York: Wiley, 1971, 812–838.

Gibb, Jack, "The Effects of Human Relations Training," in Allen Bergin and Sol Garfield (Eds.), *Handbook of Psychotherapy and Behavior Change: An Empirical Analysis.* New York: Wiley, 1971, 839–862.

Ohlsen, Merle, *Group Counseling.* New York: Holt, Rinehart and Winston, 1970. Chapter 12, "Appraisal of Group Counseling."

Patterson, G. R., "Behavioral Intervention Procedures in the Classroom and in the Home," in Allen Bergin and Sol Garfield (Eds.), *Handbook of Psychotherapy and Behavior Change: An Empirical Analysis.* New York: Wiley, 1971, 751–775.

Periodicals

Anderson, Alan, "Group Counseling," *Review of Educational Research,* 1969, **39**, 209–226.

Matheny, Kenneth, "The Periodical Literature of Group Work," *Personnel and Guidance Journal,* 1971, **49**, 649–651.

Mermis, William, "Bibliography of Group Literature," *Personnel and Guidance Journal,* 1971, **49**, 652–656.

Mermis, William, "The Small Group: Bibliography of Bibliographies," *Comparative Group Studies,* 1970, **1**, 91–92.

VII. C(1). COUNSELING—ELEMENTARY SCHOOL PUPILS

Books

Caulfield, Thomas, *The Effects of Using Video Taped Social Models in Elementary School Group Counseling with Low Sociometric Status Students.* Unpublished doctoral dissertation. State University of New York at Buffalo, 1969. Abstract in *Dissertation Abstracts International,* 1969, **30**, 1813–1814A.

Niland, Thomas, *A Utilization of Rotter's Social Learning Theory to Lower Minimal Goal Discrepancies of Elementary School Children.* Unpublished doctoral dissertation. State University of New York at Buffalo, 1969. Abstract in *Dissertation Abstracts International,* 1969, **30**, 1826–1827A.

Schmidt, Robert, *Effects of Group Counseling on Reading Achievement and Sociometric Status.* Unpublished doctoral dissertation. Arizona State University, 1969. Abstract in *Dissertation Abstracts International,* 1969, **30**, 1406–A.

Periodicals

Bigelow, Gordon, and Thorne, John, "Reality Versus Client-Centered Model in Group Counseling," *School Counselor,* 1969, **16**, 191–194.

Hansen, James, Niland, Thomas, and Zani, Leonard, "Model Reinforcement in Group Counseling with Elementary School Children," *Personnel and Guidance Journal,* 1969, **47**, 741–744.

Hinds, William, and Roehlke, Helen, "A Learning Theory Approach to Group Counseling with Elementary School Children," *Journal of Counseling Psychology,* 1970, **17**, 49–55.

Kelly, Eugene, and Matthews, Doris, "Group Counseling with Discipline-Problem Children at the Elementary School Level," *School Counselor,* 1971, **18**, 273–278.

Mann, Philip, "Modifying the Behavior of Negro Educable Mentally Retarded Boys Through Group Counseling Procedures," *Journal of Negro Education,* 1969, **38**, 135–142.

Stormer, G. E., and Kirby, J. H., "Adlerian Group Counseling in the Elementary School: Report of a Program," *Journal of Individual Psychology,* 1969, **25**, 155–163.

Tosi, Donald, Swanson, Carl, and McLean, Pat, "Group Counseling with Non-verbalizing Elementary School Children," *Elementary School Guidance and Counseling*, 1970, 4, 260–266.

Warner, Richard, Niland, Thomas, and Maynard, Peter, "Model Reinforcement Group Counseling with Elementary School Children," *Elementary School Guidance and Counseling*, 1971, 5, 248–255.

VII. C(2). COUNSELING—JUNIOR AND SENIOR HIGH SCHOOL STUDENTS

Books

Beach, Alice, "Overcoming Underachievement," in John Krumboltz and Carl Thoresen (Eds.), *Behavioral Counseling*. New York: Holt, Rinehart and Winston, 1969, 241–248.

Berryman, Berle, *The Effects of Group Counseling Upon Visual Perception and Its Relationship to Other Forms of Perception*. Unpublished doctoral dissertation. North Texas State University, 1969. Abstract in *Dissertation Abstracts International*, 1970, 30, 2793–2794A.

Cook, Frances, *The Use of Three Types of Group Procedures with Ninth Grade Underachieving Students and Their Parents*. Unpublished doctoral dissertation. Kent State University, 1970. Abstract in *Dissertation Abstracts International*, 1970, 31, 3869–A.

Delworth, Ursula, *A Comparison of Professional Counselors and Counselor Support Personnel in Group Counseling with Junior High School Students*. Unpublished doctoral dissertation. University of Oregon, 1969. Abstract in *Dissertation Abstracts International*, 1970, 30, 5230–A.

Edwards, William, *The Use of Focused Audio Feedback in Group Counseling with Adolescent Boys*. Unpublished doctoral dissertation. University of Georgia, 1969. Abstract in *Dissertation Abstracts International*, 1970, 30, 5232–A.

Gourley, Martha, *The Effects of Individual Counseling, Group Guidance, and Verbal Reinforcement on the Academic Progress of Underachievers*. Unpublished doctoral dissertation. University of North Carolina, 1970. Abstract in *Dissertation Abstracts International*, 1970, 31, 3873–A.

Hamilton, Jack, *Encouraging Career Decision-Making with Group Modeling and Structured Group Counseling*. Unpublished doctoral dissertation. Stanford University, 1969. Abstract in *Dissertation Abstracts International*, 1970, 30, 2799–A.

Hess, Tyler, *A Comparison of Group Counseling with Individual Counseling in the Modification of Self-Adjustment and Social Adjustment of Fifteen Year Old Males Identified as Potential Dropouts*. Unpublished doctoral dissertation. University of Virginia, 1969. Abstract in *Dissertation Abstracts International*, 1970, 31, 998–A.

Hum, Sterling, *An Investigation of the Use of Focused Video Tape Feedback in High School Group Counseling*. Unpublished doctoral dissertation. University of Southern California, 1969. Abstract in *Dissertation Abstracts,* 1969, **29**, 4284–A.

Kauffman, John, *The Effects of Group Composition on an Experimental Group Counseling Program.* Unpublished doctoral dissertation. University of Iowa, 1970. Abstract in *Dissertation Abstracts International,* 1970, **31**, 2685–A.

MacDougall, David, *The Effects of Group Counseling and Improved Student-Teacher Communications on the Anxiety Level of Students Entering Junior High School.* Unpublished doctoral dissertation. University of Oregon, 1969. Abstract in *Dissertation Abstracts International,* 1970, **30**, 5241–A.

Perkins, John, *Group Counseling with Bright Underachievers and Their Mothers.* Unpublished doctoral dissertation. University of Connecticut, 1969. Abstract in *Dissertation Abstracts International,* 1970, **30**, 2809–A.

Potts, John, *Selected Effects of Required Group Counseling in the Regular Curriculum for Disadvantaged Ninth Grade Students.* Unpublished doctoral dissertation. Arizona State University, 1969. Abstract in *Dissertation Abstracts International,* 1970, **30**, 3736–A.

Richardson, Duane, *Use of Small Group Confrontation for Changing Attitudes Between Ethnic Groups in a Senior High School.* Unpublished doctoral dissertation. Washington State University, 1969. Abstract in *Dissertation Abstracts International,* 1970, **30**, 4233–A.

Sanchez, Marion, *The Effects of Client-Centered Group Counseling on Self-Concept and Certain Attitudes of Seventh and Eighth Grade Students.* Unpublished doctoral dissertation. United States International University, 1969. Abstract in *Dissertation Abstracts International,* 1970, **30**, 3283–A.

Schmidt, Robert, *Effects of Group Counseling on Reading Achievement and Sociometric Status.* Unpublished doctoral dissertation. Arizona State University, 1969. Abstract in *Dissertation Abstracts International,* 1969, **30**, 1406–A.

Stewart, Norman, "Exploring and Processing Information About Educational and Vocational Opportunities in Groups," in John Krumboltz and Carl Thoresen (Eds.), *Behavioral Counseling.* New York: Holt, Rinehart and Winston, 1969, 213–234.

Stewart, Ronald, *The Effects of Group Counseling on Acceptance of Self, Acceptance of Others, Grade Point Averages, and Teacher Rated Behavior of Failing Tenth Grade Students.* Unpublished doctoral dissertation. University of Tulsa, 1969. Abstract in *Dissertation Abstracts International,* 1970, **30**, 4236–A.

Tang, Kendel, *Inducing Achievement Behavior Through a Planned Group Counseling Program.* Unpublished doctoral dissertation. University of Hawaii, 1970. Abstract in *Dissertation Abstracts International,* 1970, **31**, 3888–A.

Taylor, Theodore, *Effects of Group Counseling on Self-Concept and Academic Achievement of Selected High School Sophomore Health Classes.* Unpublished doctoral dissertation. Oregon State University, 1970. Abstract in *Dissertation Abstracts International,* 1970, **31**, 1582–A.

Warner, Richard, *An Investigation of the Effectiveness of Verbal Reinforcement and Model Reinforcement Counseling on Alienated High School Students.* Unpublished doctoral dissertation. State University of New York at Buffalo, 1969. Abstract in *Dissertation Abstracts International,* 1969, **30**, 1831–1832A.

Zani, Leonard, *Intensive versus Protracted Counselor Directed Group Counseling with Underachieving Secondary School Students.* Unpublished doctoral dissertation. State University of New York at Buffalo, 1969. Abstract in *Dissertation Abstracts International,* 1969, **30**, 1834–1835A.

Periodicals

Cormany, Robert, "Returning Special Education Students to Regular Classes," *Personnel and Guidance Journal,* 1970, **48**, 641–646.

Creange, Norman, "Group Counseling for Underachieving Ninth Graders," *School Counselor,* 1971, **18**, 279–285.

Finney, Ben, and Van Dalsem, Elizabeth, "Group Counseling for Gifted Underachieving High School Students," *Journal of Counseling Psychology,* 1969, **16**, 87–94.

Klitgaard, Guy, "A Gap is Bridged: Successful Group Counseling of College Potential Mexican-Americans," *Journal of Secondary Education,* 1969, **44**, 55–57.

Laxer, Robert, Quarter, Jack, Kooman, Ann, and Walker, Keith, "Systematic Desensitization and Relaxation of High Test Anxious Secondary School Students," *Journal of Counseling Psychology,* 1969, **16**, 446–451.

Light, Louise, and Alexakos, C. E., "Effect of Individual and Group Counseling on Study Habits," *Journal of Educational Research,* 1970, **63**, 450–454.

Mann, Philip, "Modifying the Behavior of Negro Educable Mentally Retarded Boys Through Group Counseling Procedures," *Journal of Negro Education,* 1969, **38**, 135–142.

Maynard, Peter, Warner, Richard, and Lazzaro, Joseph, "Group Counseling with Emotionally Disturbed Students in a School Setting," *Journal of Secondary Education,* 1969, **44**, 358–365.

McWhirter, J. Jeffries, "Group Counseling with Transfer Students," *School Counselor,* 1969, **16**, 300–302.

Meyer, James, and Strowig, Wray, "Behavioral Reinforcement Counseling with Rural High School Youth," *Journal of Counseling Psychology,* 1970, **17**, 127–132.

Moore, Lorraine, "A Developmental Approach to Group Guidance With Seventh Graders," *School Counselor,* 1969, **16**, 272–275.

Prediger, Dale, and Baumann, Reemt, "Developmental Group Counseling: An Outcome Study," *Journal of Counseling Psychology,* 1970, **17**, 527–533.

Shaffer, Marcia, "Group Counseling in a Senior High School," *School Counselor,* 1969, **17**, 22–25.

Vriend, Thelma, "High Performing Inner-City Adolescents Assist Low-Performing Peers in Counseling Groups," *Personnel and Guidance Journal,* 1969, **47**, 897–904.

Warner, Richard, and Hansen, James, "Verbal Reinforcement and Model Reinforcement Group Counseling with Alienated Students," *Journal of Counseling Psychology*, 1970, **17**, 168–172.

VII. C(3). COUNSELING–COLLEGE STUDENTS

Books

Casstevens, Marilyn, *Effects of Modeling Procedures in Group Counseling in the Modification of Disruptive School Behavior with Eighth Grade Students*. Unpublished doctoral dissertation. Arizona State University, 1969. Abstract in *Dissertation Abstracts International*, 1969, **30**, 2325–A.

Goodson, William, *A Study to Determine the Value of Vocational College Orientation Classes by a Comparison of Various Approaches*. Unpublished doctoral dissertation. Brigham Young University, 1969. Abstract in *Dissertation Abstracts International*, 1969, **30**, 1820–A.

Harper, John, *The Relative Effect of Group Counseling versus Individual Counseling as Indicated by Change in Grade-Point Average and Client Insight*. Unpublished doctoral dissertation. Auburn University, 1969. Abstract in *Dissertation Abstracts International*, 1969, **30**, 1821–1822A.

Jones, G. Brian, "Improving Study Behaviors," in John Krumboltz and Carl Thoresen (Eds.), *Behavioral Counseling*. New York: Holt, Rinehart and Winston, 1969, 486–498.

Lundquist, Gerald, *Utilization of Simulation and Group Counseling in the Training of Prospective Elementary School Teachers*. Unpublished doctoral dissertation. Arizona State University, 1969. Abstract in *Dissertation Abstracts International*, 1969, **30**, 2338–A.

Smith, James, "Encouraging Constructive Use of Time," in John Krumboltz and Carl Thoresen (Eds.), *Behavioral Counseling*. New York: Holt, Rinehart and Winston, 1969, 234–241.

Weinstein, Francine, "Reducing Test Anxiety," in John Krumboltz and Carl Thoresen (Eds.), *Behavioral Counseling*. New York: Holt, Rinehart and Winston, 1969, 471–485.

Periodicals

Brown, Robert, "Effects of Structured and Unstructured Group Counseling with High- and Low-Anxious College Underachievers," *Journal of Counseling Psychology*, 1969, **16**, 209–214.

Chestnut, William, and Gilbreath, Stuart, "Differential Group Counseling with Male College Underachievers: A Three-Year Followup," *Journal of Counseling Psychology*, 1969, **16**, 365–367.

Giffin, Kim, and Bradley, Kendall, "An Exploratory Study of Group Counseling for Speech Anxiety," *Journal of Clinical Psychology*, 1969, **25**, 98–101.

Hedquist, Francis, and Weinhold, Barry, "Behavioral Group Counseling with Socially Anxious and Unassertive College Students," *Journal of Counseling Psychology*, 1970, **17**, 237–242.

Jones, G. Brian, Trimble, Marilynne, and Altman, Harold, "Improving College Students' Performance Through Group Counseling," *Journal of College Student Personnel,* 1970, **11**, 373–382.

Lewinsohn, Peter, Weinstein, Malcolm, and Alper, Ted, "A Behavioral Approach to the Group Treatment of Depressed Persons: A Methodological Contribution," *Journal of Clinical Psychology,* 1970, **26**, 525–532.

Sprague, Douglas, and Strong, Donald, "Vocational Choice Group Counseling," *Journal of College Student Personnel,* 1970, **11**, 35–36 and 45.

Welter, Paul, and Hudson, Wellborn, "The Assessment of Affective Learning in Counseling Groups Utilizing the Taxonomy of Educational Objectives: Affective Domain," *SPATE Journal,* 1970, **8**, 37–51.

VII. C(4). COUNSELING: OTHER SETTINGS AND CLIENTS

Books

Cerra, Patrick, *The Effects of T-Group Training and Group Video Recall Procedures on Affective Sensitivity, Openmindedness and Self-Perception Change in Counselors.* Unpublished doctoral dissertation. Indiana University, 1969. Abstract in *Dissertation Abstracts International,* 1969, **30**, 1814–1815A.

Davis, Joe, *The Effect of Group Counseling on Teacher Affectiveness.* Unpublished doctoral dissertation. University of South Dakota, 1969. Abstract in *Dissertation Abstracts International,* 1969, **30**, 2328–2329A.

Henderson, Ann, *Small Group Treatment Effects on Behaviors and Perceptions of Secondary School Counselors.* Unpublished doctoral dissertation. Arizona State University, 1969. Abstract in *Dissertation Abstracts International,* 1969, **30**, 2333–A.

Rye, Donald, *A Comparative Study of Three Small Group Treatments and Their Effects on Accurate Communication Between Counselor Trainees and Their Clients.* Unpublished doctoral dissertation. Indiana University, 1969. Abstract in *Dissertation Abstracts International,* 1969, **30**, 554–A.

Sarason, Irwin, and Ganzer, Victor, "Developing Appropriate Social Behaviors of Juvenile Delinquents," in John Krumboltz and Carl Thoresen (Eds.), *Behavioral Counseling.* New York: Holt, Rinehart and Winston, 1969, 178–193.

Periodicals

Apostal, Robert, and Muro, James, "Effects of Group Counseling on Self-Reports and on Self-Recognition Abilities of Counselors in Training," *Counselor Education and Supervision,* 1970, **10**, 56–63.

Betz, Robert, "Effects of Group Counseling as an Adjunctive Practicum Experience," *Journal of Counseling Psychology,* 1969, **16**, 528–533.

Blank, Leonard, Wilker, Paulina, and Grundfest, Sandra, "Intense Encounters in Human Relations Training," *Personnel and Guidance Journal,* 1969, **48**, 56–57.

Cadden, James, Flach, Frederic, Blakeslee, Sara, and Charlton, Randolph,

"Growth in Medical Students Through Group Process," *American Journal of Psychiatry*, 1969, **126**, 862–868.

DeRoo, William, and Binner, William, "Group Vocational Counseling in the Rehabilitation of Emotionally Disturbed Adolescents," *Rehabilitation Counseling Bulletin*, 1969, **13**, 280–287.

Fraleigh, Patrick, and Buchheimer, Arnold, "The Use of Peer Groups in Practicum Supervision," *Counselor Education and Supervision*, 1969, **8**, 284–288.

Grand, Sheldon, and Stockin, Bruce, "The Effects of Group Therapy on Rehabilitation Counselor Trainee's Empathy," *Rehabilitation Counseling Bulletin*, 1970, **14**, 36–41.

Hoffnung, Robert, and Mills, Robert, "Situational Group Counseling with Disadvantaged Youth," *Personnel and Guidance Journal*, 1970, **48**, 458–464.

Hurst, James, and Fenner, Robert, "Extended-session Group as a Predictive Technique for Counselor Training," *Journal of Counseling Psychology*, 1969, **16**, 358–360.

Jones, B. A., and Karraker, R., "The Elementary Counselor and Behavior Modification," *Elementary School Guidance and Counseling*, 1969, 4, 28–34.

Kelley, Jan, "Reinforcement in Microcounseling," *Journal of Counseling Psychology*, 1971, **18**, 268–272.

McKinnon, Dan, "Group Counseling with Student Counselors," *Counselor Education and Supervision*, 1969, **8**, 195–200.

Seligman, Milton, and Sterne, David, "Verbal Behavior in Therapist-Led, Leaderless, and Alternating Group Psychotherapy Sessions," *Journal of Counseling Psychology*, 1969, **16**, 325–328.

Truax, Charles, Wargo, Donald, and Volksdorf, Norman, "Antecedents to Outcome in Group Counseling with Institutionalized Juvenile Delinquents: Effects of Therapeutic Conditions, Patient Self-Exploration, Alternate Sessions and Vicarious Therapy Pretraining," *Journal of Abnormal Psychology*, 1970, **76**, 235–242.

Wirt, Michael, Betz, Robert, and Engle, Kenneth, "The Effects of Group Counseling on the Self Concepts of Counselor Candidates," *Counselor Education and Supervision*, 1969, **8**, 189–194.

Woody, Robert, "Self-Understanding Seminars: The Effects of Group Psychotherapy in Counselor Training," *Counselor Education and Supervision*, 1971, **10**, 112–119.

VII. D. ORIENTATION

Books

Bowlsbey, Leonard, *An Evaluation of the Effectiveness of Two Approaches to Freshman Orientation.* Unpublished doctoral dissertation. University of Iowa, 1969. Abstract in *Dissertation Abstracts International*, 1970, **30**, 546–547A.

Kopecek, Robert, "Freshmen Orientation Programs: A Comparison," *Journal of College Student Personnel*, 1971, **12**, 54–57.

Myrick, Robert, Anthony, John, and Haldin, William, "The Student Handbook as an Aid in Orientation: A Comparative Study," *School Counselor,* 1970, **18**, 61–65.

VII. E. TESTING INFORMATION

Books

Gibian, Edward, *The Effects of Two Methods of Interpretation of Objective Test Data Upon Self-Appraisal of Scholastic Ability.* Unpublished doctoral dissertation. New York University, 1969. Abstract in *Dissertation Abstracts International,* 1969, **30**, 2331–2332A.

Holthouse, Rita, *A Comparison of the Effects of Four Methods of Test Interpretation on the Self-Understanding of Secondary School Students.* Unpublished doctoral dissertation. Ohio University, 1970. Abstract in *Dissertation Abstracts International,* 1970, **31**, 2684–A.

VII. F. GROUP GUIDANCE; GUIDANCE COURSES

Books

Foreman, Florence, *Study of Self-Reinforcement and Study Skills Programs with Bright College Underachievers.* Unpublished doctoral dissertation. University of Nebraska, 1969. Abstract in *Dissertation Abstracts International,* 1969, **30**, 1430–A.

Marshall, Marvin, *The Tenth Grade Guidance Course in the Los Angeles City High Schools.* Unpublished doctoral dissertation. University of Southern California, 1969. Abstract in *Dissertation Abstracts,* 1969, **29**, 4288–A.

McCormick, Roger, *The Influences of Dissimilar Group Guidance Activities Upon the Vocational Interests of Eighth Grade Pupils.* Unpublished doctoral dissertation. Ohio State University, 1969. Abstract in *Dissertation Abstracts International,* 1970, **30**, 5243–A.

Periodicals

Anandam, K., Davis, M., and Poppen, W. A., "Feelings . . . To Fear or to Free?" *Elementary School Guidance and Counseling,* 1971, **5**, 181–189.

Bedrosian, Oscar, Sara, Nathir, and Pearlman, Judith, "A Pilot Study to Determine the Effectiveness of Guidance Classes in Developing Self Understanding in Elementary School Children," *Elementary School Guidance and Counseling,* 1970, **5**, 124–134.

Drumheller, Sidney, "Using Group Work in Developing Functional Concepts in an Individualized Instruction Setting," *Journal of Secondary Education,* 1970, **45**, 230–236.

Giffin, Kim, and Bradley, Kendall, "An Exploratory Study of Group Counseling for Speech Anxiety," *Journal of Clinical Psychology,* 1969, **25**, 98–101.

Hoppock, R., and Brown, S. H., "Occupational Group Conferences in Grade Two," *Elementary School Guidance and Counseling,* 1969, **4**, 150–151.

Kelly, Gary, "Group Guidance on Sex Education," *Personnel and Guidance Journal*, 1971, **49**, 809–814.

Neel, Elsie, "Preparing Students for Employment," *School Counselor*, 1971, **18**, 294–296.

Patzan, Christine, "An Experiment in Group Guidance with the Whole Class," *Elementary School Guidance and Counseling*, 1971, **5**, 205–214.

Stetter, Richard, "A Group Guidance Technique for the Classroom Teacher," *School Counselor*, 1969, **16**, 179–184.

Swisher, John, and Crawford, James, "An Evaluation of a Short-Term Drug Education Program," *School Counselor*, 1971, **18**, 265–272.

VII. G. PLAY THERAPY

Periodicals

Moulin, Eugene, "The Effects of Client-Centered Group Counseling Using Play Media on the Intelligence, Achievement, and Psycholinguistic Abilities of Underachieving Primary School Children," *Elementary School Guidance and Counseling*, 1970, **5**, 85–98.

VIII. COMPARISONS OF TREATMENTS

VIII. A. GROUP WITH OTHER THAN GROUP TREATMENTS

Books

Gourley, Martha, *The Effects of Individual Counseling, Group Guidance, and Verbal Reinforcement on the Academic Progress of Underachievers.* Unpublished doctoral dissertation. University of North Carolina, 1970. Abstract in *Dissertation Abstracts International*, 1970, **31**, 3873–A.

Harper, John, *The Relative Effect of Group Counseling versus Individual Counseling as Indicated by Change in Grade-Point Average and Client Insight.* Unpublished doctoral dissertation. Auburn University, 1969. Abstract in *Dissertation Abstracts International*, 1969, **30**, 1821–1822A.

Hess, Tyler, *A Comparison of Group Counseling with Individual Counseling in the Modification of Self-Adjustment and Social Adjustment of Fifteen Year Old Males Identified as Potential Dropouts.* Unpublished doctoral dissertation. University of Virginia, 1969. Abstract in *Dissertation Abstracts International*, 1970, **31**, 998–A.

Potts, John, *Selected Effects of Required Group Counseling in the Regular Curriculum for Disadvantaged Ninth Grade Students.* Unpublished doctoral dissertation. Arizona State University, 1969. Abstract in *Dissertation Abstracts International*, 1970, **30**, 3736–A.

Rye, Donald, *A Comparative Study of Three Small Group Treatments and Their Effects on Accurate Communication Between Counselor Trainees and Their Clients.* Unpublished doctoral dissertation. Indiana University, 1969. Abstract in *Dissertation Abstracts International*, 1969, **30**, 554–A.

Schmidt, Robert, *Effects of Group Counseling on Reading Achievement and Sociometric Status.* Unpublished doctoral dissertation. Arizona State University, 1969. Abstract in *Dissertation Abstracts International,* 1969, **30,** 1406–A.

Periodicals

Kopecek, Robert, "Freshmen Orientation Programs: A Comparison," *Journal of College Student Personnel,* 1971, **12,** 54–57.

Light, Louise, and Alexakos, C. E., "Effect of Individual and Group Counseling on Study Habits," *Journal of Educational Research,* 1970, **63,** 450–454.

Mann, Philip, "Modifying the Behavior of Negro Educable Mentally Retarded Boys Through Group Counseling Procedures," *Journal of Negro Education,* 1969, **38,** 135–142.

Meyer, James, and Strowig, Wray, "Behavioral Reinforcement Counseling with Rural High School Youth," *Journal of Counseling Psychology,* 1970, **17,** 127–132.

Rotter, George, and Portugal, Stephen, "Group and Individual Effects in Problem Solving," *Journal of Applied Psychology,* 1969, **53,** 338–341.

VIII. B. BETWEEN DIFFERENT KINDS OF GROUP EXPERIENCE

Books

Bowlsbey, Leonard, *An Evaluation of the Effectiveness of Two Approaches to Freshman Orientation.* Unpublished doctoral dissertation. University of Iowa, 1969. Abstract in *Dissertation Abstracts International,* 1970, **30,** 546–547A.

Casstevens, Marilyn, *Effects of Modeling Procedures in Group Counseling in the Modification of Disruptive School Behavior with Eighth Grade Students.* Unpublished doctoral dissertation. Arizona State University, 1969. Abstract in *Dissertation Abstracts International,* 1969, **30,** 2325–A.

Caulfield, Thomas, *The Effects of Using Video Taped Social Models in Elementary School Group Counseling with Low Sociometric Status Students.* Unpublished doctoral dissertation. State University of New York at Buffalo, 1969. Abstract in *Dissertation Abstracts International,* 1969, **30,** 1813–1814A.

Cerra, Patrick, *The Effects of T-Group Training and Group Video Recall Procedures on Affective Sensitivity, Openmindedness and Self-Perception Change in Counselors.* Unpublished doctoral dissertation. Indiana University, 1969. Abstract in *Dissertation Abstracts International,* 1969, **30,** 1814–1815A.

Cook, Frances, *The Use of Three Types of Group Procedures with Ninth Grade Underachieving Students and Their Parents.* Unpublished doctoral dissertation. Kent State University, 1970. Abstract in *Dissertation Abstracts International,* 1970, **31,** 3869–A.

Delworth, Ursula, *A Comparison of Professional Counselors and Counselor Support Personnel in Group Counseling with Junior High School Students.* Unpublished doctoral dissertation. University of Oregon, 1969. Abstract in *Dissertation Abstracts International,* 1970, **30,** 5230–A.

Edwards, William, *The Use of Focused Audio Feedback in Group Counseling with Adolescent Boys.* Unpublished doctoral dissertation. University of Georgia, 1969. Abstract in *Dissertation Abstracts International,* 1970, **30,** 5232–A.

Foreman, Florence, *Study of Self-Reinforcement and Study Skills Programs with Bright College Underachievers.* Unpublished doctoral dissertation. University of Nebraska, 1969. Abstract in *Dissertation Abstracts International,* 1969, **30,** 1430–A.

Gibian, Edward, *The Effects of Two Methods of Interpretation of Objective Test Data Upon Self-Appraisal of Scholastic Ability.* Unpublished doctoral dissertation. New York University, 1969. Abstract in *Dissertation Abstracts International,* 1969, **30,** 2331–2332A.

Goodson, William, *A Study to Determine the Value of Vocational College Orientation Classes by a Comparison of Various Approaches.* Unpublished doctoral dissertation. Brigham Young University, 1969. Abstract in *Dissertation Abstracts International,* 1969, **30,** 1820–A.

Gourley, Martha, *The Effects of Individual Counseling, Group Guidance, and Verbal Reinforcement on the Academic Progress of Underachievers.* Unpublished doctoral dissertation. University of North Carolina, 1970. Abstract in *Dissertation Abstracts International,* 1970, **31,** 3873–A.

Hamilton, Jack, *Encouraging Career Decision-Making with Group Modeling and Structured Group Counseling.* Unpublished doctoral dissertation. Stanford University, 1969. Abstract in *Dissertation Abstracts International,* 1970, **30,** 2799–A.

Hess, Tyler, *A Comparison of Group Counseling with Individual Counseling in the Modification of Self-Adjustment and Social Adjustment of Fifteen Year Old Males Identified as Potential Dropouts.* Unpublished doctoral dissertation. University of Virginia, 1969. Abstract in *Dissertation Abstracts International,* 1970, **31,** 998–A.

Holthouse, Rita, *A Comparison of the Effects of Four Methods of Test Interpretation on the Self-Understanding of Secondary School Students.* Unpublished doctoral dissertation. Ohio University, 1970. Abstract in *Dissertation Abstracts International,* 1970, **31,** 2684–A.

McCormick, Roger, *The Influences of Dissimilar Group Guidance Activities Upon the Vocational Interests of Eighth Grade Pupils.* Unpublished doctoral dissertation. Ohio State University, 1969. Abstract in *Dissertation Abstracts International,* 1970, **30,** 5243–A.

Niland, Thomas, *A Utilization of Rotter's Social Learning Theory to Lower Minimal Goal Discrepancies of Elementary School Children.* Unpublished doctoral dissertation. State University of New York at Buffalo, 1969. Abstract in *Dissertation Abstracts International,* 1969, **30,** 1826–1827A.

Perkins, John, *Group Counseling with Bright Underachievers and Their Mothers.* Unpublished doctoral dissertation. University of Connecticut, 1969. Abstract in *Dissertation Abstracts International,* 1970, **30,** 2809–A.

Rye, Donald, *A Comparative Study of Three Small Group Treatments and Their Effects on Accurate Communication Between Counselor Trainees and Their*

Clients. Unpublished doctoral dissertation. Indiana University, 1969. Abstract in *Dissertation Abstracts International,* 1969, **30**, 554–A.

Taylor, Theodore, *Effects of Group Counseling on Self-Concept and Academic Achievement of Selected High School Sophomore Health Classes.* Unpublished doctoral dissertation. Oregon State University, 1970. Abstract in *Dissertation Abstracts International,* 1970, **31**, 1582–A.

Warner, Richard, *An Investigation of the Effectiveness of Verbal Reinforcement and Model Reinforcement Counseling on Alienated High School Students.* Unpublished doctoral dissertation. State University of New York at Buffalo, 1969. Abstract in *Dissertation Abstracts International,* 1969, **30**, 1831–1832A.

Zani, Leonard, *Intensive versus Protracted Counselor Directed Group Counseling with Underachieving Secondary School Students.* Unpublished doctoral dissertation. State University of New York at Buffalo, 1969. Abstract in *Dissertation Abstracts International,* 1969, **30**, 1834–1835A.

Periodicals

Anandam, K., Davis, M. and Poppen, W. A., "Feelings . . . To Fear or to Free?" *Elementary School Guidance and Counseling,* 1971, **5**, 181–189.

Bedrosian, Oscar, Sara, Nathir, and Pearlman, Judith, "A Pilot Study to Determine the Effectiveness of Guidance Classes in Developing Self Understanding in Elementary School Children," *Elementary School Guidance and Counseling,* 1970, **5**, 124–134.

Betz, Robert, "Effects of Group Counseling as an Adjunctive Practicum Experience," *Journal of Counseling Psychology,* 1969, **16**, 528–533.

Bigelow, Gordon, and Thorne, John, "Reality Versus Client-Centered Model in Group Counseling," *School Counselor,* 1969, **16**, 191–194.

Brown, Robert, "Effects of Structured and Unstructured Group Counseling With High- and Low-Anxious College Underachievers," *Journal of Counseling Psychology,* 1969, **16**, 209–214.

Chestnut, William, and Gilbreath, Stuart, "Differential Group Counseling with Male College Underachievers: A Three-Year Followup," *Journal of Counseling Psychology,* 1969, **16**, 365–367.

Grant, W. Harold, and Eigenbrod, Frederick, "Behavioral Changes Influenced by Structured Peer Group Activities," *Journal of College Student Personnel,* 1970, **11**, 291–295.

Hansen, James, Niland, Thomas, and Zani, Leonard, "Model Reinforcement in Group Counseling with Elementary School Children," *Personnel and Guidance Journal,* 1969, **47**, 741–744.

Hedquist, Francis, and Weinhold, Barry, "Behavioral Group Counseling with Socially Anxious and Unassertive College Students," *Journal of Counseling Psychology,* 1970, **17**, 237–242.

Hoffnung, Robert, and Mills, Robert, "Situational Group Counseling with Disadvantaged Youth," *Personnel and Guidance Journal,* 1970, **48**, 458–464.

Jones, G. Brian, Trimble, Marilynne, and Altman, Harold, "Improving College Students' Performance Through Group Counseling," *Journal of College Student Personnel,* 1970, **11**, 373–382.

Kelley, Jan, "Reinforcement in Microcounseling," *Journal of Counseling Psychology,* 1971, **18**, 268–272.

Kopecek, Robert, "Freshmen Orientation Programs: A Comparison," *Journal of College Student Personnel,* 1971, **12**, 54–57.

Laxer, Robert, Quarter, Jack, Kooman, Ann, and Walker, Keith, "Systematic Desensitization and Relaxation of High Test Anxious Secondary School Students," *Journal of Counseling Psychology,* 1969, **16**, 446–451.

Maynard, Peter, Warner, Richard, Jr., and Lazzaro, Joseph, "Group Counseling with Emotionally Disturbed Students in a School Setting," *Journal of Secondary Education,* 1969, **44**, 358–365.

Meyer, James, and Strowig, Wray, "Behavioral Reinforcement Counseling with Rural High School Youth," *Journal of Counseling Psychology,* 1970, **17**, 127–132.

Perkins, John, and Wicas, Edward, "Group Counseling of Bright Underachievers and Their Mothers," *Journal of Counseling Psychology,* 1971, **18**, 273–278.

Rand, Leonard, and Carew, Donald, "Comparison of T-Group Didactic Approaches to Training Undergraduate Resident Assistants," *Journal of College Student Personnel,* 1970, **11**, 432–438.

Seligman, Milton, and Sterne, David, "Verbal Behavior in Therapist-Led, Leaderless, and Alternating Group Psychotherapy Sessions," *Journal of Counseling Psychology,* 1969, **16**, 325–328.

Swisher, John, and Crawford, James, "An Evaluation of a Short-Term Drug Education Program," *School Counselor,* 1971, **18**, 265–272.

Warner, Richard, and Hansen, James, "Verbal Reinforcement and Model Reinforcement Group Counseling with Alienated Students," *Journal of Counseling Psychology,* 1970, **17**, 168–172.

Warner, Richard, Niland, Thomas, and Maynard, Peter, "Model Reinforcement Group Counseling with Elementary School Children," *Elementary School Guidance and Counseling,* 1971, **5**, 248–255.

IX. NEW DIRECTIONS

IX. A. MILIEU APPROACHES AND WORK WITH SIGNIFICANT OTHERS

Books

Bernard, Harold, and Fullmer, Daniel, *Principles of Guidance.* Scranton, Pennsylvania: International Textbook, 1969. Chapter 15, "Family Group Consultation," 307–325.

Cook, Frances, *The Use of Three Types of Group Procedures with Ninth Grade Underachieving Students and Their Parents.* Unpublished doctoral dissertation. Kent State University, 1970. Abstract in *Dissertation Abstracts International,* 1970, **31**, 3869–A.

Fullmer, Daniel, *Counseling: Group Theory and System.* Scranton: Pennsylvania: International Textbook, 1971. Chapter 13, "Family Group Consultation"; Chapter 14, "Cultural Exchange in Family Consultation: A Case Study."

Fullmer, Daniel, "Family Group Consultation," in George Gazda (Ed.), *Theories and Methods of Group Counseling in the Schools.* Springfield, Illinois: Thomas, 1969. Chapter 7.

Fullmer, Daniel, and Bernard, Harold, *Family Consultation.* Boston: Houghton Mifflin, 1969.

Kavanaugh, Michelle, *An Investigation Into the Relative Effectiveness of the Teacher-Counselor Team Method versus Counseling in Facilitating Classroom Behavior Change.* Unpublished doctoral dissertation. University of Miami, 1969. Abstract in *Dissertation Abstracts International,* 1969, **30,** 1868–1869A.

MacDougall, David, *The Effects of Group Counseling and Improved Student-Teacher Communications on the Anxiety Level of Students Entering Junior High School.* Unpublished doctoral dissertation. University of Oregon, 1969. Abstract in *Dissertation Abstracts International,* 1970, **30,** 5241–A.

Moates, Hugh, *The Effects of Activity Group Counseling on the Self-Concept, Peer-Acceptance and Grade Point Average of Disadvantaged Seventh Grade Negro Boys and Girls.* Unpublished doctoral dissertation. Auburn University, 1969. Abstract in *Dissertation Abstracts International,* 1970, **30,** 3795–A.

Perkins, John, *Group Counseling with Bright Underachievers and Their Mothers.* Unpublished doctoral dissertation. University of Connecticut, 1969. Abstract in *Dissertation Abstracts International,* 1970, **30,** 2809–A.

Schmidt, Wesley, Rovin, Ronald, Stanowski, Richard, and Widlowski, Charles, "A Marathon Counseling Session for Parents of Underachieving High School Students," in Robert Berg and James Johnson (Eds.), *Group Counseling: A Source Book of Theory and Practice.* Fort Worth: American Continental Publishing, 1971, 251–257.

Sloan, Nancy, *Family Counseling.* Ann Arbor, Michigan: ERIC Clearinghouse on Counseling and Personnel Services. Series 3: Human Resources in the Guidance Programs, 1970.

Zani, Leonard, *Intensive versus Protracted Counselor Directed Group Counseling with Underachieving Secondary School Students.* Unpublished doctoral dissertation. State University of New York at Buffalo, 1969. Abstract in *Dissertation Abstracts International,* 1969, **30,** 1834–1835A.

Periodicals

Bartoletti, Mario, "Conjoint Family Therapy with Clinic Team in a Shopping Plaza," *Group Psychotherapy,* 1969, **22,** 203–211.

Carkhuff, Robert, and Banks, George, "Training as a Preferred Mode of Facilitating Relations Between Races and Generations," *Journal of Counseling Psychology,* 1970, **17,** 413–418.

Carkhuff, Robert, and Bierman, Robert, "Training as a Preferred Mode of Treatment of Parents of Emotionally Disturbed Children," *Journal of Counseling Psychology,* 1970, **17,** 157–161.

Carlson, Jon, "Case Analysis: Parent Group Consultation," *Elementary School Guidance and Counseling,* 1969, 4, 136–141.

Danforth, Joyce, Miller, Diane, Day, Anne, and Steiner, George, "Group

Services for Unmarried Mothers: An Interdisciplinary Approach," *Children*, 1971, **18**, 59–64.

Pearson, John, "A Differential Use of Group Homes for Delinquent Boys," *Children*, 1970, **17**, 143–148.

Perkins, John, and Wicas, Edward, "Group Counseling of Bright Underachievers and Their Mothers," *Journal of Counseling Psychology*, 1971, **18**, 273–278.

Sauber, S. Richard, "Multiple-family Group Counseling," *Personnel and Guidance Journal*, 1971, **49**, 459–465.

Shaw, Merville, "The Feasibility of Parent Group Counseling in Elementary Schools," *Elementary School Guidance and Counseling*, 1969, 4, 43–53.

Watson, Drage, "Group Work With Principals: Implications for Elementary Counselors," *Elementary School Guidance and Counseling*, 1969, **3**, 234–241.

IX. B. HUMAN POTENTIAL, ENCOUNTER, SENSITIVITY, T-GROUP AND CONFRONTATION EXPERIENCES IN EDUCATION: PROCESS AND OUTCOME STUDIES

Books

Cecere, Gerald, *Change in Certain Personality Variables of Counselor Education Candidates as a Function of T Group*. Unpublished doctoral dissertation. Rutgers—The State University, 1969. Abstract in *Dissertation Abstracts International*, 1969, **30**, 1427–1428A.

Cerra, Patrick, *The Effects of T-Group Training and Group Video Recall Procedures on Affective Sensitivity, Openmindedness and Self-Perception Change in Counselors*. Unpublished doctoral dissertation. Indiana University, 1969. Abstract in *Dissertation Abstracts International*, 1969, **30**, 1814–1815A.

Howard, Rosalie, *The Effects of Structured Laboratory Learning on the Interpersonal Behavior of College Students*. Unpublished doctoral dissertation. University of Oregon, 1969. Abstract in *Dissertation Abstracts International*, 1969, **30**, 1433–A.

Lee, Robert, *Relationship Between Basic Encounter Group and Change in Self Concepts and Interpersonal Relationships of College Low Achievers*. Unpublished doctoral dissertation. United States International University, 1969. Abstract in *Dissertation Abstracts International*, 1969, **30**, 2336–2337A.

Leventer, Esther, *The Interrelation of Self Esteem, Fear, Emotionality, and Behavior in Training Laboratories*. Unpublished doctoral dissertation. University of California, 1969. Abstract in *Dissertation Abstracts International*, 1969, **30**, 588–A.

Winger, Leland, *A Study of the Otto Self-Concept Improvement Counseling Technique (OSCICT) Applied to Dropouts*. Unpublished doctoral dissertation. University of Utah, 1969. Abstract in *Dissertation Abstracts International*, 1969, **30**, 1883–1884A.

Periodicals

Danish, Steven, "Factors Influencing Changes in Empathy Following a Group Experience," *Journal of Counseling Psychology*, 1971, **18**, 262–267.

Jones, G. Brian, Trimble, Marilynne, and Altman, Harold, "Improving College Students' Performance Through Group Counseling," *Journal of College Student Personnel,* 1970, 11, 373–382.

Meador, Betty, "Individual Process in a Basic Encounter Group," *Journal of Counseling Psychology,* 1971, 18, 70–76.

IX. C. COORDINATED MEETINGS; ALTERNATE MEETINGS
Periodicals

Blank, Leonard, Wilker, Paulina, and Grundfest, Sandra, "Intense Encounters in Human Relations Training," *Personnel and Guidance Journal,* 1969, 48, 56–57.

Seligman, Milton, and Sterne, David, "Verbal Behavior in Therapist-Led, Leaderless, and Alternating Group Psychotherapy Sessions," *Journal of Counseling Psychology,* 1969, 16, 325–328.

Truax, Charles, Wargo, Donald, and Volksdorf, Norman, "Antecedents to Outcome in Group Counseling with Institutionalized Juvenile Delinquents: Effects of Therapeutic Conditions, Patient Self-Exploration, Alternate Sessions and Vicarious Therapy Pretraining," *Journal of Abnormal Psychology,* 1970, 76, 235–242.

IX. D. MULTILEADER APPROACHES; CO-COUNSELING WITH GROUPS (EDUCATIONAL INSTITUTIONS ONLY)
Books

Howard, Rosalie, *The Effects of Structured Laboratory Learning on the Interpersonal Behavior of College Students.* Unpublished doctoral dissertation. University of Oregon, 1969. Abstract in *Dissertation Abstracts International,* 1969, 30, 1433–A.

Miller, Juliet, *Co-Counseling.* Ann Arbor, Michigan: ERIC Clearinghouse on Counseling and Personnel Services. Series 1: Innovations in the Training and Supervision of Counselors, 1970.

Rye, Donald, *A Comparative Study of Three Small Group Treatments and Their Effects on Accurate Communication Between Counselor Trainees and Their Clients.* Unpublished doctoral dissertation. Indiana University, 1969. Abstract in *Dissertation Abstracts International,* 1969, 30, 554–A.

Treppa, Jerry, *An Investigation of Some of the Dynamics of the Interpersonal Relationship Between Pairs of Multiple Therapists.* Unpublished doctoral dissertation. Michigan State University, 1969. Abstract in *Dissertation Abstracts International,* 1969, 30, 1909–B.

Zimpfer, David, "Multi-leader Approaches to Groups in Counseling and Therapy," in Stanley Cramer and James Hansen, *Group Guidance and Counseling in the Schools.* New York: Appleton, 1971, 305–320.

Periodicals

Hinds, William, and Roehlke, Helen, "A Learning Theory Approach to Group Counseling with Elementary School Children," *Journal of Counseling Psychology,* 1970, 17, 49–55.

Hurst, James, and Robert Fenner, "Extended-session Group as a Predictive Technique for Counselor Training," *Journal of Counseling Psychology,* 1969, **16**, 358–360.

Warner, Richard, Niland, Thomas, and Maynard, Peter, "Model Reinforcement Group Counseling with Elementary School Children," *Elementary School Guidance and Counseling,* 1971, **5**, 248–255.

IX. E. LARGE GROUP APPROACHES

Periodicals

Collingwood, Thomas, "The Effects of Large Group Training on Facilitative Interpersonal Communication," *Journal of Clinical Psychology,* 1969, **25**, 461–462.

IX. F. TRANSACTIONAL THERAPY

Periodicals

Johnson, Robert, and Chatowsky, Anthony, "Game Theory and Short-Term Group Counseling," *Personnel and Guidance Journal,* 1969, **47**, 758–761.

IX. G. MARATHON GROUP EXPERIENCES

Books

Demos, George, "Marathon Therapy—A Psychotherapeutic Modality," in P. Gallagher and G. Demos (Eds.), *The Counseling Center in Higher Education.* Springfield, Illinois: Thomas, 1970, 337–351.

Schmidt, Wesley, Rovin, Ronald, Stanowski, Richard, and Widlowski, Charles, "A Marathon Counseling Session for Parents of Underachieving High School Students," in Robert Berg and James Johnson (Eds.), *Group Counseling: A Source Book of Theory and Practice.* Fort Worth: American Continental Publishing, 1971, 251–257.

Stoller, Frederick, "Videotape Feedback in the Marathon and Encounter Group," in M. Berger (Ed.), *Videotape Techniques in Psychiatric Training and Treatment.* New York: Brunner-Mazel, 1970, 170–178.

Periodicals

Foulds, Melvin, Wright, James, and Guinan, James, "Marathon Group: A Six Month Follow-up," *Journal of College Student Personnel,* 1970, **11**, 426–431.

Guinan, James, and Foulds, Melvin, "Marathon Group: Facilitator of Personal Growth," *Journal of Counseling Psychology,* 1970, **17**, 145–149.

Hurst, James, and Fenner, Robert, "Extended-session Group as a Predictive Technique for Counselor Training," *Journal of Counseling Psychology,* 1969, **16**, 358–360.

Young, Edward, and Jacobson, Leonard, "Effects of Time-Extended Marathon Group Experiences on Personality Characteristics," *Journal of Counseling Psychology,* 1970, **17**, 247–251.

IX. H. SIMULATION IN GUIDANCE

Books

Gordon, Alice, *Games for Growth: Educational Games in the Classroom*. Chicago: Science Research Associates, 1970.

Kersch, Susan, *Simulation Gaming*. Ann Arbor, Michigan: ERIC Clearinghouse on Counseling and Personnel Services. Series 1: Innovations in the Training and Supervision of Counselors, 1970.

Lundquist, Gerald, *Utilization of Simulation and Group Counseling in the Training of Prospective Elementary School Teachers*. Unpublished doctoral dissertation. Arizona State University, 1969. Abstract in *Dissertation Abstracts International*, 1969, **30**, 2338–A.

McHenry, William, *A Study of the Use of the Life Career Game in Junior High School Group Guidance*. Unpublished doctoral dissertation. George Washington University, 1969. Abstract in *Dissertation Abstracts International*, 1970, **31**, 610–A.

Varenhorst, Barbara, "Learning the Consequences of Life's Decisions," in John Krumboltz and Carl Thoresen (Eds.), *Behavioral Counseling*. New York: Holt, Rinehart and Winston, 1969, 306–319.

IX. I. LEADERLESS GROUPS

Books

Brown, Jerome, *Some Factors in Response to Criticism in Group Therapy*. Unpublished doctoral dissertation. University of Houston, 1969. Abstract in *Dissertation Abstracts International*, 1969, **30**, 376–B.

Solomon, Lawrence, and Berzon, Betty, "The Self-directed Group: A New Direction in Personal Growth Learning," in J. T. Hart and T. M. Tomlinson (Eds.), *New Directions in Client-Centered Psychotherapy*. Boston: Houghton Mifflin, 1970.

Periodicals

Banta, Trudy, and McCormick, Jane, "Using the Leaderless Group Discussion Technique for the Selection of Residence Hall Counselors," *Journal of the National Association of Women Deans and Counselors*, 1969, **33**, 30–33.

Grant, W. Harold, and Eigenbrod, Frederick, "Behavioral Changes Influenced by Structured Peer Group Activities," *Journal of College Student Personnel*, 1970, **11**, 291–295.

Lucas, Richard, and Jaffee, Cabot, "Effects of High-Rate Talkers on Group Voting Behavior in the Leaderless-Group Problem-Solving Situation," *Psychological Reports*, 1969, **25**, 471–477.

Zimet, Carl, and Schneider, Carol, "Effects of Group Size on Interaction in a Small Group," *Journal of Social Psychology*, 1969, **77**, 177–187.

IX. J. USE OF PARAPROFESSIONALS, LAYMEN, PEERS, PARENTS, AND VOLUNTEERS AS GROUP LEADERS

Books

Chinsky, Jack, *Nonprofessionals in a Mental Hospital: A Study of the College Student Volunteer.* Unpublished doctoral dissertation. University of Rochester, 1969. Abstract in *Dissertation Abstracts International,* 1970, **30,** 1355–B.

Delworth, Ursula, *A Comparison of Professional Counselors and Counselor Support Personnel in Group Counseling with Junior High School Students.* Unpublished doctoral dissertation. University of Oregon, 1969. Abstract in *Dissertation Abstracts International,* 1970, **30,** 5230–A.

Rappaport, Julian, *Nonprofessionals in a Mental Hospital: College Students as Group Leaders with Chronic Patients.* Unpublished doctoral dissertation. University of Rochester, 1969. Abstract in *Dissertation Abstracts International,* 1969, **30,** 1365–B.

Sloan, Nancy, *Students in Helping Roles.* Ann Arbor, Michigan: ERIC Clearinghouse on Counseling and Personnel Services. Series 3: Human Resources in The Guidance Programs, 1970.

Smith, James, "Encouraging Constructive Use of Time," in John Krumboltz and Carl Thoresen (Eds.), *Behavioral Counseling.* New York: Holt, Rinehart and Winston, 1969, 234–241.

Periodicals

Vriend, Thelma, "High Performing Inner-City Adolescents Assist Low-Performing Peers in Counseling Groups," *Personnel and Guidance Journal,* 1969, **47,** 897–904.

Winters, Wilbur, and Arent, Ruth, "The Use of High School Students to Enrich an Elementary Guidance and Counseling Program," *Elementary School Guidance and Counseling,* 1969, **3,** 198–205.

IX. K. OBLIGATORY GROUPS

Books

Potts, John, *Selected Effects of Required Group Counseling in the Regular Curriculum for Disadvantaged Ninth Grade Students.* Unpublished doctoral dissertation. Arizona State University. Abstract in *Dissertation Abstracts International,* 1970, **30,** 3736–A.

Periodicals

Wyers, Norman, "Adaptations of the Social Group Work Method," *Social Casework,* 1969, **50,** 513–518.

IX. L. OTHER NEW DIRECTIONS IN GROUPS

Periodicals

Barrick, James, Remer, Rory, Blair, Margery, and Sewall, Priscilla, "A Behavioral Approach to Lack of Friendships," *School Counselor,* 1971, **18,** 260–264.

X. PROFESSIONAL ISSUES IN GROUPS

Books

Golembiewski, Robert, and Blumberg, Arthur (Eds.), *Sensitivity Training and the Laboratory Approach*. Itasca, Illinois: Peacock, 1970. Part IV, "What Concerns Are There About T-Groups? Goals, Methods, and Results."

Howard, June, *Please Touch: A Guided Tour of the Human Potential Movement*. New York: McGraw-Hill, 1970, "The Plaint of the Patriotic Letter Writers," 226–237.

Ohlsen, Merle, "Professional Issues in Use of Group Procedures," in George Gazda and Thomas Porter (Eds.), *Proceedings of a Symposium on Training Groups*. Athens, Georgia: University of Georgia, College of Education, 1970, 111–117.

Periodicals

Beymer, Lawrence, "Confrontation Groups: Hula Hoops?" *Counselor Education and Supervision*, 1970, **9**, 75–86.

Blanchard, William, "Ecstasy Without Agony Is Baloney," *Psychology Today*, 1970, **3**(8), 8–10 and 64.

Cranshaw, Ralph, "How Sensitive Is Sensitivity Training?" *American Journal of Psychiatry*, 1969, **126**, 868–873.

Dreyfus, Edward, and Kremenliev, Elva, "Innovative Group Techniques: Handle with Care," *Personnel and Guidance Journal*, 1970, **49**, 279–283.

Gazda, George, Duncan, J. A., and Sisson, P. J., "Professional Issues in Group Work," *Personnel and Guidance Journal*, 1971, **49**, 637–643.

Halleck, Seymour, "You Can Go to Hell with Style," *Psychology Today*, 1969, **3**(6), 16 and 70–73.

Hurewitz, Paul, "Ethical Considerations in Leading Therapeutic and Quasitherapeutic Groups: Encounter and Sensitivity Groups," *Group Psychotherapy and Psychodrama*, 1970, **23**, 17–20.

Kuehn, John, and Crinella, Francis, "Sensitivity Training: Interpersonal 'Overkill' and Other Problems," *American Journal of Psychiatry*, 1969, **126**, 840–845.

Lakin, Martin, "Group Sensitivity Training and Encounter: Uses and Abuses of a Method," *Counseling Psychologist*, 1970, **2**(2), 66–70.

Lakin, Martin, "Some Ethical Issues in Sensitivity Training," *American Psychologist*, 1969, **24**, 923–928.

Maliver, Bruce, "Encounter Groups Up Against the Wall," *New York Times Magazine*, January 3, 1971. Pp. 4–5, 37–40, and 43.

Nelson, Richard, and Callao, Maximo, "Groups and Accountability," *Elementary School Guidance and Counseling*, 1970, **4**, 291–294.

Pancrazio, J. J., "A Group Experience—for What?" *Student Personnel Association for Teacher Education Journal*, 1970, **8**, 52–55.

Schrank, Robert, and Stein, Susan, "Sensitivity Training: Uses and Abuses," *Manpower*, 1970, **2**(7), 2–7.

Shostrom, Everett, "Group Therapy: Let the Buyer Beware," *Psychology Today,* 1969, 2(12), 36–40.

Verplanck, William, "Trainers, Trainees and Ethics," *Counseling Psychologist,* 1970, 2(2), 71–75.

Zimpfer, David, "Needed: Professional Ethics in Working with Groups," *Personnel and Guidance Journal,* 1971, 50, 280–287.

XI. EDUCATION OF GROUP WORKERS

Books

Dimock, Hedley, *Selecting and Training Group Leaders.* Montreal, Quebec: Centre for Human Relations and Community Studies, Sir George Williams University, 1970.

Glass, Sheldon, *The Prac.. l Handbook of Group Counseling.* Baltimore: BCS Publishing, 1969. Chapter 12, "Group Supervision."

Kemp, C. Gratton, *Foundations of Group Counseling.* New York: McGraw-Hill, 1970. Part Five, "Preparation of the Group Counselor," 207–258.

Rogers, Carl, *Carl Rogers on Encounter Groups.* New York: Harper and Row, 1970. Chapter 9, "Building Facilitative Skills."

Zimpfer, David, "Multi-leader Approaches to Groups in Counseling and Therapy," in Stanley Cramer and James Hansen, *Group Guidance and Counseling in the Schools.* New York: Appleton, 1971, 305–320.

Periodicals

Andersen, Dale, and Cabianca, William, "The 'Micro-Lab': An Introduction to Group Process," *Counselor Education and Supervision,* 1970, 9, 299–300.

Collingwood, Thomas, "The Effects of Large Group Training on Facilitative Interpersonal Communication," *Journal of Clinical Psychology,* 1969, 25, 461–462.

Lacks, Patricia, Landsbaum, Jane, and Stern, Michael, "Workshop in Communication for Members of a Psychiatric Team," *Psychological Reports,* 1970, 26, 423–430.

McGee, Thomas, "Comprehensive Preparation for Group Psychotherapy," *American Journal of Psychotherapy,* 1969, 23, 303–312.

Rand, Leonard, and Carew, Donald, "Comparison of T-Group Didactic Approaches to Training Undergraduate Resident Assistants," *Journal of College Student Personnel,* 1970, 11, 432–438.

Sollinger, Irwin, Yarosz, Edward, Loughran, Genevieve, and Sebald, Dorothy, "Training for Group Work," *Journal of Employment Counseling,* 1971, 8, 19–25.

Wolf, Alexander, Schwartz, Emanuel, McCarty, Gerald, and Goldberg, Irving, "Training in Psychoanalysis in Groups Without Face-to-Face Contact," *American Journal of Psychotherapy,* 1969, 23, 488–494.

XII. TRANSCRIPTS OF GROUP MEETINGS; CASE DESCRIPTIONS AND PROTOCOLS

Books

Dinkmeyer, Don, and Muro, James, *Group Counseling: Theory and Practice.* Itasca, Illinois: Peacock, 1971, 228–243 and passim.

Gazda, George (Ed.), *Proceedings of a Symposium on Group Procedures for the Disadvantaged.* Athens, Georgia: University of Georgia, Center for Continuing Education, 1969, passim.

Gazda, George, and Porter, Thomas (Eds.), *Proceedings of a Symposium on Training Groups.* Athens, Georgia: University of Georgia, College of Education, 1970, passim.

Klaw, Spencer, "Two Weeks in a T-Group," in Robert Golembiewski and Arthur Blumberg (Eds.), *Sensitivity Training and the Laboratory Approach.* Itasca, Illinois: Peacock, 1970, 24–38.

Perls, Fritz, *Gestalt Therapy Verbatim.* Lafayette, California: Real People Press, 1969, passim.

Periodicals

Berger, Milton, "Experiential and Didactic Aspects of Training in Therapeutic Group Approaches," *American Journal of Psychiatry,* 1969, **126**, 845–850.

LISTING OF PERIODICALS SEARCHED SYSTEMATICALLY THROUGH MAY, 1971

Adult Education
Adult Leadership
American Journal of Orthopsychiatry
American Journal of Psychiatry
American Journal of Psychoanalysis
American Journal of Psychotherapy
American Psychologist
American Vocational Journal
Archives of General Psychiatry
Behavior Research and Therapy
British Journal of Educational Study
Clearing House
Counseling Psychologist
Counselor Education and Supervision
Dissertation Abstracts International (formerly Dissertation Abstracts)
Educational Leadership
Educational and Psychological Measurement
Educational Sociology
Elementary School Guidance and Counseling
Employment Service Review
The Group
Group Psychotherapy and Psychodrama (formerly Group Psychotherapy)
High School Journal
Human Relations
International Journal of Group Psychotherapy
Journal of Abnormal Psychology
Journal of Applied Behavioral Science
Journal of Applied Psychology
Journal of Clinical Psychology
Journal of College Student Personnel
Journal of Consulting and Clinical Psychology
Journal of Counseling Psychology
Journal of Educational Psychology
Journal of Educational Research
Journal of Employment Counseling
Journal of Experimental Education
Journal of Nervous and Mental Disease
Journal of Personality
Journal of Psychological Studies
Journal of Psychology
Journal of Secondary Education
Journal of Social Issues
Journal of Social Psychology

Mental Hygiene
National Association of Secondary School Principals Bulletin
National Association of Women Deans and Counselors Journal
Personnel and Guidance Journal
Personnel Psychology
Phi Delta Kappan
Psychiatric Quarterly
Psychiatry
Psychological Bulletin
Psychological Reports
Psychology Today
The Record (formerly Teachers College Record)
Rehabilitation Counseling Bulletin
Review of Educational Research
School Counselor
School Review
Social Forces
Sociology of Education (formerly Journal of Educational Sociology)
Sociometry
Vocational Guidance Quarterly

Author Index

Subject Index